LIFE STYLE
French Style

Some other related titles

France: A Handbook for New Residents
The one book on France you cannot do without
M. Michael Brady

A French Restoration
The story of two people who bought and restored
their own mini chateau
Clive Kristen and David Johnson

Going to Live on the French Riviera
Whether you are going to the Côte d'Azur to study, retire or work
this book will tell you all you need to know
Charles Davey

Starting a Business in France
A step by step guide to turning your dream of self-employment
in France into successful reality
Richard Whiting

Starting & Running a B & B in France
How to make money and enjoy a new lifestyle running your
own chambres d'hôtes
Deborah Hunt

howtobooks

Please send for a free copy of the latest catalogue:
Spring Hill
Spring Hill House, Spring Hill Road,
Begbroke, Oxford OX5 1RX, United Kingdom
info@howtobooks.co.uk
www.howtobooks.co.uk

LIFE STYLE
French Style

ALL YOU NEED TO KNOW ABOUT
MAKING A HOME IN FRANCE
INCLUDES REGIONAL GUIDE TO WHERE TO LIVE

ELIZABETH MORGAN

SPRING HILL

Published by Spring Hill

Spring Hill is an imprint of
How To Books Ltd
Spring Hill House, Spring Hill Road,
Begbroke, Oxford OX5 1RX, United Kingdom
Tel: (01865) 375794 Fax: (01865) 379162
info@howtobooks.co.uk
www.howtobooks.co.uk

British Library Cataloguing in Publication Data
A catalogue record for this book is available from
the British Library.

First published 2007

ISBN: 978 1 905862 09 2

Photo Gallery: pp 1, 2, 4(b), 6(b) © *specialist* publishing services ltd;
3 © iStockphoto.com/Heinz Linke; 4(t) © iStockphoto.com/Jean-Yves Benedeyt;
5 © iStockphoto.com/Frank Mark Serge; 7 © iStockphoto.com/Jacques Croizer;
8 © iStockphoto.com/David Hughes; 6(t) © Elizabeth Morgan
Chapter opening photos: 1, 2, 4, 5, 7–11, 13–17, 21, 23, 24 © *specialist* publishing services ltd;
3, 18 © iStockphoto.com/anzeletti; 19 © iStockphoto.com/Lambert Parren;
20 © iStockphoto.com/Karen Phillips; 22 © iStockphoto.com/Francois Sachs;
6 © Elizabeth Morgan

With grateful thanks to Le Point for permission to reproduce the information on pp114–19.

Produced for Spring Hill Books by Deer Park Productions, Tavistock
Typeset by *specialist* publishing services ltd, Montgomery
Printed and bound by Bell and Bain Ltd, Glasgow

CONTENTS

Take more of your money with you

If you're planning a move to France it's likely that the last thing on your mind is foreign exchange. However, at some point you will have to change your hard earned money into euros. Unfortunately, exchange rates are constantly moving and as a result can have a big impact on the amount of money you have to create your dream home.

For example, if you look at the euro during 2006 you can see how this movement can affect your capital. Sterling against the euro was as high as 1.4992 and as low as 1.4243. This meant that if you had £200,000 to transfer you could have ended up with as much as €299,840 or as little as €284,860, a difference of over €14,000.

It is possible to avoid this pitfall by fixing a rate through a **forward contract**. A small deposit will secure you a rate for anywhere up to 2 years in advance and by doing so provides the security of having the currency you need at a guaranteed cost.

Another option if you have time on your side is a **limit order**. This is used when you want to achieve a rate that is currently not available. You set the rate that you want and the market is then monitored. As soon as that rate is achieved the currency is purchased for you.

If you need to act swiftly and your capital is readily available then it is most likely that you will use a **spot transaction**. This is the *Buy now, Pay now* option where you get the most competitive rate on the day.

To ensure you get the most for your money it's a good idea to use a foreign exchange specialist such as Currencies Direct. As an alternative to your bank, Currencies Direct is able to offer you extremely competitive exchange rates, no commission charges and free transfers*. This can mean considerable savings on your transfer when compared to using a bank.

*Over £5,000

Information provided by Currencies Direct.
Website: *www.currenciesdirect.com*
Email: *info@currenciesdirect.com*
Tel: 0845 389 1729

INTRODUCTION

This book is aimed at those who are thinking of buying, or are about to buy, a house in France, whether it is a holiday home, a semi-permanent home or, indeed, a permanent home. It is also for those who have already bought, but who are contemplating moving on.

For all, the question to be asked is 'Where?' The right location is vital to the life style most appropriate for you. Therefore it is hoped this book will offer sufficient information to serve as a guide when such a choice needs to be made. Where in France you decide to go finally is influenced by personal factors, and gut reaction. Maybe you are mad about snow sports, swimming or rambling, and you have already researched the centres. Maybe you have friends who have found four walls and a roof near to their pad that need complete renovation, and have offered enthusiastic help and support. Maybe you had a fabulous holiday in a rural *gîte* two years ago, and wouldn't it be wonderful to have your own place in that very village? However unless you already know your location in advance, the pertinent question remains, 'Where?' France is a big country; three times bigger than the UK, offering a bewildering variation of life style and climate. I am always amazed to find so many people, particularly on those property shows which flood television screens daily, happily going off to buy a home in France without really having an idea of the life style the village/town/area has to offer.

There are certain naïve assumptions about the country, which I have heard voiced quite seriously on television: that Calais is always warmer than the English south coast; that the sun is always shining in France from north to south like a sub tropical haven; that most people speak English and there is no need to know any French; that because alcohol is infinitely cheaper everything else has to be.

1

One interviewed couple were emigrating to France because they had found a cheap house in Normandy. When asked if they knew the country or even the Department, alas they did not, and had visited only Calais – but dozens of times, they added in justification, on day trips to pick up cheap alcohol and cigarettes. Neither of them knew a word of French, although to my mind that would have been the least serious deficit in this scenario.

France, the old enemy, only twenty-two miles away; the home of the great Bogey Man Napoleon, God rest his soul; the home of the 1066 invader, the occupier who remained and intermarried and left us a rich linguistic legacy of some 12,000 French words. Some thousand years later, the Conqueror's native land remains not only our most visited holiday destination and holiday home choice, but also over recent years the most popular location for *émigré* Brits.

Maybe we should have effected a straight swap at the time.

Several hundred-thousand British families have holiday homes in France and over past years that number has increased to include the thousands who have decided to make the country their home. For those who move lock, stock and barrel to France the reasons for doing so are frequently complex and personal, but one tends to hear the same catalogue of general complaints and disenchantment with life in the UK which always includes lager-louts, health, education and the cost of quality living. However justified, these are negative reasons, and for such a mega upheaval there should be positive reasons too, to keep spirits buoyant in those inevitable moments of doubt. It follows that unless the choice of location is really considered carefully, the consequence of error can be totally dispiriting, if not disastrous. You might just as well stick a pin in a map. Buying in haste, on impulse, could mean selling in haste, thereby losing far too much on a capital investment. First find the location, and with care. Consider carefully where you want to live. Remember it's your life and with capital at stake you cannot make a catastrophic mistake. Nothing is perfect, and there are always compromises to be made. In an ideal world you would like a *château* (wouldn't we all?) with built-in staff, but we settle for the very best our cash can buy.

When you think you have found your patch, make a couple of visits, at different times of the year if possible. A hot sun in August, with the scent of lavender and the sound of crickets, is very different from a cold rainy day in mid-winter. Having to drive two kilometres to buy a *baguette* may be fun when you are 40, but a chore when you are 60. Try asking each member of the family – if they are old enough – to write down or tell you the things they would like in a holiday home. Even if you discard most of it, at least you will have an idea of the family's requirements, and it could help crystallise your own shortlist of locations. In the UK, if you want a Putney life style you would not go to Pitlochrie, Pewsey or Perranporth, just because houses are cheaper.

Finding a house after all the location pros and cons is the easy part.

It is not difficult to follow the progression from the two-week holiday, sunning or skiing, to the search for a modest holiday home so long as it is affordable and can be minimally worked-on to provide a base for the family during the school holidays. A two-week family package holiday can cost on average about £4,000. A small patch of France will cost you more than that, but you will be able to stay there whenever you wish. Dream cottages are usually run-down and in need of some restoration, or they would never be cheap enough for us to buy. Therefore expect the first holiday, possibly even years, to turn into a circus of blood, sweat, toil and tears, with a generous helping of arguments and laughs thrown in.

The ratio of laughs is in direct proportion to the state of dilapidation. I know this to my cost. When the children wanted to be taken swimming a good half-hour away, I would be up to my armpits in cement, racing to get over yet another DIY hurdle before the end of the school vacation. They still remember.

It is a great temptation, but try to avoid taking on too much unless there is a reliable labour force prepared to continue renovations in your absence if necessary. Irrespective of country, finding a workforce anywhere that labours with consistent effort for the absentee owner is always a gamble. Withholding most of the payment is one solution; an unscheduled flying visit is another, so be thankful you are renovating in France and not in Tasmania.

Pacing the work is essential, otherwise the holiday home turns into a nightmare especially if there is no eagle eye to monitor the bank balance. But working together as family, to make your own modest paradise, can be immensely rewarding in every way and for a blissful period, replaces the need today's children have for the pap of television with far more instructive activities. There is a great deal to be said for a 'Swiss Family Robinson' approach when it comes to holiday home-making!

Prefacing the section in this book devoted to regional exploration there are chapters to guide the prospective purchaser through house finding and buying, renovations, where to find the most reasonably priced DIY, permissions, planning applications, furniture, organising the various services, and finally moving on with the problem of French capital gains tax. Throughout, there are cautionary tales and advice on how to work your way through the bureaucratic minefield.

To simplify this general guide to choice of location and for the purposes of this book only, I have partitioned France into ten regions (see map).

West

1. Brittany, Normandy, Picardie, Nord-Pas-de-Calais
2. Paris and the Île-de-France
3. The Loire Valley, Orléans, Chartres to Nantes, Loire-Atlantique
4. Poitou, Charentes, Dordogne, Limousin, Cher
5. Aquitaine, Midi-Pyrénées, Pyrénées-Atlantique, Haut-Pyrénées

The author's regions of France as used in this book.

East

6. Champagne, Ardennes, Lorraine, Alsace

7. Burgundy, Franche-Comté

8. Auvergne, Rhône-Alpes

9. Languedoc

10. Provence

You will find regional differences in house prices, amenities, and aspects of community life. There are interviews with ex-pats, local dignitaries, holiday-home owners and estate agents. Local voices are usually more reliable than any brochure. You could find any number of social-geography books or travel guides giving perfect descriptions of the selected regions, but few will document the honest opinions of those who have chosen to live and work there. This is essentially a 'hands on' book, all suggestions and words of advice are based on the experiences of people, some of whom are beginners, and some who, at this point in their lives, are wearing the proverbial T shirt. Incorporated in the chapters is relevant updated material from my book *Can We Afford the Bidet?*, which includes the list of specialist and non-specialist markets throughout France.

In the mid seventies we bought a small patch of France. Since then, through changes in family life, I have moved house and town five times. Had I been advised and thought it through, maybe I could have made the right decision first time.

Although intended primarily as an aid to location when buying a house in France – the questions to be asked, the problems that arise, and the parameters of general caution that are best observed – this book should also provide a guiding infrastructure wherever you choose to buy, be it Tuscany, Seville or Sofia.

ELIZABETH MORGAN

1
First things first

Life, unfortunately, brims with pitfalls and problems of varying degrees, and it is as well to be forewarned. But, whatever befalls in the acquiring and refurbishment of your *chez vous*, don't give up. Nothing is impossible, except to lawyers. Whenever I have asked a French workforce 'Is that going to be possible?' the answer has always been '*Rien est impossible madame*'. Therefore always be positive, keep the objective alive and, unless you are particularly unlucky, you will achieve it.

Wherever you finally choose to hang your hat, it is a good idea to narrow the search to one of your chosen region's larger centres where you will find a higher concentration of estate agents. As all leading estate agents are listed with their websites, email addresses and telephone numbers, you may think it unnecessary these days to make personal visits, because of Internet communication. Think again! When I was looking for my present house, admittedly in an expensive area of France, I combed dozens of websites for something in my price range. Each time I found nothing available for my money, except perhaps a sprinkling of one- or two-bedroom flats. Gradually it dawned that only the top of the range properties were given screen space. Naturally this depends on the region.

I know a few people who have bought quite successfully on the Internet, but always in rural areas where property is cheaper. Horses for courses.

YOU, YOUR ESTATE AGENT (*IMMOBILIER*)AND YOUR *NOTAIRE'S* FEES

The bad news as a buyer is that you pay the *notaire's* fee plus that demanded by the state, rather like our stamp duty. So always count on paying about 6.5–7% of the agreed purchase price in addition. French *notaires'* fees are amongst the highest in Europe, which is probably why French people do not move as often as we Brits.

House price	French *notaires'* fees	Average UK city solicitors' fees
€100,000	€1,344	€850
€300,000	€3,307	€1,250
€400,000	€4,294	€1,500
€600,000	€6,268	€1,800
€800,000	€8,241	€2,400

In addition to the *notaire's* personal fee will be the equivalent to our stamp duty plus house registration fees, both of which go straight to the government. The *notaire's* fee is regulated by the government, unlike in the UK and many other EU countries, where fees are set freely according to the market and the solicitor's office. When deregulation occurred in Holland, conveyancing fees dropped by 65%. Austria is also abolishing fixed fees and soon Italy, Greece, Spain and Portugal will follow suit. There is growing pressure on France to fall in line, but although it hasn't happened yet it seems likely that it will eventually.

The good news when you sell is that you, the vendor, pay nothing. The price you want for the property will be *nett vendeur*. Estate agents' commission in France is high, can vary between 5 and 8% and is added to the vendor's price before it goes in the window. When buying, it is worthwhile spending time gazing into as many other *immobiliers'* windows as possible in your chosen spot as it is likely you will find the same gem with an agency which has a lower commission charge. This does not mean you have no room for some aggressive market trading. A friendly agency will often either lower its commission, or split the difference with the vendor in order to effect a sale. When buying, always make sure the house price advertised *does* include commission. Although this is standard practice, *ipso facto* there are swindlers (*arnaquers*) throughout France, so ask anyway.

On one disastrous occasion I was told by the senior negotiator of an established agency that the house sale commission in that particular *departement* was always an added extra to the house price, thus increasing the total purchase price of the house I wanted to buy. As a somewhat naïve newcomer I had no instant means of checking. However, worrying weeks later I discovered the scam: he was personally pocketing the extra agency commission. Although he was dismissed from his agency I had to wait months for the return of my deposit from the *notaire*.

Generally speaking, estate agents in France – once you are sitting there in the office – are far more willing to put themselves out for you than many in the UK. Of course you find a few too pushy, and a few too young and too laid back but, most of the time, both men and women are helpful and courteous. Telephoning a few agents is the next best thing to a personal visit, but to do this you should have a fair understanding of French, particularly in country areas where it is unlikely the agents speak any English – and why should they?

I remember telephoning about twenty agents in the area in which I wanted to live. Most of them responded with a selection of informative faxes and sheaves of smudgy black and white pictures. That was a start! But do not expect any follow-up. To get results you have to keep badgering. On more than one occasion I have become quite excited about a house as it seemed to correspond precisely to my requirements, only to find another agent had already sold it. Notwithstanding, from the combined efforts of several negotiators you will be able to make a list of at least a dozen houses that meet your specifications.

There is no avoiding it, now is the time for a visit, but here comes the hard part, unless you happen to have a personal assistant. I gave myself ten days, during which time I saw 23 houses once only, and the one I finally bought, twice. That is not hard. The hard part lies in tying the agency's negotiators down to viewing times, keeping a tight schedule and sticking to it. Do not be put off by the agent who asks you to telephone when you get there; he just can't be bothered to pull out the office diary.

This is a popular scenario.

YOU   I shall be arriving next week, but only for a few days and I should like to view five of the properties you sent me.

E.A.   Of course. Please call me when you get here.

YOU   But I have a limited time, and I wish to make definite appointments.

E.A.   Good. So we will make all the appointments when you arrive. OK?

YOU   No! I have other houses to see with other agents, and I have no time to make several visits to France. I wish to buy a house and it could be one of yours. I particularly like 'Villa Fromage'.

At this point he grabs the diary and promises to call you back when he has contacted the owners and arranged a viewing.

With prospects of a sale, he will call you back. But always be prepared to call him again the following day.

It is a polite French estate agency tradition, to collect and return you from your hotel/lodging, so you will not need a car.

If you have any friends in your chosen area ask them to send you a copy of the local estate agents' free magazines, to be found on stands outside their offices, as well as at newsagents and supermarkets. This way you will find a vast selection of property in and around the *arrière pays* (surrounding area) plus a useful comparative price range. Alternatively when you make the initial area visit, bring back several copies. They make fascinating reading.

Even before you decide to visit the dream home you have spotted in the estate agent's window, there are questions you should ask.

Find out about the vendors. The obvious questions are 'Have they already bought?', 'Are they in a hurry?' and 'How long has the house been on the market?' This incidentally could be quite a long time. In country areas houses take a year to sell on average. Remember this in the future if you decide to put *chez vous* on the market.

> My current house had already been 'sold' to local people who pulled out suddenly, leaving the British vendors understandably annoyed as they had plans for the house proceeds back in the UK. However, it left me delighted at finding the right house in the right area quite by chance. Plus of course, second time around the vendors were prepared to negotiate the price.

But by far the most important question is whether the property is an inheritance the family is selling off. If so, are they all in agreement? The estate agent may tell you they are, of course. Do not accept his word. Check on it. If possible contact the deceased's offspring. All members of the inherited property **must** agree upon its disposal, and must be ready to sign the *compromis* (contract). To illustrate this very important point, here is a sad cautionary tale.

> A few years ago I set my heart on a particular house. It was truly *Belle Epoque*, slightly over the top in its ornamentation, and in a perfect position, close to sea and town. The trouble was the price was over my limit. However, the estate agency's chief negotiator was a laughing, amiable chap who looked like Fernandel, and appeared to have his finger on the business pulse. Adjoining the house and part of the estate was

a sizeable piece of land extraneous to my needs, which already had building planning permission. Not only had this latter-day Fernandel a builder in tow, but also the builder had a client, complete with architect, ready to buy the land from me. Even at the going rate this meant I would be paying an astonishingly reasonable sum for my *Belle Epoque* dream. We all met at the house just before I was to sign the *compromis*; the builder, who had acquainted himself with the renovations needed to perfect my dream house and had even prepared an estimate (*devis*) of essential work; my future neighbours, a delightful couple; a surveyor (*geometre*) to measure out the land allocated for the new construction, and smiling benignly over us all, Fernandel himself. I knew the house was an inheritance, and that it was being disposed of by two sisters, one living in the USA, the other a local doctor. I had been told that the local doctor was a monster and that the two sisters were ready to kill each other on sight. However I also knew they had both signed the necessary mandate to sell the house and had agreed on the price, otherwise it would never have appeared on the market.

Months later after signing the *compromis*, and paying out my 5% deposit to a lawyer local to the area and used by the estate agency, my prospective neighbour, whilst telephoning for an up-date, asked a very simple question: had both sisters signed the contract? The possibility of doubt had never crossed my mind; it was something I had taken for granted, and even the delays gave no cause for alarm given the to-ing and fro-ing of documents to the USA. But, upon persistent investigation, the answer was a shocking and emphatic 'no'. Only the USA sister had signed, the other had refused.

The lawyers knew this, Fernandel knew it. The builder, the architect, the future neighbour and I, were the only ones conveniently kept in the dark. Perhaps Fernandel hoped he could persuade the local monster, but in any case he assured us all he was bringing a case against her. This, along with so many other pronouncements we found later, were fabrications. The case was being brought against him for proceeding with an illegal sale. Soon after, Fernandel disappeared without trace, leaving his employer, a gentle woman, minus her car and several thousands in debt.

The builder who had entered into a business partnership with our laughing cavalier was nearly bankrupted and the prospective neighbours had to set about finding another piece of land on which to build their retirement home. Finally, so relieved was I to see my 5% deposit returned, that the money spent on extra air trips and the few artefacts I had already bought for my Belle Epoque, had to be written off to experience. Meanwhile the agency proprietor is still apparently attempting to claim the agency's percentage of the abortive sale and the house remains unsold, Goneril acidly determined to keep her sibling bereft of inherited euros. Through such shabby human behaviour this beautiful house with Italienate frescoes and large turquoise stones studding the frieze has fallen into total disrepair. A lesson to remember.

These days you are more likely to find a property sale handled solely by the *notaire* in country towns and large villages. Usually it is the house of a family known to him for generations, with no current inheritor. The last time I saw property advertised in a *notaire*'s window was at Langres, a delightful town in the Haute-Marne, popular with sailing enthusiasts because of the lakes near-by. It is worthwhile considering this type of property because the price asked is usually less than the estate agent's. But you have to be quick as word spreads in small communities.

In many areas it is the *notaire* who also handles house auctions, and if ever you have the opportunity to view one, take it. You will be watching a piece of historical tradition, unchanged for centuries. Prospective purchasers sit round a tall candle in the lawyer's office. The candle is lit, the bidding starts. I remember watching in breathless silence whilst bids were mumbled, the faces of those involved creased with anxiety and auction fever. Tension mounts as the candle becomes smaller, and as the flame gutters before finally extinguishing itself the last bids come tumbling in. When the flame is no more, the auction is over. Whoever managed the last bid of the live flame wins. I don't think I could buy a house that way, the tension would be unbearable, but on the other hand you would no doubt come away with a bargain and, quite possibly, a heart condition.

Again mostly in country areas, house-sellers reluctant to involve estate agents will advertise with hand-painted notice boards nailed to a tree or fence outside the domicile. Buying this way you could avoid a number of expenses, so why not hire a car for the day and drive around? The *notaire* as we know will demand about 5–8% on top of the asking price, so it is in everyone's interest to reduce the price, in order to reduce the percentage paid to the *notaire*. In this situation, the house would be bought on paper only, at a lower price, but if ever sold on for a hefty profit could work against the purchaser if it is deemed a second home (*maison secondaire*). French capital gains tax, the *plus-valu* could then take a chunk out of the profit, but more on this tax later. Whichever way you do it, disguising the real cost of the purchase is strictly speaking against the law, but it is still done, in town and country alike, so if you do it, be French, keep quiet. I was tutored in this sort of deal some 25 years ago, I well remember sitting on a park bench facing the *notaire's* office, ten minutes ahead of our appointment, with my husband and the vendor, an old peasant farmer.

A wad of notes was slipped from my husband's hand to the farmer's, under cover as I recall of my headscarf (not on my head at the time). We shook hands and then walked into the lawyer's office with an air of supreme innocence, where papers were signed for the purchase of our first *ruine*, at half the real price. Heady stuff.

A more sophisticated approach but with the same objective and result, of which I again have personal experience, is where the *notaire* knows the sub plot but pretends he does not.

Imagine the scenario. After the signing of papers, the legal man begins over-acting by crossing and uncrossing his legs or, depending upon his acting ability, suddenly develops an unstoppable cough, and leaves the room. Immediately a wad of notes is flashed before the expectant eyes of the vendor. Simultaneously the arms of both vendor and buyer disappear under the desk, as if in clandestine embrace. After a second of fumbling, one avid pair of sticky hands belonging to the vendor emerges triumphant, money tightly grasped in fist, from whence it is quickly stuffed it into the bag/suitcase, depending on the quantity, opened ready and waiting. After a few minutes the *notaire* makes a nonchalant re-entry, avoiding two or three pairs of shifty eyes. I have frequently marvelled at the perfect timing. Perhaps it's a keyhole job. In case of doubt check to see if he has a portrait hanging in the office. If the eyes move you will know. I well remember a legal man returning whistling tunelessly and doing up his top fly button: a confirmation he had left the room for a real purpose.

Although these lovable spongy parameters of French law are beginning to dry up, because of strangulating government control, you should still be able to negotiate a part cash payment to the estate agent, and even better if you have an understanding *notaire*. For example if the vendors wish to say they are leaving you 30,000€ of furniture, they make a list and, providing he approves, the purchase price on paper is 30,000€ less. In fact all fixtures and fittings can be calculated quite legally, paid for in cash exchanged in a private deal between vendor and purchaser and be deducted from the sale price, although the *Fisc* (French inland revenue Gestapo) have the right to make an inspection and check on the value of the furniture purportedly being sold. But are they there on moving out day?

It is so important to find the right *notaire*. The agency may have its favourite but he may not be yours. Ask around in cafés and bars, and you will quickly work out which local lawman is *sympa* – straight and unstuffy. In the smaller towns, lawyers usually spend their lives in the same practice, rather like our old family doctors, so each of them is well known, warts and all. But some of the younger *notaires*, fresh-faced and without the gravitas and, frequently, the professional girth of the older country lawyer, can be very pernickety. For example, if you buy in joint names with your British offspring, it is normal practice that the purchase documents have to be signed by them and witnessed by a British lawyer back in the UK, one who is a qualified notary.

One thing that does seem to vary with French house purchases is having to obtain an *'Apostille'* on top of everything else. Confused? So was I. This would seem to be a somewhat unnecessary obfuscation in which the British solicitor is obliged to send off all the signed and witnessed French house purchase documents along with individual passport details to the Foreign Office in London (or French Consulate), who then run down the list of qualified solicitors, stick a piece of paper, the *'Apostille'*, on the back of each document, attesting that the British solicitor who witnessed your offspring's signature and duly provided his/her stamp and seal, is *bone fide* and a real lawperson. Bureaucracy gone mad I fear! Not only does this question the legality of the beagle, but it costs at the time of writing about £19 per attestation. My UK solicitor, also a public notary and who has been witnessing French house purchase signatures for many years, explained that this demand was unusual for France, and all depends on your French *notaire*. Furthermore if you happen to be selling your French house and the house ownership is shared with offspring, and your *notaire* demands an *'Apostille'*, you will have the same rigmarole to go through. Of course if you are both selling and buying, there is twice the pain if your French *notaire* happens to be a nervous *'Apostille'* chap. There is only one solution, leave him.

THE BUYING SCENARIO

With the best will in the world you cannot be sure if the house/flat you have set your heart on will be for ever more the holiday/semi permanent/permanent home: the best laid plans ... as we all know. Nonetheless ensuring enough space for immediate family is often not enough. I was forced to move out of my *bijou* town house, when my daughters started bringing oversized boy friends and their friends down for the summer. The ideal as a first timer is to play safe and find a house with an undeveloped attic (*grenier*), or an outhouse (*remise*), which you will find in older houses. If you feel there is a possibility you could put down permanent roots in the region my advice would be to go for a property with the largest space possible that you can afford, with areas for conversion (*aménagement*). To that end, make a special note of the properties you see containing the phrase *à aménager,* and so long as you have an immediate, and potentially comfortable living space for you and the family, the rest can all come later. If you want to make the house work for you straight away, as a letting property or *gîte*, areas for *aménagement* are crucial and, depending on the region, not difficult to find. If you want to build any extension, then make sure the property has a *cos residuel*, which will tell you how many square metres you have left for construction.

There are plenty of legal books that will guide you with boring precision through the convolutions of a French house purchase. If you use a UK-based lawyer who deals with French law, you could be charged the earth, possibly to pay for the extra legal course he took. I once had to have my signature on a document relating to my French house (not even a purchase) witnessed by an English lawyer who also practised French law. There are several to be found advertising in Anglo-French journals. As I was in the UK at the time I found one such lawyer living nearby. No problem. Yes of course he would witness my signature, and that would cost me £58. I found this unacceptable, so I telephoned my *notaire* in France. I don't think we realise in the UK the power and esteem in which the French *Mairie* is held, so when my *notaire*'s clerk told me that in France I could go to my local *Mairie* to get it witnessed, I hot-footed it to my local British Town Hall, and the signature was witnessed free of charge. Don't let them forget the official stamp. It may be a throwback to Napoleon's sheaves of law-making documentation that must have cluttered his office, but the official stamp seems to be vital in all French legal transactions. A word of caution: this service may not be available in every town hall in the UK.

French *Mairies* have become potent forces since the massive upheaval some years back within the French civil service, which de-centralised many Paris-based decisions, in favour of municipal power. Anyone living in France will find out just how influential they are.

Another example of French republican democracy is the fact there is no form of property ownership that is labelled either leasehold or freehold. You own the parcel of land upon which your house is built or you jointly own the parcel of land upon which the building housing your flat is built. And you really own it, not as in the UK where, although we may think we own our freeholds, the land – every square inch (rivers too) – is, in fact owned by our royal masters, HRH and co.

The house/bijou cottage/château

Having now made your choice, make your offer. An *immobilier* told me quite recently that one should immediately take off 10% as that was the margin allowed for debate. It is not the normal practice to employ a surveyor to check the premises, unless you are taking out a mortgage, and even then the officials sent round (and sometimes they are not), appear to be far more laid back than their UK equivalents.

If there is work to be done it is a good idea to find a local builder or ex pat with renovation experience to cast a careful eye over your prospective home. Once your offer is accepted a date will be made for signing the *compromis* (exchange of contracts). Often in France it is the vendors who choose the *notaire* but there are no set rules. As in the UK you will be expected to pay a 5–10% deposit when you sign and a date will be agreed for completion. Probably because of the size of the Hexagon, and the distances to be travelled, there is no legal necessity to move in and move out on the same day, with all done and dusted before the banks shut shop in the early afternoon, as is usual in the UK. There is a breathing space of a couple of days allowed after the purchase money has changed hands and, although this may not seem important the first time around, it will be should you ever sell up in Normandy and move south to Montpellier. A word of caution: in the event of moving on, do not assume your friendly *notaire* will give you a cut price if you use him for both selling and buying. As the French Government controls the *notaire's* fees there can be no juggling with figures.

APARTMENTS

Many UK homemakers like the idea of an apartment in a block, an *immeuble*, rather than a house. An *immeuble de standing*, means it is of a superior quality. An apartment is certainly less of a responsibility if you are an infrequent visitor. Paying for interior and exterior maintenance is normal; the downside is you may be paying for services you are not using, like hot water, and central heating.

An apartment in a '*Residence*' is somewhat different. This is the upmarket version of apartment life. Generally built upon a sizeable swathe of green with trees, copses, lush flowerbeds and, frequently, a pool and tennis courts, many residences are luxuriously appointed with marble entrance halls and soft lighting in silent lifts. The great appeal of a *residence* for many householders is the absolute security. Electric gates, high walls and enclosed garages are the norm. A *residence* is a protected fortress of comfort and the ones I have known benefit from their own lively community life. The best Bastille Day party I have been invited to was in a *residence*. Everybody brought a consumable contribution, and the dancing went on into the wee small hours. My feeling is, if you want an apartment plus a sense of community, go for a *residence*. Here you will be paying for the janitors, the handymen, the gardeners, pool boys, and probably the communal hot water, but it's worth looking into, particularly if you buy with friends; that way you can ensure one of you will be using the place outside the annual summer hols.

DOMAINE

A *domaine* is an estate of houses, some detached some semi. They are usually rather stately residential areas with electric gates, and quiet, well-manicured meandering roads. Hedges and tended flower-beds provide a cosy seclusion; almost a small village atmosphere without the shops.

For this you pay, on average 30–45 euros per calendar month. The plus side is undoubtedly the safety factor, but you may be disinclined to pay the substantial monthly outgoing for this.

EN VIAGER

An unusual arrangement this, but more common than you might think.

In order to release income on property the householder, usually of advanced years and with no inheriting family, will sell the house for an annuity based on the property value. When the owner dies, the property falls legally into the hands of the purchasers. This obviously is a gamble; a gamble based rather unkindly on the imminent death of the ageing incumbent. But be warned. There have been many cases where the purchaser has shuffled off before the aged householder, who will thereby have gained the income as well as retaining the property.

Well, it is a gamble.

CO-PROPRIÉTÉ

This refers to a plot of land on which several houses have been built, and which could also be called a *residence*. The houses are usually of quality, all quite individual but adhering to certain rules of conduct; for example, you cannot operate a small business like a car workshop, and there are usually rules about what colour to paint the shutters, as there are in conservation areas, and no washing should hang on the front balconies. Nothing extreme, but rules nevertheless. Sometimes there is a small annual charge if the rubbish collectors have to make a special detour into the enclave.

Advertisers' jargon

Property advertisements need a little clarification. The number of rooms specified never includes kitchen and bathrooms. Thus a *4P* will provide three bedrooms, and a living room, plus kitchen and bathroom. A *6P* would give you four bedrooms, a salon and a dining room. A *salle de bains* is the bathroom while a *salle d'eau* is a shower room; *chauffage centrale* (central heating); *tout à l'égout* (mains drainage); *fosse septique* (septic tank) ; *poss. piscine* (room for a pool).

If you see the word *parc* don't get carried away; it simply means an extra large garden, so a *parc arboré* is a garden with trees. *Proche commodités* (near shops); *villa individuelle* (detached) *villa jumulée* (semi-detached; literally 'joined'); *villa mitoyenne* (terraced house); *hôtel particulier* (detached town house/mansion); *cuisine americaine* (kitchen/diner); *vue dégagée* (open view); *rez-de-chaussée* (street level); *rez-de-jardin* (garden level); *à ravaler* (to do up); *à saisir* (a property to snatch up).

This basic *immobilier's* vocabulary will serve as an introduction. The rest will depend entirely on his/her literary flights of fancy.

Useful French

alimentation en eau	water supply
aménager	to alter or convert
assainissement	disposal of sewage
bâtiment	building
cabinet	small room or office
cellier	store room
chaudière	boiler
cheminée	chimney or fireplace
double vitrage	double glazing
escalier	staircase
étage	*storey*

fuel	heating oil
grenier	attic
jardin d'hiver	conservatory
maison d'amis	second home
offre d'achat	offer to buy
pavillon	small, detached house
porte-fenêtre	French window
rangements	storage areas
salle de séjour	living room
vendeur	vendor
visite d'expert	property survey
volets	shutters

How about trying to learn a few?

Quelle barbe !   What a drag!

2
YOU AND YOUR BANK

Before the love affair with your dream goes any further, you will have to have a bank account. There are several types to choose from, with varying charges, but by and large they are all more expensive than in the UK. Throughout the country most small towns will have a Credit Lyonnais, Credit Agricole, and BNP Paribas and there are smaller regional banks, like the Banque Populaire du Midi in the south. The Caisse d'Epargne is more of a mutual building society than a bank, but can be found everywhere. They take deposits from nationals and foreigners alike and have a mortgage section for house purchases. In the UK we expect our high street banks to have the same interest rates and charges wherever the branches are located. Not so in France. Banks may have the same name, like Credit Agricole, but regional branches are autonomous, each with their own rules and scales of charges. There is a financial consumer website *www.testepourvous.com* which offers a click-on map showing regional banking costs. The post office (*La Poste*) also offers a banking service, which is noticeably one of the cheapest providers.

USING YOUR BRITISH BANK CARDS

French card machines are called *distributeurs,* just in case you have no cash and no dictionary. Incidentally Barclays Bank debit cards incur no charge when used in a BNP machine.

All British credit cards are surcharged at 2.75% for purchases. In addition there is a cash withdrawal fee for all ATM withdrawals in a foreign currency of 1.5–2%. For debit card cash withdrawals and purchases there is a surprising variation not only in the withdrawal fee but also in the extra currency conversion fee. See the table below for a few examples.

	Nation-wide	NatWest	HSBC	LloydsTSB	Barclays	Halifax
ATM charges	Free	2.65% +2.25% (£4 max)	2.75% +1.5% (£1.75 min)	2.75% +1.5% (£4.50 max)	2.75% +1.5%	2.75% +£1.50
Retail purchases	Free	2.65% +75p	2.75%	2.75%	2.75%	2.75% +£1.50
On top of this Nat West charges 75p per transaction, and the Halifax £1.50.						

Not difficult to see how banks make so much money out of us.

The most satisfying characteristic of the French bank for any foreigner is the wave of empathy you will sense from the first moment you talk to a bank clerk. Nowadays many are delighted to try out their English, and will lose no time in telling you of their sister/son/daughter who has visited the UK. Don't hurry away, be prudent. Take time to establish a relationship, whether it is with a personal banker, the foreign clerk, or the manager him- or herself. There may well be a moment in the future when you will want a sympathetic ear, help or advice.

There was a time when we could obtain this personal service from our English banks but, alas, it has all but disappeared. Fortunately it still exists in France even in the larger cities. You will fill in the usual application for a chequebook, and be asked for your address, which is printed on each cheque. There are hidden advantages if you choose to use your French address. You immediately become a part of the community, and your foreign-ness need no longer be underlined with a UK home base emblazoned on each page. In the old days it was imperative to use the UK address in order that statements were posted to you, but with Internet banking this is now unnecessary. Depending on how much money you are prepared to put in the new account you may be offered a debit card. Please note there are no credit cards in France, at least not as we know them in the UK. There is a system of 'deferred debit', i.e. you may store up debts incurred during the month, and on a particular date at the end of the month (each bank has its own set date) your debts will be debited from your balance, with no interest to pay. Should you be overdrawn, dash *post haste* to see your friendly banker, and have plenty of reasons ready. If friendship has lapsed, your account will be blocked.

The French take banking very seriously, and an overdraft is no laughing matter: it can be a criminal offence. No one is permitted to overdraw, particularly a foreigner, without first having an arrangement with the bank. For a small monthly fee you can take out an overdraft (*découvert*) facility and it is well worth it. Without it, you are given 15 days to clear any overdraft or the account is frozen for a year. But even with it, I would never advocate splashing out on that television without first chatting to your friendly cashier.

Hot news: BNP Paribas has just started a new scheme allied to debit cards and as the service is completely free, you just have to sign up for it. If you need to overstep your balance for the purchase of a large item of furniture for example, they will spread the cost over a few months at 1% per month. However experience still dictates they should know in advance!

Many years ago, before setting out from France on a Balkan holiday I paid off a few service bills for my French house thinking I could just about cover them. Alas I was unknowingly £30 in the red. It mattered not that I could clear the debt immediately I returned to France, my chequebook was withheld for a year, and my account frozen. Fortunately the bank

25

clerk with whom I used to have enthusiastic chats about Welsh and French rugby – (he used to turn up for work with various parts of his body *hors de combat* after each Saturday game) – paid all the service bills from my account directly from the bank. See what I mean about finding a chum in the chequebooks?

One final word about cheques; they cannot be stopped, so if you have made a dreadful mistake in a purchase, you will have to think up other means of getting your money back.

Some banks, like BNP Paribas, will create two accounts at the outset, your current account and a *compte d'epargne* which is a savings account paying interest, with no tax deducted if you are a foreigner. If the current account runs short you can transfer. I suppose it is the bank's way of making sure you have something to fall back on. Twenty euros is the minimum you may leave in your savings account. If you have money lying around not being used, the bank will suggest a number of interest-paying accounts, and if you are still a UK resident there will be no tax payable on the interest. Once you become a French resident you will have to pay some tax to the French fiscal system, which is not so bad as it sounds because it could serve you in good stead – but more of that later.

French debit cards are very useful, particularly if you are in the process of renovation and refurbishment. But even if you have several thousands in the bank designated for the task, don't think you can necessarily pay for all that serious bathroom equipment you have amassed on your king-sized trolley, on your debit card. Several times I have been embarrassingly either turned away from the check-out of a big DIY store, my card rejected, and either had to pay the difference on my British card, or use the French chequebook. According to the bank, rejection should only occur if you have been making cash withdrawals over your monthly limit, and not when paying by card for purchases. In my experience that is not necessarily so. These debit cards are easily confused. But it's banks again. They have a universally cunning method of squeezing as much out of you as possible.

BNP Paribas, for example, has currently three types of debit card, each one giving you a different cash facility related to the monthly charge for your particular card. Top card is gold, *(Premier)* which can turn somersaults, and give you a cash withdrawal facility of 1,500€ per month, but for this you pay 18.30€ per month. The ordinary Visa debit card allows you to draw out 500€ per month and costs 9.55€. In the middle there is *Amplio*, a card they constantly threaten to withdraw, but mine is still going strong after three years.

A final cautionary word about your French debit card *(Carte Bleue)*. Personally I can just about manage adding up, and long division if it is really necessary, but I do have trouble with numbers: numerical dyslexia I call it. Telephone numbers are a pain, but bank card numbers can be a disaster. I know they tell you to chew and swallow the paper on which your special digits are written, but life can't be all James Bond, so I have to write the figures down in a small corner of a diary which no one would recognise but me. The French card number has always been the problem, because used less than the British card, the digits were like strangers. Once I had them in my head and could use them with ease, I felt a smug triumph just like passing an exam. But one day, I must have been particularly tired, I tried three times to get them in the right order, and failed. As a result my card was blocked for three days. I therefore made a huge effort to learn them, but that didn't stop the knee-wobbling anxiety the next time I punched in the code. My hands trembled as the finger hovered over an 8, or was it a 9? It worked, but my nerves were so shredded I really felt like a lie down.

As well as your French chequebook always remember to take your passport with you when shopping, if you wish to pay on your British card. Even though French stores will chip and pin more recent UK debit/credit cards, you may still be asked for identification.

I have never really understood the value of having a safe deposit box at the bank, neither in the UK and certainly not in France – largely because I have never had anything valuable to deposit. But a few years ago when

27

I had sold our first *ruine* and could not be present to receive some cash, the estate agent volunteered to stand proxy and accept the cash for me, but insisted I open a *coffre* where the loot could be deposited, not by herself, too unethical, but by one of my friends. This I did and gave the friend the key. Alas, when said friend turned up with the money my banker – who had been apprised of the plan – was off sick, nursing a rugby pummelling and his understudy sent the friend packing. She sensibly banked the money in her own account and sent me a cheque. All was well, until she informed me a year later, she had lost the key to the *coffre*. Naturally I asked the bank for a duplicate. There was no duplicate, so for a few years I forgot about my *coffre* until I discovered I was paying a not insubstantial bank charge for this unused hole in the wall. Action was needed. No key, so the manager told me he would have to summon an explosives expert all the way from Montpellier. It seemed like overkill, but there was apparently no alternative. There would be a charge, of course, but I reasoned it would be cheaper than an annual payment for an empty box. All was arranged, and at precisely 11am on the chosen day a small dapper man carrying a large attaché case marched into the bank's reception area. 'You have lost the key *madame*?' he asked admonishingly. Head lowered, I nodded. The manager took us to a hidden staircase located behind pillars, unlocked an iron door, so impregnable it could have come from the Bastille, and escorted the explosives expert down into a vault. I was instructed to wait at the top of the stairs. Some time later the manager called. 'Please come down *madame*, *monsieur* is waiting for you.' My imagination ran riot.

The vault was thickly carpeted, and so luxurious you could have moved in. 'I shall leave you now *madame*', said the manager who climbed the stairs and with what looked like a sly smirk, locked us in.

Monsieur the explosives had already taken off his jacket and was examining a *coffre* that I assumed was mine. His attaché case open on the floor was crammed with gadgetry, presumably a professional exploder's kit. While he fiddled he chatted, non stop. This was uncomfortably similar to that Roman emperor, and there was no escape from this palace. He recounted how he had been summoned to a London city bank to perform a spot of exploding, and another time to a large insurance company in the city. Not daring to ask, I hoped he had been summoned by management on each occasion and that he was in the exploders' 'Who's Who'. Suitably serious he explained how much explosive he would need to use, because too much and we could both be blown up. He laughed. I wilted.

'Stand back' he commanded, whilst executing some deft surgery on the lock. I needed no commanding. I was already cowering in a corner. There was a small 'pouff' and it was over. The empty box sprang open, we shook hands and that was that.

All told I had paid about £300 for this pleasure.

TRANSFERRING FUNDS

The moment you become hell-bent on buying a French home, and have found a friendly bank, now is the time to think about transferring funds from the UK. British bank charges for this service vary, but as a general rule the more you transfer the better the rate, although they all make a buck or two.

On a transfer sum of £10,000, paid in euros into a designated French bank, the following rates apply.

1. From Barclays Bank

You may only transfer £5,000 at any one time on a standard transfer. This will cost you £20 and take about three working days, provided the bank begins proceedings by 4pm. A priority transfer – usually effective the next day – costs £35.

2. From Lloyds TSB

Up to £10,000, through their Euro money-mover service, will take up to three working days, and cost £20. The exchange rate will be tourist. Over

£10,000 any sum costs a flat rate of £30 to transfer. They have other rapid transfer schemes, and on a larger sum, you are given the commercial rate.

3. From the Co-operative Bank

They offer transfers for a flat rate of £8, through their Tipanet scheme. No more the endless form filling for this very reasonable service, the bank does it all internally. There is a stipulation, however, that you have a bank account with them. Tipanet allows you to transfer only € 12,500 (£9,000) at any one time, and the operation takes up to six working days.

Exchange rates

Exchange rates are a positive pain. We all want to have a good deal and having to decide on Monday a rate that could go up or down on Tuesday is like playing roulette. There are other ways of securing the rate you would like to have but which may not be currently available. It is called a Limit Order. You set the rate and the money will be transferred when the market achieves it. It could take time, but if you are in no hurry it is worth the waiting. The other option for money transfer is with an established foreign exchange expert. Their rates are extremely competitive.

With the constant fear of money laundering, if you are transferring hefty sums say from the sale of a UK property, your receiving French bank will require a fax of the completion statement and a signed letter from your solicitor, which should avoid your having a Maigret-type grilling.

Specialists

Here are a few reputable companies prepared to transfer without commission, promising to refund any bank receiving fees, and guaranteeing a better rate than any bank.

1. World First *www.worldfirst.com*. They promise same day transfers.

2. Currencies Direct email *info@currenciesdirect.com* (0845 130 8152). Sums of over £5,000 are transferred free of any charge, but they specify that only certain banks have no receiving fees.

3. Hifx *www.hifx.co.uk* (0845 880 1130). No commission and no bank receiving fees.

4. Money Corp *www.moneycorp.com* (0207589 3000). No commission, fast transfer, and no receiving fees, and their exchange rate at the time of writing is impressive.

Did you know that one in ten Brits lives abroad? We have the third largest number of expatriates, beaten at the finishing post by the Chinese in second place and the Indians coming first. Now there's food for thought.

Another way of transferring smaller sums of money is with old-fashioned cash.

There are a number of outlets in the UK that make no charge for exchanging sterling into euros, and if you spread withdrawals you could collect a sizeable sum. Great so far, because you have avoided bank charges. But now comes the problem; how to pay it into your French bank account without being stripped and searched as a terrorist arms dealer, even though your pocketful would just about cover a few headscarves. It all depends on the sum, and how well the bank knows you. For example, I have friends who spend a few months of the year in their French home. Each time they bring with them euro cash, usually about 2,000€ which they bank, and there is never any problem. I, on the other hand, once sold a car for cash – as one generally does – but buying another from a Peugeot garage was a different story. Nowadays garages can only accept a small percentage in cash for a sale, and the rest must be paid for with either a cheque or debit card. I took my sales cash to the bank to pay into my account, but was obliged to explain its provenance to the cashier who was most apologetic at having to ask.

Times have changed. Be prepared.

Here's another cash scenario. If like some friends of mine, you have recently withdrawn funds in the UK, and have arranged to keep a euro float in your pocket to pay for moving, workmen, helpers, emergency plumbing, etc., ask your solicitor to write a note to your bank confirming that you have had a reshuffle of funds, exact figures are unnecessary, and to forewarn them that you could well be putting sums of cash into your French account, just in case you decide to bank it.

MORTGAGES

Mortgages are obtainable through any bank and, in France at the time of writing, they are very reasonable. There are of course other ways of raising a mortgage than through a French bank. Adding to a UK mortgage is one possibility, but I would urge you to look at the French offers first. They could be far cheaper.

For those who feel safer when doing deals in the mother tongue, try *www.moltd.co.uk*, specialists in French mortgages or *www.frenchmortgage.com*, tel. 01869 278181.

Another company specialising in the expatriate loan market and wholly English speaking is *www.offshoreonline.org*, an expatriate fast track mortgage service; email: *info@offshoreonline.org*; tel. +44 (0)20 8333 9125.

I was once faced with the prospect of having to have a bridging loan in France. An English one would have been scary enough, but a French bridge was, I thought, one too far; so I tried my UK bank and, as a client of some 30 years, I assumed there would be no problem – after all they would have the collateral on my UK house, and the new French home. Their attitude was frankly extraordinary, considering my loss would have been their substantial gain in the event of an unforeseen catastrophe. To comply with their demands for this temporary help my income would have to have been £100,000 per annum. This particular high street bank would not even consider a mortgage for such a short span either. In fact, after 30 years as a client, I was so appalled with such dastardly, unscrupulous dealing I withdrew my account.

Whilst continuing the frantic search I found a French mortgage broker who was able to facilitate the loan, and tailor repayments to suit my pocket. Furthermore a board-room salary was quite unnecessary. They needed merely an assurance from my accountant that I could pay back interest.

In moments like these one really appreciates the full impact of the French Revolution.

USEFUL FRENCH

Au poil !	Great! Super!
Je m'en fous	I don't give a damn
Des clous !	No way!
Bande d'idiots	Bunch of idiots
Archi	Extremely
Archi-degeuelasse	Extremely disgusting
Et alors ?	So what?
Faire une gaffe	To make a mistake
Avoir du bol	To be lucky

3

PLANNING PERMISSION AND

SERVICES

Any alterations to the domicile requiring planning permission are dealt with either by the *mairie*, or by the local municipal authority, and a *Certificat d'Urbanism* is valid for a year. In rural areas the mayor will be the source of permission for most alterations, even for a swimming pool (see the last chapter about the *mairie's* power). Getting to know the mayor of your commune is always a vital piece of networking, and so much the better if he/she happens to be a sociable person. I had no trouble whatsoever in obtaining permission to convert a barn adjoining my village farm house into a *gîte*, nor in converting the old farm courtyard into a swimming pool. The mayor was invited round for a drink, taken on a tour of the crumbing remnants of two barns, and was very pleased at the idea of restoration. The only stipulation made was regarding the pool that in the event of fire, the *pompiers* (firemen) could use the water.

Opening up old windows and doors that have been bricked up, as in the UK, generally presents no problem, but if your window overlooks another's property, there is. It is all to do with the Napoleonic Code.

I first came across a reference to Napoleon's code through Stanley Kowalski's rantings in *A Streetcar Named Desire* and at the time dismissed it as literary licence. Not so. Napoleon spent years formulating social structure and citizens' responsibilities, and you are likely to find it rearing up where you least expect.

The code forbids open windows overlooking someone's land lest rubbish and worse be tipped out, and I can see his point, particularly with relation to the eighteenth century.

In our first *ruine*, a disused *bergerie* (housing for sheep and shepherd), situated in an old Protestant hamlet, the back of the building had no windows, only three slits in the thick stone wall wide enough to poke a rifle through. This was apparently a seventeenth century defence strategy, designed to pop passing Catholics. As a home firing range was never on our agenda we naïvely measured up for the smallest windows, and they were really small. Behind the house was a strip of wasteland, with tall weeds overlooked by our gun turrets. The land belonged to Madame, next door. It lay derelict and was used for nothing, not even her livestock. She was a very unpopular woman, known as the 'Village Poisoner' and certainly not a bundle of laughs. This was not a good start.

Early one morning I plucked up the courage to ask for her permission. I could hear her sandals flapping on the courtyard cobbles as bolts and chains were slowly released inside her forbidding outside door. She stood no more than one and half metres tall, and probably as wide. Dressed completely in black, she held in her hand the end of a long rope. At the other end and at the back of the courtyard, a large goat stood. His legs coquettishly crossed, he wore a straw hat at a jaunty angle. She waited and stared threateningly. Finally I managed to stutter the request for three small windows, hoping she would agree, as the weeds on her precious patch were as high as the gun turrets. In the silence that ensued the goat with consummate elegance strolled over and stood behind his mistress. They made a charming couple. I waited for her reply. She took a deep breath.

'Non', she snapped.

The goat as if on cue, snapped his mandibles in sympathy, and proceeded to chomp and digest every sunflower head in the luxurious patch behind her. The visual effect was mesmeric. I could say nothing.

Oblivious to the background scenario, Madame continued.

'Non! Non! Absolument non!' and slammed the door.

I barely saw her again, but the builder sneakily chipped away at the slits until they were big enough for very small windows. We were lucky.

In a different house some time later, I turned one large bedroom into two, leaving one half without a window, and the only place to make the opening was on the side of the house overlooking a neighbour's lean-to garage–cum–chicken run. I went to see them, hoping there would not be a re-run of the Poisoner and her goat.

They agreed yes of course I could have the window. No problem. A week later they changed their minds, so I went to see the mayor, and this time the law was on my side. All rooms have a right to have daylight. Overlooking someone else's land, opaque glass bricks must be used, but you may also insert an airbrick in the wall.

For more significant changes, i.e. changes that perceptibly alter the look of the building, permission is usually given by the local authority.

Some years later living in a town house, I created a terrace by taking off the roof of the back bedroom. As I was overlooking my own garden it did not occur to me that I should need planning permission until my neighbour, a charming Parisian whose holiday home was the mansion of our district, explained that as we were in a conservation area permission was necessary. He must have seen my look of despair. 'Don't worry', he smiled, 'I shall say nothing but perhaps you would be kind enough to add another half metre to your terrace wall.'

His balustrade and pillared stone staircase, fit for any Romeo, backed onto my garden wall and he obviously did not wish to be seen tripping down to breakfast in his dressing gown. Naturally we complied. Another learning curve.

Back again in a rural village I wanted to take off the front part of the attic roof to make a terrace, but not knowing who to ask I went to the Department's imposing planning offices in our nearby city, and collected sheaves of forms. I returned with the forms filled, photographs of the façade and three copies of a drawing showing how the proposed alterations would affect the aspect, plus three copies of a plan of the terrace. An architect friend suggested I made drawings from the photograph, adding a couple of sun umbrellas where once the roof had been. Because there was no significant change to the general aspect of the house, the municipal planners regarded my request as such small potatoes, they directed me back to my village mayor, happy for him to give his seal of approval, which he did.

Roof terrace walls must be 1.8m high if they overlook someone else's land; otherwise the regulation height is 1m. But always check first. Regulations have a way of changing overnight and it is not worth trying to go it alone. Somebody somewhere will complain about debris, dust and scaffolding, and there is no come back without permission, only aggravation.

I once complained about an accumulation of nine months' building debris from a house being massively renovated and practically rebuilt, within three metres of my front gate. We were in mistral country and the builder's lorry had tipped out loads of sand, cement and gravel, leaving disfiguring hillocks uncovered and open to the elements outside the site, thus blocking the three metre wide area between us. Permission had been obtained for this barricade from our genial mayor. Unfortunately he had not assessed the havoc the loose, swirling cement could create when blown into my pool.

After one weekend of mistral there were lumps of the stuff fixed firmly to the pool's base. Everyone knew what had caused this disaster, even the site builders. I asked the boss if they could please chip it away for me, but was refused. There was no redress and certainly no good will by that time. Apart from cement on the pool's smooth floor, while the mistral raged Lawrence of Arabia would have felt quite at home in our sand-covered courtyard.

The horse had left the stable, but to prevent a recurrence of neighbour problems with me, the boss finally put weighted tarpaulins over the offending building supplies. Common sense at last, but too late.

Mistral terrain or not, make sure delivered building supplies, whether your own or a neighbour's are covered up from the start. You will have no redress if high winds wreak mayhem, and the damage that could ensue, could be costly to put right.

There was a time when a builder could put Velux windows in your roof without the problem of planning permission, but no more. It certainly does not alter the aspect of the house, unless you are viewed from a low flying aircraft. Nevertheless two young relatives of mine living in a very rural area near Limoges were obliged to wait several weeks while the *mairie* decided whether or not they could put in two Velux windows on the back slope of their roof. Eventually they had their permission.

Although the same regulations pertain throughout the country, interpretation is a completely different ball game. Therefore if you are in a country district take time to get to know people, especially the mayor. We should never forget we are the foreigners. Be sociable, and don't worry about making mistakes in French. French people make mistakes in French, so use the words you have, however limited, and try to learn a few more.

Permission for any building addition in towns is another thing. Sometimes large conurbations have sub *mairies* that afford easier access and swifter replies to building demands. If you are in this situation don't forget to ask your estate agent. They usually know which button to press and whom you should see. And don't forget to find out first whether your house has any *cos residuel* (see previous chapter).

POOLS

If you intend to have B&Bs or start *gîte* holidays, a pool is fairly essential. Even if you are on the coast the beach may not be sandy, and most parents prefer to have the children within easy watching distance.

Permission for a swimming pool is relatively easy in the country provided you have the space; the minimum land required in most communities is 500m^2. In a town the waiting time is several months, and then much will depend on the urban density zone in which your house is situated, even if you have the land.

There are many companies that supply pools in 'kit' form. Had I known the problems this entailed I should have gone with a company that did it all and, quite frankly, the difference in cost would have been relatively insubstantial, if personal stress is taken into account. The forms to fill in are in triplicate, and complicated. Fortunately the 'kit' suppliers did that, and took the five photographs showing the proposed site from all angles.

Buying in 'kit' means you have to do all the rest of the organisation yourself, but in my case that was never really spelled out. First find the *terrassier* who arrives in his JCB and digs the big hole. My 'kit' man buzzed around like a demented mosquito when he found the hole was 12cm too deep. Naturally he blamed me, despite the fact that these two *mecs* (chaps) had had a long telephone conversation settling the finer points, as I thought, of the work in hand. Then there is the *gravier* (gravel) – enough, I thought, to reconstruct several bomb sites – and, of course, you have to employ workmen with muscle to throw a 10cm coverage into the hole. Someone else meanwhile is spreading the redundant soil over the rest of the garden like marmite, which you are not really supposed to do, but everybody does it as it is very expensive to get soil carted off. In any case my garden had a slope that needed straightening up. You see what I mean by escalating costs.

I had bought a pre-formed pool. Having previously had a constructed concrete pool, the pre-formed variety is certainly easier to clean. The pool's arrival is a moment of truth. The neighbours converge in little groups gasping with awe as the crane lifts the carcass over the hedge. It floats suspended like a deflated barrage balloon over the hole into which it is expected to slot like a piece in a jigsaw. Meanwhile cars wishing to get into work cannot pass. Neighbours' gasps are well-founded for the suspended object lurches twice, causing a volley of loud French expletives from both driver and the man with the kit. Finally the pool sits in place. But that is not the end. More sand, gravel and cement has to be delivered for your builder to make a solid collar around the pool, upon which your *piscinier* (the pool man) will place, not *pose* (fix), the surrounding tiles *(margelles)*: fixing them down is for someone else. Now it's the turn of your electrician/plumber to drill out channels for both services in order to make the pool active, and to fix the timing box on the wall of the cubby hole where the controls *(locale technique)* hide. The costs are never ending, but installing a pool is like having a baby, you forget all the discomfort of giving birth because it's so lovely when you finally see it.

Next time I shall buy a house with a ready-made pool.

Regulations vary depending on the *endroit* (location). In a low density urban area the pool has to be a minimum of fifteen metres from your neighbour's land and cannot be nearer the road than the outer wall of your house. Some towns stipulate the colour of the pool's shell. Nice, for example, insists on white, so if you want blue, move somewhere else. Above all make sure the plan submitted is punctiliously correct.

On one occasion a pool supplier to some friends of mine drew up the plan as part of the deal, but made a slight error regarding the positioning of the pool-house. When told of this by the *mairie* he submitted a corrected page. A month or two went by before being told the *mairie* could not accept redrawn pages, so the whole application had to be resubmitted. A further three months elapsed before the outline permission came through, and another month before the dossier was returned from the architects' department. Why involve an architect? Apparently to make sure the pool looked attractive in its surroundings! Bearing in mind this large area had been ignored from a horticultural point of view for years, the previous owner having used it as his private car park with ramp, the current owners were sure the city planners would be delighted with the changes that had been made; shoring up a palm tree, a protected species; transforming the raised scrub section into a terrace with vines along the border and plans to turn the area surrounding the pool into lawn. The pool company had already received a verbal 'oui' on their clients' behalf. Alas the day the pool was delivered the city men changed their minds and insisted the area had to be 50% vegetation, and the terrace demolished. A difficult situation.

After a few Gallic shrugs poring over the city planners' letter, a solution was found. A piece of plastic grass would be bought to cover half the terrace, where it would be left in place for a year then taken up. The total length of time on this project was about nine months, and left the pool owners with a nervous twitch, each time they walked past the city's Hotel de Ville (*mairie*) from thereon.

Be prepared for anything.

There are now even further regulations for pool builders. From 2004 all new pools must have an alarm system, either a sound or a sensor light and a cover. Existing pools, in hotels or in private B&B establishments are obliged to erect some type of fencing as a safety barrier. This new regulation has come about because 30 children were drowned in pools in 2003. Tragically accidents happen even with the most watchful parents. But one cannot help feeling this swimming pool regulation is a hammer to crack a nut in relation to the consistently high toll in road deaths about which very little is done that is effective.

CONSERVATION AREAS

If you buy a house in a conservation area find out about the approved house colours before you dab any paint on a shutter. I remember when Uzès in the Gard was quite rightly given historical status. Overnight the down-at-heel areas of the old town were spruced up, their grubby façades sandblasted to creamy white, and poorer properties with no bathrooms and no central heating muscled in on generous government grants. Stunning 16th century mansions were given makeovers, their beauty restored to exactly the same standard as it must have been when they were built. My house had been in the right *quartier* for a grant, and given the time and effort I could have filled in all the forms and enlisted the obligatory services of an architect but, as I had already sandblasted the house façade and was about to move back into the country, there was little point. However, if you find yourself in a conservation area there are always grants around to aid with refurbishment, so it is worthwhile talking to the *mairie*. But nothing is for nothing, and it probably means staying put for a specified number of years. All quite fair if that is what you want.

SERVICES

You will need a form of heating, even in the sunny south, and the central type will be the most comfortable and, if you intend to use *chez vous* frequently, the most economical as not only will you be able to visit throughout the year, but you also have the possibility of a winter let, which at least keeps the house aired. If you intend using the house only for the school summer holidays it will be a rather heavy initial expenditure. Better to wait until you decide to spend more time in *chez vous*. We managed for years, even with flying winter visits with oil-filled electric radiators. Depending on location you are unlikely to require heating for two thirds of the year but, even on the Riviera, from November to March, mornings and evenings need bursts of warm air. Effective heating varies with the type of house. Old stone houses, wonderfully cool in summer take longer to heat in winter, so electric radiators are expensive. It appears the insulation in some old houses – especially if the rooms are quite large – is so poor that it can reduce the heat generated by radiators by as much as 50%. Modern houses use electric heating far more efficiently.

The most economic form of heating in country areas is gas, the sort that comes in very large containers: expensive to install but relatively cheap to run. The trouble is you have to have a suitably large space a specified distance from the house in which to bury the monster. Cooking using portable gas bottles is very cost effective; they last a long time, and are used extensively. Even in a *baguette*-less hamlet there will be always be someone who sells gas bottles. But do remember to have a spare at the ready: nothing will drive you to the drinks cupboard faster than a table full of hungry youngsters and an oven full of uncooked food.

You will find that a high percentage of gas cookers (*cuisinières*) for sale in any hypermarket will have an integral bottle housing.

In the country I once had oil (*mazout/fuel*) central heating. It was reasonable to install, and run, but I had my doubts about the age of the boiler. It looked battered though it was supposed to be new, and from its size would not have looked out of place on the Graf Spee. It certainly did the job, but when it fired up the noise was horrendous. It reverberated throughout the village echoing like a heavy bombardment. Apart from my boiler being an embarrassment, the industrial-sized chimney the plumber had erected on the roof was worse. Villagers would stop and stare at this house turned factory.

So I was more than pleased when someone else in the village installed a similar system and with an equally earth shattering boiler. Hers would fire up regularly at 3am waking the village without fail, so quite naturally it became the focus of the boulangerie's gossip. At least mine kept more civilised hours.

Town gas (*gaz de ville*), if you are in the supplied areas, provides by far the cheapest form of cooking and heating, and the most efficient type of boiler is the combination. If the house you are buying has central heating, but has been empty for some time, don't forget to ask the owner to fire the system up for you, as the pipes may be too furred for efficiency, and buying a new boiler may not be in the budget. If it is, a combi boiler (*chaudière*) with installation, for a five/six bedroom house costs approximately 1,300€, assuming the radiators are all *in situ*.

As both electricity and gas are controlled by the same organisation EDF/GDF (*Electricité de France/Gaz de France*) reconnecting both is simple and quick with none of the worries about which company is responsible for what that are now encountered in the UK.

Bills come in every two months and meters are read every six months, but if you are not sure where you will be it may be safer to set up an arrangement with the bank (see page 76 for methods of payment). The best place for all meters is outside the property, but to change a meter's location is costly.

Many country domiciles have wood burning stoves for central heating, hot water and cooking and curiously, for some, the fuel appears to be free. Weekly excursions into the surrounding countryside to forage for wood can be a way of life. A neighbour I once had, Eli, built a long low-slung trailer for the sole purpose of collecting logs. The whine of his chain saw was heard throughout the village for days after a haul. His house was so small I could never believe that all those neatly stacked logs, crammed into his workshop leaving barely room to stand, were for his personal use. Every year he declared he was ready for the next ice age.

In some parts of France purchased wood is sold by the tonne and cut to any length. I have been told of a curious standard of measurement, which relates to the arm length of the man buying it. Should you come across this old tradition make sure you have a de Gaulle with you and not a Napoleon.

Wood burning stoves make a really potent focal point and can throw out incredible heat. The sight and sound of a burning log fire is evocative of peace and comfort and can be a satisfying, though frequently labour-intensive, form of heating.

WATER

Meters to cover the costs of household water usage plus town/village cleansing (*Eau et Assainissement*) are the norm in France, and charges between regions vary considerably. But be aware that mistakes, and serious ones, can be, and are made by water companies, so make sure you feel satisfied with what you are being asked to pay before you write that cheque.

Some years ago when I was about to move from the town into the country, like a good citizen I called at the water office to give them the name of the new owner. Within minutes a jubilant *madame* told me I had the equivalent of £450 to pay in retrospective water charges. I laughed thinking she was joking, but she was quite serious, adamant that this money was owed. By this time several office staff had gathered around her by way of support. It was impossible, I protested. I had made only two flying visits in the past eighteen months and alone. It would have been cheaper to bathe in asses' milk. I laughed again. They did not. I would have to write out a cheque for the amount or the new owners would have no water. This was particularly serious as my account was flat broke and, although I was due to return to the UK the following day, it would take a few days to transfer money. However the shadow of the guillotine loomed large so my trembling hand wrote out a post-dated promise which, surprisingly, they took. I should add this is not thought to be an acceptable business practice in France, but on this occasion they really had no choice. With no time to lose I leapt upstairs to the *mairie's* central office, where the same set of figures came up on a computer. All my counterfoils of bills paid to the water department, my only means of defence, were in the UK, so I took the name of the head of department to call him immediately I returned.

Justice finally prevailed. Not only did I have all my water bills, fully paid up, but also I was also able to check them against old chequebook stubs.

Jubilantly I telephoned the office. There was some coughing and an embarrassed silence. The chief was not available, but yes they had confused me with another family of the same name, and of course I had nothing to pay, and my post-dated cheque would be torn up.

But just like government ministers there was no apology, which proves that bureaucracy is the same insensitive animal everywhere.

The lesson to be learned here is be prudent about throwing anything away, at least until you move. The general advice is to keep all old cheque stubs for thirty years, because they are proof of payment and because a civil action, in case of litigation takes that long to be launched! Mortgage contracts, bank statements, house and car insurance, and all bills of work carried out should be kept for ten years. So you will need that extra room.

I moved into my present town house at the end of August a few years back, alone, except for an intermittently visiting builder. He would work for an hour or two in the morning, break for lunch, leaving his sweetly inefficient minions to slog on in the heat and eat their baguettes on the hoof. He would always return about 4pm completely blotto, and attempt to drive them home an hour later in his clapped out old van. Fortunately the work had been almost finished when I asked him to take himself off permanently. I remained on site using only a washing machine from time to time, and the daily shower.

Two weeks before leaving in mid September, I received a bill from the local water board for €2,500. Flabbergasted was an understatement. I telephoned. Surely there had been a mistake. No, that was what I had consumed. Was I a hotel? Did I have an enormous family bathing several times a day? Absolutely not.

Perhaps the meter had not been paid by the out-going proprietor? It had been. After several worrying days and nights an agent of the water board came to see me. Fortunately the water meter is outside the house, so each week during my subsequent absence, the agent, a gentle soul called Monsieur Poésie regularly monitored the meter for leaks. There were none. Finally in March I was sent a very modest bill quite in keeping with the modest amount of water used. I paid the bill personally at the water board office, and asked about the alarming mistake. They were very sorry, but it had been a computer error.

Remember to take a reading of your meter when you move in, and when you receive your first bill. It is worth taking time to calculate roughly your usage against the regional charge per cubic metre. Water authorities reckon the average adult uses 500 cubic metres per week.

Useful French

Il est nul !	He's useless!
Manquer de bol	To be unlucky
Chiper	To nick (steal)
C'est vache	That's too bad/that's rotten
Quelle mouche te pique ?	What's got into you?
Il y a un os	There's a hitch
à l'oeil	Free/gratis
Une fine bouche	A gourmet
Au dodo !	Off to bed!
Le nounours	The teddy bear
Une bonne affaire	A good bargain
L'epargne	Thrift

4
GETTING STARTED

If you have four walls standing, a roof, one solid floor, and running water you have the basic necessities for a summer camp. A spring camp can be a disaster.

We made a big mistake in our first hovel by assuming that March south of Lyons, would be as balmy as an English summer. It was so bitterly cold we had to put the camp beds together at one end of the large kitchen-diner in order to share the heat from one electric fire and a fan heater. There was no hot water at that point, and a cold shower (that particular piece of apparatus was installed and working, likewise the loo), was out of the question. Strip washes were *de rigueur* and were taken sitting in the shower tray with a bowl of hot water. By late afternoon the temperature in our communal igloo began to rise, and by nightfall we would retire to the camp beds, the children warm and tired, whilst we clambered between the sheets in a roseate haze induced by wine and good food. The mornings were quite the reverse, requiring all the enthusiasm of a Girl Guide camp to expose even one toe to the savage elements. The previous incumbents had fared far better.

They were sheep.

Be warned and be prudent

It is easy to be carried away with your *chez vous*; what you would like to do/install/embellish/demolish. But soft! Make a short list, really short, of the absolute basics required. Obviously if you find a domicile with water and a bathroom, no matter how primitive, you have a head start. Providing the roof is reasonable, take your time, and concentrate on the things you can do yourself, like cleaning and painting. There is nothing like transforming a grimy, gloomy room into something sparkly clean to give you heart for the next step.

Essential basics

Electrics

Older houses usually need rewiring. You may have done the electrics at home quite successfully, but French electrics are not the same, so it is best to leave it to the French electrician even if you are a professional. EDF regulations are far tougher than ours and if the system has to be rewired it will have to be inspected by the EDF. They could be even tougher if you are not French. Extensions to a previously approved system are different. I know dozens of Britons who have extended their own power and light with no problem and no interference. The electrician will ask you how much power you would like. The lowest is 6kW. This is usually enough for a small household, particularly in summer. In winter, if you are using a number of electric heaters, the electric kettle and start the washing machine all at the same time, you will probably be plunged into darkness until something is turned off, and you locate the trip-switch. Just be sure you always have a ready supply of candles and you can find them in the dark. In country areas storms also play havoc with the electricity supply, as so many cables festoon the skyline just inviting a lightning party. Putting cables underground is now top of the agenda in many rural communes, and something a prospective purchaser should ask about.

The next power stage is 9kW, and then 12kW each up-grade having an increased standing charge. If your four-bedroom house with a couple of bathrooms is served solely by electricity you will need 12kW, certainly in winter.

Plumbing

French plumbing used to be and, to a degree, still is, a joke to the British, despite the fact that it is excellent, highly sophisticated and with more choice of ultra modern bathroom equipment than you could dream about. I suppose it is because in some isolated areas you can still find a wayside café with a squatting loo, as indeed you do in the odd motorway lay-by. Nonetheless, when it comes to putting in your state of the art bathroom, France will offer more choice and at a far more reasonable price than the UK. I know a few families who make sorties to DIY shops in Calais for the sole purpose of buying bits for the kitchen and bathhroom.

Main drainage is called *tout à l'égout,* and nowadays even small hamlets have their main drainage but, if a house is not connected, a linking *branchement* (connecting pipe) will have to be dug in, and that means re-plumbing the whole system. This may well be an unforeseen expenditure for a new buyer. In more isolated parts of the country you will have to go for a *fosse septique* (septic tank). Putting in a *fosse septique* is a specialised skill, because if it goes wrong the village knows about it. It's also something that the *mairie* is now responsible for supervising: all properties not on mains drainage receive a visit from a private company acting on behalf of the *mairie* and they have the power to advise, and ultimately impose, improvements.

Our first *ruine* had no water, and the hamlet no mains drainage therefore once the water had been brought in the only way to take it out was through a *fosse septique.* Our self-styled architect seemed to know exactly what size was needed and that it would be placed under the window of the projected shower room on the street side of the ground floor, with the loo directly above it on the first floor.

I could understand that bit.

Several months later we were all looking forward to returning, not to a pile of bricks but to the beginnings of our holiday home.

The local plumber had done a splendid job. We had an excellent shower with plenty of hot water and a super flushing loo. But the fosse? It was the size of a burial vault, and although there was plenty of room for it under the shower room window, it was the smell. Unused to septic tanks we thought the smell was normal, until the villagers, charming and polite as they were, could be seen holding their noses as they walked past the house. The fact our hamlet had only one narrow street made it worse. We were given advice, told what disinfectants to buy, what powder to throw down.

This we did to absolutely no avail. We, and possibly our diet, were the topics of conversation throughout the village. Smells would emanate from the burial chamber each time the loo was flushed, never mind being used. We sprayed air fresheners in the house, outside the house, up the village street, on our persons. It was a nightmare. Finally, our increasingly angry complaints to the self-styled architect about the anti-social behaviour of the fosse, forced him into action. A tall thin tin chimney, taken off a Romany caravan I suspected, was erected on our roof terrace presumably to foul up the ozone layer above rather than the street below.

We were assured this would do the trick. The result was worse. Not only did the shower room continue to smell – we were closing all windows by this time – but suddenly in the middle of a gentle siesta on the roof terrace depending on the prevailing breeze, a pungent aroma of boiled onions would assail the nostrils.

The village suffered with us. Our fosse was their fosse. Noses were gripped even tighter between thumb and forefinger each time they walked down the street. We took to using loos in restaurants, cafés, anywhere but at home. At the end of that first holiday we decided something had to be done. It was the fosse or us.

A few days before we were due to return to the UK, my husband fell victim to a touch of Montezuma's Revenge. Gallantly at 4am, he staggered out of bed saying he couldn't possibly use the loo; think of the children, think of the village, we almost thought of France. So saying, in slippers and dressing gown he walked out of the house like Captain Oates of the Midi to find a quiet patch in a foreign field. We were surrounded by dense shrubbery, trees and garrigue, and with dawn breaking he found a suitable site. As he was proceeding to descend groundwards in a crouching position, a deafening salvo blasted forth from within touching distance. There was a moment of silence, then a frantic rustling in the near-by bushes. About ten local men whom he knew emerged from the camouflage brandishing shotguns hip flasks and bottles of wine. Nothing was better designed to put a bung in nature. In a flash he had rearranged his garments, and attempted to create the impression he was taking a sunrise stroll. 'Bonjour Monsieur' followed by hand shaking, introductions, and liberal quantities of alcohol. Had monsieur forgotten this was the first day of the chasse? Monsieur had certainly forgotten.

The fosse was having unforeseen knock-on effects.

We drove back to the UK and mains drainage but the fosse was never out of mind. When we returned the following spring, we found the village street inaccessible. The road was up. Within minutes a posse of jubilant villagers greeted us with the best news since Ghent communicated with Aix. Our fosse had created such havoc in the village even without being used that a deputation of the whole village – all sixteen inhabitants – had been to see the mayor of the commune. He arrived, sniffed, and that was that. A few days later a sewage pipe was ceremonially laid. That night, chains were pulled with abandon. The cost for us was 2500F (£250) and worth every sous.

DIY (BRICOLAGE)

There are scores of DIY shops in every town in France. It is a national pastime. These shops are bursting with every conceivable type of gadgetry to help the *bricoleur* (the DIY enthusiast). There is one particularly large chain, Castorama, which is now part of our own B&Q. You will find similarities in stock even down to the shape and size of their proprietary brand of paint. Although paint is cheaper in the UK, there are always exceptionally good special offers, worthwhile buying even if you are not ready to use it just yet.

Of course DIY shopping can be not only exhausting but it can drive the mildest souls into doing something completely out of character. Castorama, for example, should have a B&B attached to it or at least a good bistrot, because there time passes at a rate that would have made Einstein raise his eyebrows. The problem is, there are plenty of goods on display, all very good value and, in my opinion, it is the best place to find kitchens, bathrooms, flooring and paint under one roof, but the first task is finding an assistant.

You arrive at 9am. ready to buy for the new bathroom, and search out a member of staff in the *salle de bains* (bathrooms) section. This could take time, but at least there is plenty to look at. Once you have communicated, been advised – they are always helpful – he/she will then go to his/her computer point, and type out a *bon de commande* (order form). Unfortunately there are other assistants queuing up for the same point, or worse still, the computer doesn't work. It is now 11.30am and so far you have only bought a shower tray. With your feet ready to lash out – your tongue remains paralysed because you don't have a flow of French invective – you decide to buy all you need for the kitchen and the floor, and get it all delivered; you cannot waste any more precious time.

Eventually you are asked for your address, and a delivery date is fixed. Clutching the *bon de commande*, damp from your nervous grasp, you go to the desk of that particular department, join a queue and pay, telling the cashier that you wish to add more items to your delivery. She prints out more sheaves of paper and gives you a duplicate with a stapled receipt.

You go to *carrelages* (tiles), search for an assistant; tricky, because by now it is the holy hour when French hearts and minds are grittily concentrated on food, and anyone with a lean and hungry look will not give you the attention you require. Be patient. A post lunch-break assistant is easy to spot. If he looks replete, flushed and smiles easily, he's your man, so grab him. You make your choice of tiles, he calculates the number of boxes, but he needs his computer point. Impossible, they are all taken. You wait. Your feet chomp the floor, your tongue is swollen with immobility and anger. Finally a computer point is free, but guess what, they have no stock of your tile choice, but there are some in a store 200km away. Too far, go back and select another tile.

More than an hour later, with more sheaves of paper printed from a machine that has intermittent paralysis resulting in the printing process having to be aborted and restarted several times, you arrive at the *carrelages* checkout. You pay for the tiles, all added to your delivery.

With more sheaves, stapled receipts and satisfying surges of something accomplished, you make for the *cuisines* (kitchens) department. Glory be: it is almost empty, and not an assistant in sight. However, you make your choice from the ample display units, gravitate towards the central desk which is obviously the epicentre of transaction because there is one efficient kitchen person sitting there in control like the captain of a spacecraft surrounded by machines. More waiting while efficient kitchen person finishes giving answers in French naturally, to a queue of other bewildered/anxious/cross customers. Finally you get to sit down, she buries herself in the computer, tells you what's in stock and what you will have to wait a month for. You decide to buy whatever there is available, because by now you don't care. Desperation has set in. You need food and need the loo. Neither is at hand. You grit your teeth and wait.

With a new '*bon de commande*' you proceed to the checkout queue. Your new purchases will be added to the delivery. Great. You have more sheaves of paper and another receipt stapled to your impressive collection. But now, your DIY enthusiast remembers he must buy some plasterboard, might as well buy it all together, on the one delivery charge. With a folio of flapping papers you grimly go to the brick and plaster department outside. Your DIY enthusiast chooses large pieces of toy-town bricks with which to build the extra bathroom, and you proceed to the paying shed where an assistant sits at a computer. You pay, present your sheaves of paper and ask to add the toy-town bricks to the delivery, only to be told that the last person you paid closed off the delivery and that you have to start all over again.

At this point the moon has risen, your bladder is in turmoil, your stomach has dropped out and your tongue has shrivelled. You could try fainting, but it's better to muster all the finer bits of your emotional makeup, with great fortitude subdue your feelings, and whilst trying to appear the victim, plead ignorance, you don't need many words for this, and blame the last checkout assistant, adding a hopeless Gallic shrug and wan smile. This generally works because they, like you, are also victims, and before long the shed person will be confiding in you about all the internal organisational problems that drive them crazy too.

A final word about major DIY shopping, avoid the summer if possible. Everyone wants to make their house improvements during the summer holidays, and if equipment has to be ordered it isn't likely to come through in August, when France and its factories close down.

One of the many endearing characteristics of the French generally, is no matter how affluent or well established they may appear, to a man and woman they are commendably aware of costs and of guarding the 'sous'. Always remember a Frenchman's home is his *château*, and knowing where to find the best DIY deals is an essential component of life. You have only to ask, and you will be told.

HOUSE INSURANCE

Don't ever think you will not need house insurance. You will! If you are able to inherit a house *assurance*, take it and be thankful. Many insurance companies in France do not like second homeowners. There are some British companies who offer a second home insurance but, just like a car breakdown, it can take a while to sort out, meanwhile you have to pay. On the other hand if you have a 50/50 existence between the UK and Britain, or your neighbour has the key, or you have someone in your apartment/*gîte*, there is generally not much of a problem. For a large 6– 7 room house you would pay about 37€ per month. If you have kept a *pied a terre* in the UK then your French house is your *domicile principale*. If you expect to be absent for several months you'll need to arrange for a neighbour or your *femme de ménage* to make weekly house visits. Any sudden problem within an apartment is likely to make its presence known to neighbours quickly, so always be contactable. Should catastrophe strike when you are *in situ* the emergency services will arrive promptly and should they ask if you would like them to call up your insurance company for you, let them. In distress the brain of even a competent French speaker plummets into a catatonic torpor.

I once awoke, fortunately quite early one bright morning to feel the blistering waves of a sauna outside my bedroom door. This was unnerving as I did not have a sauna. I soon discovered the source of heat was coming from the family bathroom, currently unused. Gallons of hot water were cascading down the stairs into the hall and kitchen below.

Water, water everywhere, I had enough sense to turn off the water supply and to telephone the nearest plumber. Thankfully he offered to telephone the insurance company as soon as he arrived. My brain was dead. Three hours later the plumber and his three apprentices – two were no more than fifteen – had repaired the split hot water pipe in the washbasin, put in a new *robinet* (tap), punctured the ceiling several times to allow a deluge of imprisoned hot water to fall free and mopped it up. He was a cheery soul this large plumber and so he should have been with the extortionate sum he was supposedly charging my insurance company, via my chequebook in the first instance. As he left I made a weak lament about the amount of water we had lost. His large face split in a grin. 'Well *madame*, think of the water you lose when you have a baby.'

I'm still trying work that one out.

Useful French

Etre dans la merde jusqu'au cou !	To be in deep shit!
Un tacot	An old slow moving car
En bon français	To put it simply
Une histoire marseillaise	A tall story
De pied ferme	With determination
Une grande gueule	A loudmouth
Le gratin	The upper crust
Un Parigot	A Parisian
Un plouc	A country bumpkin
Un type/mec/gars	A fellow/chap
Une bonne femme	A woman
Un gamin	A kid
Un bouquin	A book
Un velo	A bike
Un coup de fil	A telephone call

5
FINDING THE WORKFORCE

Personal recommendation of a labour force is the best way to minimise disasters, and even then there is an element of lottery. The estate agent will always know someone, but may decline to recommend for self-protection. In a village/small town, the *boulangerie* is the local oracle, the hot-line to everybody, and will know of any house renovations being carried on within a sizeable radius. The same goes for the *tabac* and *bistrot*. If you are in a larger community ask the neighbours, and any British people in the area. Of course if they have found a gem and want to keep him, don't be surprised if they become oddly furtive.

It is worth remembering that prices charged to Britons can sometimes be higher than those charged to nationals, so check out any estimates with a French neighbour. In certain highly-populated areas of France you will find British builders. Some are genuine builders and excellent whilst others have hopped on the property bandwagon, and have no professional skills, other than being averagely adept at DIY and having the gift of the gab. They know how much easier it is, if your French is limited, to explain what you want to a fellow Brit. For this advantage you will probably have to pay. Ask questions before you commit to anything.

If all else fails go to the *mairie*. There they keep a list of approved artisans, and current general building costs. I wish I had known this several years and houses ago. I can think of a number of builders who would never even make the *mairie*'s waiting list.

It is always prudent to have three estimates *(devis)*. I find estimates difficult enough in English, especially if the builder has recently done a course and spills out technical jargon, but in French it is awesome, so have a dictionary handy. For example, a *télérupteur* is not someone who talks through your favourite TV programme, it is a light switch. It took me years to realise that to *pose* a wash-basin/lavatory/shower, means simply to fix it in position. On some *devis* you will find the extra words, *mise en service,* which means it will be connected up and left in working order. If these words are omitted it does not necessarily mean your loo will be left solely as a conversation piece, but it is worthwhile checking. Only if the word *fourniture* is included will the article be supplied, so if you expect the article to be supplied, and left plumbed/working, look for '*Fourniture, pose, et mise en service*'. Always check.

If *chez vous* is going to be your holiday home, for your own peace of mind you have to find a builder whom you can trust to get on with work in your absence. In my last house I was fortunate enough to find a builder who was not only a first class worker, he also had impeccable taste, so I had no worries when he had to choose tiles for a small terrace in my absence.

Many workers will want to work in the 'black'. In fact the French government have such stringent, not to say punitive, tax requirements that many small artisans find it difficult to survive, and therefore working for cash is an attractive option. It may be for you too, but it can backfire. *TVA* (VAT) is charged in exactly the same way as in the UK, on materials and labour but, aware of the problems and loopholes, the French government have sensibly reduced this tax to 5% on the restoration of old buildings. If this should apply, in my opinion it is better to bite the bullet, find a registered company, one with a '*siret*' number, pay the 5% tax and most important, keep all the bills. Should you ever decide to sell on, (see next chapter) these bills could be lifesavers or certainly money-savers.

Habit and tradition go hand in hand with the building trade, and one has to accept the fact that given our two cultures, building problems are solved in different ways, and that the two do not necessarily mix.

On one occasion I had damp walls in the sitting room and adjoining kitchen, and it appeared to be the rising kind, probably due to an old communal well, which sprang into life underneath the damp wall. I spoke to several highly competent builders, none of whom had heard of the hacking-off plaster, injecting, coating and replastering technique. I assume that this is a particularly British method of dealing with damp, no doubt due to our climate. The French solution is a 'cloison contre l'humidité', a complete dry lining damp course. It is effective but you lose several centimetres of room space. Otherwise for a small area to cover, French builders go for one of the many waterproof sealers on the market.

Having asserted that national building traditions do not necessarily mix, the following saga and its disastrous results will prove the point.

During the first August in my small townhouse in southern France, owing to work in the UK and the pressures of time, I took over a couple of British builders whose work I knew, reasoning that if I were not around, better the devil you know. Having a free weekend we hired a van into which we piled a bathroom suite, two washbasins, two loos, kitchen units and two new divan beds with their bed linen. At the time sanitary equipment and basic new furniture was far more expensive in France. They agreed to work for a weekly wage to be paid in francs, and I opened an account at the local builders' merchant. This meant they could just point to materials in the yard, as neither knew a word of French. The house already had one cold tap, and an outside loo. They agreed to fit the kitchen, put in a bathroom, washbasins in bedrooms, and a shower and loo in the top floor attic room. There was nothing here they had not done before. But I also wanted a small roof terrace created from the attic floor's separate back bedroom, which meant taking the roof off. I was assured there would be no problem. Lifting off the roof was easy and they would simply waterproof the existing tiles. Yes, but were they the proper tiles I asked? Again, with a certain amused male patronage I was assured they were. At that point I left them to it and returned to the UK. I know they worked late because much later I discovered my neighbour, the suave Parisian, had asked them to stop hammering at 10pm. Not that they had been working like slaves; unused to strong sun and cheap wine, they had lain comatose in an alcoholic haze each afternoon. However they completed the work and returned apparently squabbling and disgruntled.

Not nearly as disgruntled as I became the following January.

I received a telephone call from friends to whom I had given the house key. After a spell of heavy rain they had called at the house purely on a whim. On opening the front door a putrid smell had assaulted their nostrils. It came from upstairs.

No fosse this time and certainly no body, both builders had returned home. It was mould covering the main bedroom that lay underneath the new terrace. Ceiling and walls were covered with an evil smelling slimy layer of black, and part of the ceiling was already down, lying on rotted bedclothes and black divan beds. Even the new floor rugs had been eaten with mould. Everything had to be thrown away, and my friends gallantly covered the sodden terrace in a plastic sheet as a temporary measure. I returned a month later and found French builders to relay the terrace with correct tiles and lead waterproofing. To add insult to injury they had to re-plumb both leaking washbasins.

The moral of this tale is always use local builders especially for something as important as a terrace. They know the climate, the country and local building traditions. A costly learning curve.

USEFUL FRENCH

Degueulasse	Disgusting
Moche	Ugly/lousy
Un bordel	A balls-up/mess
Sympa	Friendly
Crevant(e)	Exhausting
Rigolo	Funny (amusing)
à la gomme	Useless
Paumer	To lose
Un salaud	A bastard (careful where you use this!)
Une salope	A bitch (this one too!)
Le vieux	The old man
Un chameau	A nasty person (lit. camel)
Putain !	(lit. whore) Oh my God! (know the company)
Un petit merdeux	A little twerp
Le palpitant	The ticker/heart

6

FURNISHING *CHEZ VOUS*

If you are a junk-a-holic, you will find the second-hand scene in France full of surprises and very rewarding. There are several centres specialising in furniture and white goods, quite apart from the more upmarket *brocante/antiquités* fairs and shops which have varying degrees of quality stock, from rusty portable tin bidets to stunning 18th century *boule* commodes, and Aubusson carpets.

The recycling of artefacts in France is remarkably well organised, and if you know where to look for your household needs it will save precious time. There are about eight main sources of supply to be found throughout the country.

Troc De L'Ile

With 75 shops resembling large warehouses dotted around France you will find anything – be it fridge, bidet, sofa or window. Once I even found an antique *lit-bateau* for 600F. In 2004 I bought a very good outdoor glass dining table with four sturdy dining chairs for 70€. Washbasins are usually cheaper than anywhere else, but every *Troc* is different. So, although it is possible to find a minor antique gem, it is also possible to find shelves of kitsch, plastic, and overpriced rubbish. The price on the ticket is what you pay and it is almost impossible to bargain. These are second-hand furniture depositories where the *Troc* takes a percentage of the sale and, although started only twenty years ago, independent franchises have now spread to Spain, Belgium and Switzerland. The *Troc* is probably the best place to dispose of your unwanted furniture.

LA TROCANTE

This is another *dépôt-vente* (second-hand shop) chain of hypermarkets with 44 warehouses throughout the country. There is a particularly good one in Valence. This again is a non-bargaining chain: prices tend to be fixed.

DÉPÔT-VENTES/GRENIERS

Every town has one, and if you are in doubt ask at the tourist office or at the *mairie*.

Prices here are far less rigid, depending on whether the owner wants a quick turnover, wants the space or is fed up with seeing the object. Generally these shops are full to bursting with the nation's domestic cast-offs: sofas, buckets, chairs, tin baths. Outside on the forecourt you usually have to pick your way through sinks, bidets, loos, shower trays, doors, windows and, possibly, farm implements. There is usually plenty of good turn-of-the-century furniture, but be prepared for elbow grease and paint stripper. The French equivalent to our Victoriana is Henri IV, a medieval king whose period style was revived in 19th century France. There used to be far more Henri IV around, but the current generation of young professionals have suddenly wised-up to its quality and have started buying.

VIDE-GRENIER

Throughout the year you will catch notices of these events usually handwritten and nailed to a tree, or stuck on a lamp post, rather like a message from the sheriff in old cowboy movies. These are generally homespun affairs like garage sales, as the name implies 'empty the attic', though increasingly they are becoming more like car boot sales. They are always worthwhile visiting and it's a great way to meet the neighbours.

EMMAUS

Another centre of second-hand everything with depots not only all over France but also some are appearing in the UK. This organisation is quite different from the others. It was started 1949 by Abbé Pierre in Paris as a humanitarian movement to help displaced victims of Europe's war from refugee camps, but now encompassing the needy, the homeless and ex-convicts.

Near each Emmaus depot is a hostel providing lodging and a small weekly wage for those who serve in the various departments. All goods are donated, and prices are really minimal, so it would be churlish to try to bargain, besides which, it is a very good cause. I bought a dozen delicate brass fingerplates for about £10. Some friends found a complete new bathroom suite with Jacuzzi bath for £30.

I doubt if you will find a missing old master in Emmaus, but for basic house furnishing it is well worth a visit.

LES PUCES

Apart from the well-documented flea markets of Paris and other large cities, you can find out about these local affairs usually by word of mouth, the local free paper, or sometimes the tourist office. They are really the French equivalent of a car boot sale, but generally with a more interesting and a greater variety of merchandise. The only trouble is that you must be there ready to bargain by about 7.30am and most of them take place on a Sunday. The true *aficionado* will have no difficulty because, as we all know, this is when the real pickings can be found.

My greatest regret was passing over a set of French wire garden furniture, four chairs and a table, for 130F (£13).

FRIPERIE

If you love crisp white bed-linen from a bygone age, lace-edged, panelled, embroidered, and even monogrammed, then go in search of your local Friperie.

Les Frips are not a country-wide chain, and are found only in certain towns. Again they are large warehouses (the one I know best resembles a wartime Stalag), and are entirely given over to textiles gathered from all over Europe, mostly Germany and Switzerland. Here you will find crimplene tat, bankrupt stock, factory clearance, mixed with Dior and Lanvin. If your local town does not have a warehouse there will surely be a *frip* stall in your local market; always worth a rummage.

BROCANTE SHOPS

Brocante means second-hand, but these shops generally go for the minor antiques, as well as hugely overpriced rubbish. Some really are rip offs, so have an idea of value before you start.

ANTIQUE/BROCANTE FAIRS

These are usually the bi-annual/annual 3–4 day events held throughout the country. Keep your eyes on notice boards and ask at the tourist office or *mairie*.

These *foires* are fascinating, fun, and a bargain hunter's paradise. Surrounding the large space designated for the event are scores of refreshment stalls for weary punters.

It is probably the one place where you can be caressing a Louis XV bureau with one hand whilst holding a Toulouse sausage in the other. No class distinction here. Plastic carriers are the norm and, although you will see stunning antiques that could well end up in a posh salon, bargains are to be found, particularly if you postpone your visit to the last day. Naturally these fairs are full of foreign dealers, and the British are well represented but, of course, the expense of the journey has to be covered by the mark up on the furniture bought, to say nothing of dealer profit. I often wonder how many times pieces change hands before they reach their optimum price ticket in an antiquarian's shop.

There are stalls overflowing with tapestries and curtains that once must have graced a château, and 19th century rococo mirrors can be bought for less than half the UK price. Remember to take cash and your French chequebook, and although cards are not welcome, the vendors will always point you in the direction of a *dispenseur*: a cash machine.

Furnishing your *chez vous* need not burn an unacceptable hole in the budget. There is a wide selection of second-hand furniture from which to choose, and for those who like the clean lines of modern furniture there is plenty of choice on the budget end too with chains like Ikea, and Basika.

In the future should you wish to replace anything, you now know where to take your unwanted goods.

But it is in the weekly markets you are likely to find good decorative artefacts for your home, especially mirrors, frames and prints. The best time to buy is not the summer when prices are geared to tourists. Incidentally, once you have a home you will cease to feel like a tourist. In fact, like the locals, you will begin to regard them with a certain benign amusement.

Some years back when the children were young we spent a night in the village of Barbizon, outside Fontainebleau, and visited the hostelry where the painters of what became known as the 'Barbizon School' and their literary friends like Georges Sand, and Alfred de Musset, lived it up when the plague hit Paris. A few years later I happened to be scavenging in a Paddington junk shop when, to my everlasting surprise, I found an original signed and dated etching of Barbizon's one and only main street showing the artists' hostelry and our hotel. The date was '51. Judging by the cobbled street I thought it had to be 1851, until a friend pointed out the delicately pencilled shape of a motorbike leaning against a tree. Well, you can't win them all!

Here are lists of some of the *brocante* markets throughout France. Depending on your interest, they could help you decide where to live.

ANNUAL AND BI-ANNUAL MARKETS

July
Amboise (Ile d'Or)
Mèze (nr Montpellier)

July-August
Avranches (Mont St Michel)
Béziers

August
Barjac
Cannes
Evian (Swiss frontier)
L'Isle-sur-la-Sorgue
Orange (Palais de la Foire)
Pont l'Eveque (Calvados)
Port de Lanne

Valbonne

September

Avignon (Parc des Expositions. A7 exit, Avignon Sud)

Cagnes-sur-Mer

Chartres (Parc des Expositions)

Clermont-Ferrand

Issoudun

Lac d'Aiguille (A7 exit Valence Nord)

Le Havre (Palais des Expositions)

Paris (Parc Floral Bois de Vincennes)

October

Paimpol (Château de Kersa Ploubazlanec)

Villefranche-en-Beaujolais

November

Paris (Espace Wagram)

And this is only the tip of the iceberg.

In Isle-sur-la-Sorgue for example, traders operate every day of the week, and at weekends this delightful town with its inviting cafés and wall-to-wall brocante/antiques, is bustling with visitors.

A SELECTED LIST OF MONTHLY ANTIQUE/*BROCANTE* MARKETS

Saturdays

Bagnols-sur-Cèze	3rd Sat
Béziers	1st Sat
Bordeaux	1st Sat
Bourg-en-Bresse (Square Lalande)	3rd Sat

Chambery	2nd Sat
Cherbourg (Place des Moulins)	1st Sat
Clermont-Ferrand (Place du 1 mai)	1st Sat
Givors	3rd Sat
Nancy (Vieille Ville)	2nd Sat
Riom	2nd Sat
Stes Maries de la Mer	1st and 3rd Sat
Valence (Parc Expositions)	2nd and 4th Sat

Sundays

Amiens (Parc Parmentier)	2nd Sun
Bergerac (Vieux)	1st Sun
Blois (Place Ave Maria)	2nd Sun
Cahors (Place Rousseau)	4th Sun
Cannes (La Bocca)	1st Sun
Chartres (Place St Pierre)	4th Sun
Dijon (Ancienne Patinoire)	Last Sun
Fréjus	4th Sun
Hyères (Marché aux Fleurs)	1st Sun
La Ciotat	3rd Sun
Le Mans	2nd Sun
Limoges	2nd Sun
Marseilles (Cours Julien)	2nd Sun
Milly la Foret	2nd Sun
Montelimar (Rue Ste Croix)	2nd Sun
Moulins	2nd Sun
Nevers (Place Mosse)	3rd Sun
Poitiers	4th Sun
Salon de Provence (Parc Expositions)	1st Sun

Reims (Zone Industrielle)	1st Sun
Toulouse	1st Sun
Troyes	3rd Sun

Mondays

| Chartres (Place St Pierre) | 4th Mon |
| Grenoble (Place St André) | 3rd Mon |

Other

| Toulouse | 1st Fri |

WEEKLY MARKETS

Saturdays	Sundays
Aix-en-Provence	Alés
Albi	Clermont-Ferrand
Angers	Hyères (Av de la Pinede)
Arles	Lille
Bordeaux	Limoges
Limoges	L'Isle-sur-la-Sorgue
L'Isle-sur-la-Sorgue	Montpellier (Espace Mosson)
Monaco	Paris (Porte de Montreuil)
Nantes	Paris (St Ouen)
Orléans	Paris (Square G. Brassens)
Paris (Porte de Montreuil)	Perpignan
Paris (St Ouen)	Rouen
Paris (Square G. Brassens)	St-Étienne
Rouen	Toulon (Parc Expositions)
Tours	

Mondays	Wednesdays
Limoges	Tours
L'Isle sur la Sorgue	
Nice	Thursdays
Nîmes	Aix-en-Provence
Paris (Porte de Montreuil)	Rennes
Paris (St Ouen)	
	Fridays
Tuesdays	Grenoble
Aix-en-Provence	Poitiers
	Vence

Many markets not listed here are for specialist collectors: old books, prints, paintings, *objets* from the 18th century, *toiles* and old fabric, toy cars, jewellery, porcelain, and the list goes on. If you are a specialist and the idea of a market on your doorstep appeals, the next time you are in France search out a copy of a magazine called 'Aladin'; the *chineur*'s (*brocante*-hunter's) bible.

Every town and large village will have its own market day for the sale of local and regional produce, where stalls groan with cheeses, and farm produced butter. Large amphorae brim with succulent olives of varying flavours, and garlands of freshly-picked vine tomatoes spill over counters, reminding us once again that France has agriculture at its roots, literally.

On Thursdays in old Antibes you will find a truly superb food market, so packed with gastronomic quality and delights, it could leave you salivating for the rest of the year.

No one should miss a French market.

USEFUL FRENCH

Tu rigoles, non ?	Are you kidding?
Une nana	A chick
Sa julie	His woman
Sa bergère	His old lady
Une fille de joie	A lady of the night
Un coureur	A womaniser
Un vieux garcon	A confirmed bachelor
Un baratineur	A smooth talker
Un pot au feu	A stay at home
Un m'as-tu-vu	A show-off

7

THE COST OF COMMUNITY LIFE

LOCAL TAXES

Wherever you live in France and however much time you spend in your *chez vous*, you have to pay your two local taxes to the *bureau de perception* (tax collecting office) at the *mairie*. One is called *taxe foncière*, the land tax, and is paid by the owner of the property, while the *taxe d'habitation* is payable by the occupier whether or not he or she is the owner.

These taxes vary according to location value and amenities, and are assessed by the *Commune*, the *Departement* and the *Région*. If you live in a hamlet with no shop, you will pay less than someone who lives in a town. Where there is local industry that pays tax (*professionel*) at a higher rate than the private householder (*particulier*), the tax paid by the local inhabitants will be comparatively less. So if you live in a small town with a municipal swimming pool, daily rubbish clearance, and a cinema you will be paying more than if you lived near an industrial estate. That is why inexpensive hotels like the Formule 1 chain like to build on or near a ZI (*zone industrielle*).

Taxe d'habitation and *taxe foncière* are paid by the householder annually. *Taxe foncière* is paid in October and *taxe d'habitation* for the year beginning January 1st. When you buy a house in the UK, the conveyancing solicitor invariably tots up the amount of council tax liable to be paid by, or reimbursed to, either party.

This is not necessarily so in France. For example, if you sell in July and you have already paid *taxe foncière* in October you have nine months to claim back. Sometimes the portion of *taxe foncière* (always the larger sum) owing may be written into your bill of sale, in any case you should ask the *notaire* to calculate it for you to avoid any dispute, but you cannot claim back from your purchasers any *taxe d'habitation*. This bill is your responsibility.

In some smaller communes tax demands have a habit of winging their way very slowly, particularly if they are sent to your UK address and you have moved. In which case you may not receive them until well after the legal pay-by date. In fact not only can they be confusing, but the results of delayed payment can be alarming.

For example I received a *taxe foncière* bill for the house that I had sold, over a year after I had moved out. Thinking I had been completely up to date with all bills prior to sale, I ignored it, convinced the previous tax office had made a mistake and would soon catch up with the new owners. At the time all bills were sent to my UK address and since I had also moved in the UK, postal efficiency and time were not on my side. Finally the tax demand somehow found its way to my new French address. Again I ignored it, but when my bank statement arrived fortuitously only a few days later, I noticed certain mystifying withdrawals which were clearly nothing to do with any personal extravagance. After several agonised telephone calls to the bank's headquarters, and calls to my new local tax office who sweetly declared I owed them nothing, my chequebook chum at the bank explained.

It's the power of the *mairie* again. The tax office controlling my previous commune had belatedly sent a bill for the year in which I sold the last house. I was responsible, and with no payment from me they had the right to freeze my bank account, and to withdraw the offending sum from it. Until I could personally authorise payment to them, my account could not be used for any withdrawals whatsoever. Of course it was rectified quickly with a couple of signatures and I was never so relieved that I had had enough money in my account to pay this covert withdrawal. The bank took the whole event with complete equanimity and smiles, which suggested I was not the first. Within seven days my account was up and running again. But this was a severe lesson with a number of alarming possible scenarios. My personal appearance at the bank was absolutely necessary to expedite matters. If I had been in the UK, the account would have been frozen for three months. Not good. Then there is the problem of persuading your purchasers that they owe you half a year's tax two years after the event. I think the British way in this area of house purchase is far clearer. So my advice would be, should you sell your domicile, work out the sums of tax owed and present it to your purchasers within a week of moving out, while memories are fresh.

PAYING BILLS

You can pay your bills by cheque, with cash at the *Bureau de Poste* (Post Office) by *virement automatique* (standing order) or by *prélèvement automatique* (direct debit) at your bank, which is the method all service companies would like, but unless you are resident it may not suit to drain your account of funds for services during a period of absence. On the other hand it saves the effort of writing out cheques and finding the correct postage stamp from the UK. Usually you are given ten days to pay so there could be a problem if the post is delayed. It is a shock to arrive at *chez vous* only to find the electricity has been cut off – and, believe me, it will be. Sometimes computers make mistakes with addresses. I used to live in the London area N1 8EH. The EDF regularly addressed the bill to N18 and forgot the EH. Somehow they filtered through but finally it took several calls to EDF HQ to correct the mistake.

TELEPHONE

These days you are not obliged to use France Telecom apart from the line rental. OneTel, as in the UK, Kast and Phone Ex-pat are just three of many new companies offering very competitive telephone rates, but direct debit is obligatory. There are a number of new companies offering broadband and free European telephone calls for around € 30 per month and you have no line rental to France Telecom to pay, although you need them to give you your telephone number and *ligne fixe* (house phone) in the first place.

It's also worth looking at VOIP (voice over internet protocol) if you regularly make calls back to the UK: with some companies at various times such calls are entirely free and others, such as Skype, offer big discounts over conventional telephone call charges.

PAYING GUESTS

If you have the separate space, e.g. a studio, or *gîte* (apartment/cottage) there is no better way of contributing towards the mortgage or, at the very least keeping the house afloat, than a seasonal let.

It's fair to say the older we get, especially after family have departed, the less inclined we are to have anyone share our home. But if you are interested in a few more euros dropping into the domestic fund, a house that offers a separate letting space (and so many of them do) is worth looking at seriously. In my view short seasonal lets are the best, because you can choose your letting dates. Not so with long local lets. In France rentals are generally much lower than they are in the UK, and tenants have protection over the winter months. Even if they turn out to be villains you cannot turf them out between November and May, no matter how many notices you serve.

Renting out your *gîte,* as a short holiday let is relatively painless, except for changeover day when it is all hands on deck. When I had a three double bedroom two-bathroom *gîte* attached to my village farm, there was no problem in finding holiday tenants; the only major problem arose during August when my wonderful *femme de ménage* took her hols. Saturdays were always frantic, even when she was there and we worked together, but when she was not, it was a non-stop marathon. The *gîte* had to be swabbed and dusted, six beds stripped and made up, bathrooms cleaned, kitchen left spotless and the cooker left gleaming, its inside festooned with kitchen foil (to keep it cleaner) in preparation for the incoming guests. I have always believed that if you set a high standard for incoming guests, the more care they take of your nest. That has usually worked, but not always.

Changeovers for six or more beds, which have to be done within a few hours, are frankly exhausting, particularly if you are sending off messy guests. There are two solutions; one is, let for a minimum of two weeks, so spacing out the frantic days, and two, make sure you have a good reliable home help, apart from the annual French exodus when you will either have to enlist family, or a jobless student. Finding a good *femme de ménage* is like finding a good builder. Ask the neighbours, as local recommendation is the best way.

I have interviewed several ladies over the years, and have made many mistakes. The genial jovial personality does not necessarily signify a conscientious attitude towards your house and its well-being, and be wary of someone who already has a fairly full workload. If you are absent, in a busy week no prizes for guessing who will be short-changed. The trouble is you will never know the standard of her efficiency in your absence unless of course guests complain.

Several years back I found a wonderful, laughing, jolly helper. She was a complete workaholic, and fitted me in with her several jobs. While she would work like a Trojan in my presence, in my absence the situation was rather different as it transpired. The beds were changed and clean, but frequently the *frigo* (refrigerator) was left untouched with bits of festering food inside, to say nothing of the rest of the house.

I should never have known this had not two old friends had the good sense to tell me. On this occasion for her five hours work only two of the beds had been changed, nothing else had been touched, so my two friends set to and cleaned up. I telephoned others who had stayed and, yes, they all confirmed lapses of various sorts. My jolly *madame* was far from pulling her weight. It was difficult to sack the lady because I liked her, so I tried to drop hints about pernickety friends who would complain to me if all was not perfect. All this was done with smiles and eyebrows shrugging up and down. Whereupon she threw up her hands and laughed until the tears rolled down her chubby red cheeks. She had never heard of friends like that, and I should not worry; she would tell them to go and sit in the sun if they didn't like the house. So *tant pis!* Not the result I had hoped for.

Someone trustworthy is essential for peace of mind, someone to whom you can give the house keys, and who will drop in from time to time in your absence and water the plants, and not least someone who is content to work madly through the summer when you are likely to be *in situ* either with family and friends or with paying guests, and who will not object to being 'laid-off' during the winter. For reasons of continuity and goodwill it is worthwhile paying a small retainer fee during your absence, for general tidying not so much in the house but around it.

Letting in Absentia

I have always drawn up a work-agenda for house help and carefully gone through it point by point, more for my French than for her comprehension. Usually it has been a complete waste of time, although there have been a few wonderful exceptions.

If you are going to let in your absence make sure your *femme de ménage* knows exactly how you want the beds made, and which sheets and towels to use. If you keep a separate shelving unit for apartment/*gîte*/studio, bed linen and towel arrangements are less likely to go wrong.

For all the care and precautions you may take, nothing is sure until your help has been tried and tested, but it is worthwhile to know that if your *femme de ménage* is regarded as *serieuse* by the neighbours, you have chosen well.

What to provide

When people rent a furnished holiday apartment they want everything, but that does not necessarily mean you will provide it. However, be aware that tastes and requirements are becoming more sophisticated and you will be competing with establishments that provide washing machines, dishwashers, televisions and video players. What is provided will be reflected in the weekly rental charge but, like your home, the apartment/studio will evolve as you exchange some rental cash for extra equipment. If you are thinking of letting your personal living quarters in your absence, don't forget to put all valuables into a locked cupboard/room, and empty all wardrobes and drawers.

The basic requirements for letting are all kitchen utensils, saucepans, frying pans, crockery, cutlery, iron, ironing board, electric kettle, clothes airer, fridge-freezer, cooker or microwave, small oven and hob, good bread-knife and paring knife. It is also a friendly gesture to provide a roll of kitchen paper, one refuse bag, and loo paper. I know many landlords do not provide sheets and towels, but I personally feel it is unfair to expect families travelling by plane to have to stuff suitcases full of sheets and towels. If it is made clear in advance visitors usually bring their own beach towels and it is a good idea to make a rule that fabric sun-loungers are covered by the sun-worshipper's towel, otherwise the oil stains are impossible to remove.

If you have stone floors leave the guests a bucket and mop with a bottle of cleaning liquid as a gentle nudge, and keep light bulbs in stock.

Essentials for holidays in the sun will be patio tables and chairs. Although sun-loungers are *de rigueur* they seem to have a short life expectancy, as much depends on the weight and care of the tenants. A couple of roistering teenagers will crack the plastic in an instant. So, be prepared to renew every couple of years. If you are a resident and are in the French fiscal system, you are allowed to earn, tax free, a certain sum each year from your home, rather like our system, but as this figure is liable to unpredictable change, it should be checked out.

When potential guests enquire about availability, and they have children, ask the ages of the offspring. Delightful though they are, children under five may not be quite 'potty trained', although the parents will swear they are. But we all know how youngsters react to new surroundings and the general excitement of a holiday. I know this to my cost having had to throw out two new mattresses. Ask the parents to bring with them a plastic sheet, or better still buy an impermeable mattress cover from the hypermarket.

LETTING CONTRACT

For your own peace of mind an agreement form should be sent out to anyone who rents your house or apartment, be they friends or strangers. These days owners should take precautionary measures against holidaymakers bitten by the American compensation bug that seems to be gaining in popularity in the UK. The French incidentally rightly scoff derisively at this unscrupulous practice.

A relevant clause written into the standard holiday let agreement makes good sense. Here is a typical example, to add to or subtract from according to personal taste.

Holiday let agreement

BETWEEN
PROPRIETOR ....
AND

TENANT ....

Whereby the latter agrees to rent furnished accommodation known as

THE *GÎTE* at *Chez Nous*

From .... arrival date

To .... departure date

At .... per week. No. of weeks .... Total ....

THE GUEST agrees to remain at THE *GÎTE* for the appointed time only, unless otherwise agreed.

HOUSE REQUESTS

To refrain from smoking in the *gîte*.
To leave by 10am, on the final day, unless previously arranged.
When using the pool help us maintain standards of hygiene by making sure feet are clean and children have been to the loo.
Sorry, no lilos or ball games.

PLEASE

Use a towel to cover terrace loungers when sunbathing.
Do not leave fabric chair covers out at night.
No house linen to be used for sunbathing.

THE PROPRIETOR agrees to provide:
Electricity
Hot water
Gas
House linen: bed and bath
Cleaning on departure

If these conditions are agreed please sign where indicated and return to the Proprietor together with a booking deposit of 50% of total ....

The balance .... to be paid six weeks before arrival and sent to ....

We shall send you a reminder at the appropriate time along with a location guide and information about the region.

Guests are requested to place a deposit of £100 with the proprietor on arrival, against any damages. This could be in the form of a sterling cheque which will be destroyed if nothing has been broken.

Please note:

1. Holiday booking deposits are non refundable.
2. In the event of cancellation, balances cannot be refunded so it is a wise precaution to take out holiday insurance. And don't forget your EHIC card.
3. Children must at all times be chaperoned by adults when using the pool. Their safety and behaviour has to be the responsibility of accompanying adults.
4. Management cannot be held responsible for personal accident or injury sustained on the premises.

Accepted and signed ....

The absence of clause 4 had some unfortunate consequences for a friend of mine.

Some young man, a newly arrived guest, tried to make his way to the loo during the night after a rather heavy dose of French wine at dinner. He slipped and caused himself a terrible injury, dealt with most efficiently at the nearby hospital. At the time all agreed he had become somewhat disorientated through tiredness and alcohol, forgetting where the electric switches were. One year later my friend received a letter from solicitors claiming damages to the tune of thousands of pounds for negligence. She was, frankly, appalled as not only had the young man in question been given every possible assistance and comfort in and outside the hospital, but also all had agreed upon the cause of the accident.

She was accused of having faulty electric switches and of having an unfriendly stone floor, which caused his unfortunate injuries. She had to

LIFE STYLE FRENCH STYLE

explain to these rapacious lawmen in the UK that young children had been going to the loo in the middle of the night from that very bedroom for many years without accident or injury, and flatly denied any personal responsibility for the young man's over consumption. And so it went on for another year until the 'no claim, no fee' merchants finally stopped pestering. But be warned. Guests have up to seven years to make a claim. She hopes now they have gone away, but cannot be sure. How absurd it is, the implication according to this compensation culture, that an able-bodied adult should have to be guided when making trips to the loo in the middle of the night.

After your first season you will quickly know what should be added to general requests but, most important, write in your own clause 4.

Advertising

Advertising these days is frequently done on the Internet. The advertiser will ask you to provide a specified number of photographs, plus a full description of the premises and its surroundings to include shops, restaurants, public transport, amenities, places of interest, and activities, particularly for youngsters. Nevertheless it is a good idea to print out your own information sheet to send to your prospective guests as most of us like to have information that can be easily referred to. There are various British journals that advertise holiday accommodation, however, with photographs – and you will want to show it off at its colourful best – it will not be cheap.

Many French estate agents have letting departments, and perhaps a longer winter let would be a good idea. For reasons already mentioned, a winter let to Brits wanting a couple of months' break would probably be less of a problem than a local let. At least you would know that your tenants had a home to return to.

Rents vary according to the region and what you can offer. Obviously you will charge more for an apartment on the Côte d'Azur, than you will in Normandy, but probably not more than Cornwall in high season. It is useful to read British magazines advertising holidays abroad to assess price structure. You will surely find something similar in your area. And swimming pools are becoming far more the norm in holiday accommodation. You have only to pick up one of the many glossies in the newsagents to see that with a pool the rent increases.

USEFUL FRENCH

Avoir du piston	To have friends in the right places – well connected
Comme il se doit	As it should be
Il est zinzin ce type !	That chap is round the twist
C'est le fin des haricots	It's the last straw
Occupe-toi de tes oignons !	Mind your own business
Ecrase !	Shut up!
Ta gueule !	Shut your face! (a bit stronger)

8
SELLING ON

As a non resident selling your *chez vous* either to buy another house in France, or to repatriate the funds will mean having to pay Capital Gains Tax, CGT in the UK and *plus-value* in France. This tax is paid on the profit you have made, i.e. the difference between the buying price and the selling price. The tax paid in France used to be the same as in the UK, but since January 2004 it has changed.

For a non resident of France, but a resident of an EU member state the *plus-value* payable on the sale of a second home is now a flat 16%. There is also the possibility of further discount. Selling within the first five years you can expect no discount except for improvements, like the installation of a pool, that have been done by an official French registered company: the costs of which are then added to the original purchase price of the house. For years 6–9 you receive 10% per annum which equals 40% discount for four years. Therefore with 40% deducted from the capital gain, your tax at 16% of the remainder will be considerably less. When *plus-value* was at the same level as the UK, there were annual allowances against inflation, but no longer. There are however building improvements (for example a new bathroom, kitchen or patio) plus renovations (perhaps an extension) that may be deducted, again provided that the work was done by a registered French company with a *siret* number, and that you can produce receipts for the figure claimed. If you are an all round DIY devotee, as seller you are supposedly allowed to add a further 15% to the original purchase price of the property as a reward for your actual labour, but don't count on this. You may claim nothing for decorative works. Furthermore the tax is dealt with by companies, sidekicks of the governmental fiscal authority who, for example, on a *plus value* (CGT) tax payment of 14,000€ charge another 2,000€ for their work in assessing you. There is no standard fee either: these companies are competitive, and one wonders whether they apply precisely the same criteria as to what constitutes 'decoration', and what constitutes genuine improvement through DIY? In other words are they unbiased or biased, and in whose favour, yours or the government's?

A few years ago under the old system I sold my converted silk-worm farm that I had restored from a village eyesore into a thing of beauty. Instead of rotting barns and a grubby courtyard, stood a delightful building around a pool, with stone walls the colour of honey, and the interior spacious and light. Many people including friends, family and jobbing British artisans either on holiday, or working their way through France, had been involved in the work. I paid in cash and to be fair they all gave me scribbled out bills and receipts. In the UK some were self-employed, but what mattered was they were not in the French fiscal system. Naturally I had kept all the bills and added them up to an astounding figure. My *notaire* instantly rejected, both the figure and the bills. This was a body blow. Hitherto bills of this sort had always been accepted. For twenty-odd years they had been accepted. No one had told me the law had changed during the previous two years. From now on only the bills of work done by registered French companies with *siret* numbers were considered valid. In desperation I visited the tax bureau for my commune. They laughed at the bills. They were not proper companies madame. Individual artisans did not exist it seemed. This now meant that I had no claims whatsoever against the full tax on the profit I had made, save a couple of years' allowances against inflation. This total amount to be paid was a staggering 44,000€.

Of course there was profit in turning a pigsty around, I pleaded. My pleas were in vain. I was even more desperate because the deposit had already been paid on my next house.

We assembled a collection of very good photographs detailing building progress over a period of a year and a half, starting from the rubble upwards, but to no avail it seemed. After a succession of sleepless nights I finally went to see the *notaire* and told him I should have to withdraw from the sale and the new purchase, despite having paid the deposit. He looked very serious and for that moment I saw some genuine concern for my plight. It seemed there was a solution.

'You will have to involve the *fisc* madame.'

'But why? All these artisans who worked on the house are British and in the EU like me.'

He smiled. 'But you are not in the euro are you?'

I was not amused. 'That's racial discrimination.'

'*Madame* I joke. The *fisc* will have to inspect your house.'

My head swam. My stomach lurched. In France to talk of the *fisc* you might just as well say the Gestapo is about to visit. I felt like Joan of Arc facing the English hordes only this time they were French. There was nothing else to be done. I stood to lose everything. So it came to pass a *rendezvous* was fixed for the inspection.

My nerves were shattered, as I waited for this latter-day Himmler.

He arrived on time, a locum, because the regular inspectors were away on holiday. He was no Himmler. He was a retired architect with a kindly face and a gentle manner. This in itself was a relief. I took him on a tour of the establishment, and then left him to it. Five hours later he emerged with all his calculations. He had assiduously measured every piece of plaster-boarding, and new construction, counted nails, screws, measured all the new pipes, assessed the costs of new bathrooms, the cost of scaffolding, terracing sandblasting and more. After another three hours of polite questioning we had some supper and he left armed with the collection of 'before' photographs that had obviously impressed him, promising he would telephone. Meanwhile I was obliged to move out of the house and, still not knowing whether I actually could complete on the new place, rented a studio in a friend's garden and put my furniture in store. I spoke to my gentle architect from the fisc a couple of times who told me that so far, according to his calculations, I would be paying far less than the original sum, but I should know officially in a week or two. Tension was high.

Finally after nearly four weeks came the call I had been waiting for. I had nothing to pay – nothing at all. All calculations showed that there had indeed been a large sum spent on restoration. The outcome was perfect; the agonies suffered were not.

I shall never again confuse the fisc with the Gestapo.

The lesson to be learned from this saga is that French law changes all the time, and, like me, you may not hear about it until it is too late. It does seem far easier and cheaper now to sell on, but just make sure you have the correct bills, from the correct type of company. Bills for materials bought if you are a DIY fan will no longer be counted, but again the law could change at any time. To be on the safe side, if you are restoring an old ruin, take dozens of photographs; they could save the day.

If you wish to sell on as a resident and the French house is your primary domicile the fiscal authorities make different demands. You may think you will have nothing to pay as the French home is your primary residence. Sorry! Think again. If you are in the French fiscal system however, and have paid your taxes in France, for a minimum of two years, then you would be exempt from any capital gains tax if the home you are selling is your primary residence, just as in the UK. Which is fair. For residents whose primary home is in France, but who still pay taxes in the UK, the same tax rules would apply as for non residents if they wish to sell on. The *plus-value* is calculated at 16%.

I have friends who in the space a few hours transferred all accounts, invoices, and returns to an accountant resident in France. So don't panic. There's no need to practise adding up in French. There are any number of English accountants working in the French system and living in France. But do remember that if you repatriate the money from the sale of your house to the UK, without paying *plus-value* in France, Her Majesty's Revenue and Customs officers could get you for more CGT than the French system would have charged.

The one important aspect of French taxation laws is that they change as rapidly as the infant's *derrière*. Therefore always take advice. I am giving you what is applicable now in 2006.

AGENTS

A note about the agent(s) who handle your sale. Don't think you will pay less commission if you restrict yourself to only one selling agent as you may in the UK. You might just as well have four because it will cost no more in the end. And don't be persuaded to go with one exclusively, but if you do just make sure it is for not more than three months, and get sets of extra keys cut.

When searching for your replacement domicile, there are good friendly agents with their agency networks manned by ex-pat Brits ready to help for a flat fee. A particularly efficient organisation is run by Elayne Murphy, the co-director of Provence Grannies. Her contact email; *elayne@provencepropertysearch.com*. Searches are undertaken throughout France, and are not as the name suggests restricted to Provence. I can assure you that having someone on the spot, to search in the region of your choice is the best time-saving investment ever. Until my last move I had always gone it alone, largely because I was staying in the same area, and knew the *immobiliers*. This time moving

20 km away I tried daily Internet searching and time consuming car trips to *immobiliers* in the new area. It was both tiring and dispiriting, largely because there were certain necessary criteria to be met, not least budgetary ones. Finally it was an agent who had my house for sale on her own books who managed to find my present house. Of course the new place was with another agent, but no problem: the hot line got to work and like long-standing buddies they split the commission.

SHUFFLING OFF

We all have to die at some point so we might just as well make it easier for our nearest and dearest.

Being a Celt, I am prone to feeling the imminence of doom and catastrophe lurking ready to pounce, so I went to see a *notaire* about making a will in order to leave the house, and what pittance I had in the bank account, to my children.

'Do you live alone *madame*?'

'Yes'

'So you have no relation apart from your children to leave anything to?'

'No.'

'Then you need do nothing. It will automatically go to your children. Most English people who live alone here leave their property to the cats' home or to donkeys.'

So far so good.

What he failed to point out was the inheritance tax my offspring would have to pay. If you have a holiday home in France, upon your demise it will be considered an overseas asset and will be added to your British estate and taxed in the UK. At the moment any estate totalling more than the present threshold of £285,000 is taxed at 40%. There are very strong rumours that this tax will rise to 50% on estates with a higher threshold.

If you have lived outside the UK for more than three fiscal years, and are taxed in France, only then will your inheritors be outside the UK inheritance tax net.

France, too, has its succession tax. If you live in France, tax will be payable on your total worldwide assets. If you are a non resident, i.e. with a holiday/part-time home, only your house will be liable to tax.

Married couples have a problem. When one of them dies the house does not automatically go to the remaining spouse as in the UK. In France assets left to the living spouse over a threshold figure of 76,000€, are liable to French succession tax. There would be exemption with jointly-owned assets and a recognised community marriage contract. Assets left to your children over and above €48,000 per child, are also liable to tax.

If you are co-habiting, please note that a certificate of concubinage which is obtainable from the *mairie*, apparently does not help the partner left behind. Contrary to popular trend, French law recognises only a legal marriage with contract. It is hoped there may be a change soon, as the majority of under-thirties seem to cohabit rather than go through the formalities of a wedding.

I read of a British woman living in France who lost her partner of 24 years. At the outset all documents of the house had been supervised correctly by the *notaire* and written *en tontine* which, so far as they understood, would protect the partner left when the other died, and allow that partner to inherit the house, without any problems. Unfortunately as they were not officially married, the one left has had to pay 60% of half the property value. These succession laws are a nightmare and are likely to change at any time. Therefore I would strongly suggest a visit to the *notaire* if you wish to put your house in order.

There is another way, which I believe to be the most satisfactory, and that is to give your house to your children during your lifetime. If you decide to do this you will have to pay to have their names inserted into the written deeds, and in effect you all share the ownership of the house for a period a few years after which time it becomes theirs. If you sell, their names are on the deeds of sale and on the new purchase deeds. In time you become the '*usifruitier*'; literally they own the tree but you use the fruit. They cannot throw you out; neither can they prevent your receiving any rent from the property, which is all to the good. When you eventually shuffle off you are leaving no assets because the house is theirs, and they will pay no death duties, neither to France nor to the UK. If they choose to sell-up before 15 years has elapsed, and have to pay capital gains tax (*plus-value*) you will be beyond caring. *Tant-pis!*

Another safeguard is to have the local *notaire* write a letter directing all your bank assets, upon your demise, to be shared equally amongst your named next of kin provided you are able to name and verify. Most of us can do that, but there are others whose life of Riley can catch up unexpectedly. Place a copy with the bank as a reference, and the *notaire* will keep the original. Banks rarely get involved with inheritance claims because they have been known to lose large sums of money when an unknown and never-before-recognised child crawls out of the woodwork. Choose your lawyer with care as there are no executors in French wills to guide the inheritors. The *notaire* does all the guiding.

Taking out an offshore bond, an *Assurance Vie* is another very good way to avoid French succession tax, and by the time you are ready to start thinking of your own mortality, financial whiz kids will have evolved several other avoidance measures.

Healthcare

We all know the fine reputation that French medical care has continued to maintain over the years. If you decide to live in France permanently, the French health service will accept you with whatever chronic disease or condition you have. In fact it will give you preferential treatment. Appointments at the surgery with any doctor can be made with ease, are usually on time, and in the case of real sickness or pain the doctor will make a visit within the hour. Any follow-up treatment like scans or x-rays are made within the day. I know this from personal experience. You should know the French are great believers in the use of the suppository, so never display signs of panic if the doctor prescribes one for your bad knee, headache, or backache. Look on it this way; they are very kind on the stomach, and they do work!

In the past we have gone to France armed with our E111 forms obtainable from the Post Office: promissory letters from the British NHS to pay about 65% of the cost of any French medical care you require during your stay. If you collected an E111 form during 2005, from 2006 you have had a plastic EHIC card in its place. Perhaps you have used this system and discovered how slow the NHS can be in reimbursing you the charges paid out of your own pocket.

But at last there is a solution for full-time and part-time French residents, in the form of 'Exclusive Healthcare Insurance' which offer three different packages to suit different needs.

For those about to join the French system on a full time basis there is the 'Gateway' plan specially designed to cover health emergencies during the period of approximately four months it takes to become fully integrated into the French system. They also provide a good top-up insurance that everyone except those in penurious circumstances pays in France. For someone in their early fifties the monthly payment for this cover is 66.60€.

The 'Argent' broad band plan (41.00€ per month) and the 'Bronze' hospitalisation plan (24.00€ per month) cover the full difference between the cost of treatment and the amount reimbursed by the state system, and they also top up the EHIC throughout Europe. There are no age limits for joining, and no medical questions asked.

All claims and assistance services are conducted in English and French paperwork is in English translation, which if you are feeling lousy makes life a lot easier. These policies are available from Exclusive Healthcare, tel. + 33 (0) 4 94 40 6670/314; email *exclusivehealthcare@wanadoo.fr*.

I have several British friends who, although living in France for a good part of the year, rely on the EHIC card for any treatment they might need. They have not taken out top-up insurance arguing that as they are generally healthy what they pay from their own pockets is at the moment considerably less than they would have paid out over several years to an insurance scheme. Plus, they know that if they are struck down with an illness whilst in France, i.e. they didn't know about it when they crossed the Channel, the NHS will pay the lot.

USEFUL FRENCH

Un lèche cul	An arse licker
Obsédé	Obsessed
Refoulé	Repressed
Volage	Fickle

Now here's useful phrase, to be used selectively.

Venez voir mes estampes japonaises !	Come and see my etchings!

9

THE LANGUAGE AND
THE SOCIAL SCENE

Should any smart-Alec tell you French is an easy language to learn, he/she is either lying or their standard is abysmally low. If you have an ear for sound, it is a wonderfully musical language. You could possibly pick up phrases without any special help, but you really need to go to conversation classes to improve your overall standard of understanding and communication: every French town will have them. The French government is now insisting that all immigrant children have a crash course in French before going to regular school. You may not think you are in that category, but this directive underlines the fact that the government is keen to integrate all newcomers, and integration is the keyword for us Brits too. Some Brits remain mum because of the language problem but, quite frankly, if people choose to holiday on a fairly permanent basis in a particular country, it is their responsibility to learn a little of the language. Unfortunately the antiquated notion that we are British and everyone else foreigners – even in their own country – still pervades in far too many cases. The other day I heard strong complaints that hoteliers on the coast of Normandy didn't speak English. The complainers spoke not a word of French and had no intention of trying. This bulldog arrogance is anathema to the French, and could well rekindle the Napoleonic Wars – and I know which side I'd be on.

French can be a formidable language in its written form, and unfortunately for the majority of Brits it presupposes a knowledge of grammar and language construction. That is why French children know how to speak properly. Grammar is taught assiduously from an early age. Alas, this applies no more to British education on the whole. I, like countless others of my generation, was lucky in that grammar was taught as a separate subject in my Grammar school – as English Language as opposed to English Literature. Ah! Those were the days. The result is that many younger Brits start to learn French with a disadvantage, i.e. they have no understanding of grammar. But don't give up; it's worth persevering even if only to read important notices, or transport timetables; you may never have to write a thing. From mid-August, in preparation for *la rentrée* (the start of the new school year, when everyone returns after the holidays), the hypermarkets burst with fabulous grammar books for French children of all ages, so start with books for the 5–7 year olds. You can always pretend it is for your child/grandchild. I keep all mine as reference books. When learning another tongue, if your grammar is shaky, begin with nouns. Knowing the names of household artefacts, and of food sold in the supermarket is one of the first challenges. From there you will have the confidence to attempt simple phrases.

BEING RUDE IN FRENCH

Listening to and copying sound is vital but, depending on the company, there are some words that would perhaps be best avoided. The French, despite being a polite nation, are often over-generous in their use of certain words which, although we hear their equivalents with tedious regularity on UK television screens, we would not use in polite conversation. Take for example the Anglo-Saxon four letter word that even the Bard himself used, c*nt. It's not likely we'd use it in conversation with the lady florist or at the checkout in Tesco to describe someone. The French equivalent is the word *con*, which though literally the equivalent is most frequently and widely used to describe 'bloody fools', or worse. The first time a complete stranger used it to describe a particular plumber to me some twenty years ago, I was really quite shocked, not realising how much part of colloquial language it was. So you need never be afraid to use the word within your peer group, but it should be accompanied by a certain force of feeling to give it weight. It has bred its own family like *un connard* (an idiot) *une connerie* (rubbish). That's why the very mention of Sean Connery always elicits a little smile.

Another word the French use frequently is *merde* (shit). In fact students wish each other *merde* as a good luck send off before an exam, rather like our 'break a leg'. This is a word for the friendly vocabulary.

Tu me fait chier, (you give me a pain in the arse/you piss me off) is a phrase you could use to a rotten builder, provided you didn't expect to see him ever again.

Je m'en fiche/Je m'en fous (I don't care/don't give a damn), are perfectly reasonable expressions and won't see you ushered out of the *bistrot*. However if you told someone to *'Va te faire foutre'*, (F**k off), yes you'd be using the same script as most of the UK's television programmes and current street parlance, but don't expect to get away with it so easily in France. Choose the subject of your venom with care. Anglo-Saxon has a lot to answer for.

J'en ai ras le bol (I've had it up to here) is perfectly polite and is accompanied by a suitable gesture to denote the extent to which you have had it.

Baiser is a word to be used with great care. Its literal meaning is to kiss, but it is usually the colloquial meaning to lay/screw/f**k/sleep with/make love to – whichever seems to be the accepted norm. For years I was innocently signing my letters with lots of big screws, and apparently with all the family. Far safer to sign off with *gros bisous* (love and kisses), though not necessarily to the bank manager. My feeling is, the word *baiser* which after all means to kiss, says something about the French attitude towards love and love-making. The Anglo Saxons invented the crudest word to describe love-making, which refers only to a physical act. There are several more unattractive phrases like 'have it off', which mean the same thing. Words like kiss, love and embrace don't enter the equation. Is it because the majority of Anglo Saxon males in particular feel their macho manhood slipping away when faced with feeling and tenderness? French men on the other hand are so unafraid and so sure of their own masculinity that emotions and tenderness present no problems. As an *immobilier* once told me, 'You know the difference between French men and English men? We French really like women as people as well as lovers'.

'Ah cherie. Je t'adore. J'ai vraiement envie de toi' (I really want you)

OR

'C'm 'ere doll. How about a quick bonk?'

Spot the difference.

Most French men have a built-in charm gene; it is used quite spontaneously to all women irrespective of age, because the French are natural romantics and enjoy being in love; furthermore they continue to be great rugby players!

There's no denying the accent in French is important, and gives the language its lyrical sound. Getting it right is only a question of listening and copying, just like a young child. For us Brits who prefix all nouns with the ubiquitous 'the', French language has an added difficulty. Nouns are either masculine or feminine, and there are no really hard and fast rules to help you remember which are which. A masculine noun is prefixed by *le* or *un* ('the' or 'a'); a feminine noun by *la* or *une*. Naturally there are blunders to be made. For example *le rein* is the kidney (a throaty rr followed by nasal snort), *la reine* ('renne') is the queen, so you could conceivably upset the balance of monarchical power by announcing the queen had a blockage. *Un retrait* (pronounced 'rutray'), masculine noun, means literally a retreat, but in common parlance refers to a withdrawal, the sort you make either at the bank or at a *dispenseur* (the hole in the wall). *Une retraite* (pronounced 'rutrett', feminine noun), means, a retirement. Confusing certainly, but try to avoid telling your neighbours you'll be spending your retirement in a hole in the wall.

Take heart: even French people get it wrong.

FAUX AMIS

There are a number of words called *faux amis* (false friends), and although they sound the same in English have quite different meanings in French.

For example, *actuellement* (at present/at the moment/currently) should not be confused with the English 'actually'. The English 'actually' is translated into French as *en fait* (in fact). And should a Frenchman call you a *biche* do not hit him, he is merely calling you his doe, his sweetie/darling, so enjoy it!

If someone has a collection of *trombones* on the office desk, don't gasp with disbelief. A *trombone* also means a paperclip. And Mrs Worthington could well have been delighted if her daughter had left home for a *stage*, meaning an intensive course of some sort, rather than for a proscenium arch.

Should someone have a *magot* under the mattress or in a *bas de laine* (a woollen stocking) it doesn't mean he necessarily keeps a filthy house. A *magot* is simply a nest-egg/savings. When you tell your neighbour that you like jam without *preservatifs* she would agree, but appear puzzled. Who would possibly put condoms in the jam? A *preservatif* is a male condom.

And if your partner is referred to as your *concubin(e)* it's not a throw back to the Ming Dynasty, but the perfectly acceptable term for common-law spouses.

The French will raise eyebrows with gleeful expectation, however, if you announce the full disclosures of your *aventures* in Paris. Who wouldn't want hear about your sexy romps?

PRONUCIATION

As for pronunciation, again it's a question of listen and copy. Just make sure you are listening to someone who speaks good, clear French. I know a couple, both in the Arts, who decided to come to France to live. At that time the husband spoke no French and finding work in his *metier* was difficult, so he became a long-distance truck driver. Unfortunately problems arose each time they went out to dinner with smart lawyer and doctor friends. His wife would constantly have to nudge him into silence. His by now effortless French was, alas, peppered with juicy phrases, slang words and expletives picked up from his truckie peer group, which frequently stunned his bourgeois hosts into silence.

Some twenty years ago I popped into the bank to see my manager, an attractive middle-aged Frenchman with a twinkle in his eye. I had found an untraceable item in a statement that needed clarifying. The word for account is *compte*, and thinking it correct did not pronounce either the p or the t, so what came out was a nasal *con* – a word already discussed. At the time I was quite surprised at the breadth of his smile when I asked to see my *com(pte)*, and further could we look at it together as I wanted him to explain it to me. At this he smiled even more and walked off in the direction of either the vaults or the washroom obviously to have a good laugh. He came out later with a colleague, both wreathed in smiles. It took several years and several more gaffes on my part, to realise why.

Be warned!

THE SOCIAL SCENE

For those who have decided to make the complete break with the UK, or who anticipate residing in both countries for periods of several months at a time, the *carte de sejour* is no longer necessary. If you wish to move your UK furniture to your French house, there are a number of UK-based removal companies that share their services with Anglo-French counterparts in various parts of the Hexagon (the common French term for France). In my opinion this is better because you would then be eligible for French insurance (*assurances*). In the case of a claim, followed by the essential visit of the insurance inspector (*l' expert*), it is so much more convenient to sort out problems closer to your new home.

Exporting your animals is easy though costly, provided they have had the rabies vaccine, have been chipped and have passports in paw. I have a friend who had a very snooty looking pedigree cat called Florence, who insisted her pet's name would be changed to Fifi once she took up residence in France. Perhaps she was thinking of smoother integration with the feline population of the village.

Having a home in France requires having a good relationship with the neighbours. French people – whether in town, village or hamlet – are at first quite reserved, so don't be put off. Newly-arrived Brits frequently complain, but have often barely nodded to their neighbours. They expect them to make the running; an attitude embarrassingly like the days of Empire. Fortunately the majority of home owners – and certainly the ones I know – are to a greater or larger extent, Francophiles. They love the country, the food and wine, make valiant attempts at the language, and strike up friendly relations with local people. That doesn't imply there is a constant exchange of cultures. Lunch and dinner parties can be very true Brit, partly because all the residents want to see the semi-residents again, and the semis want to talk to the residents about builders and plumbers. The guests of both want to talk houses and prices because they may want to join the club next year. Time was when a Brit need not have uttered one word of French at these gatherings, because generally few French were invited, and those that were, spoke English. Thankfully times have changed and now you are likely to find a good balance. Take the plunge, invite your French neighbours in to see the changes and renovations. They are genuinely interested in you and your family, and in how you are improving the house. Apart from an honest, country nosiness, they are all mad keen *bricoleurs* anyway, and will give you no end of advice.

Children are great ambassadors and will draw you into a community, especially if there are other children to play with. Once you have shown you are friendly and approachable you will be offered any number of '*coup de main*' (a helping hand), and what is more, offers are quite sincere, so learn to accept them. Don't be afraid to talk about how much you have been charged for plumbing, labouring, gardening, plastering. There is nothing that angers the French more than someone being taken for ride, especially if they like you and know that, as a foreigner, you are at a disadvantage when it comes to debating the issue. Don't worry they could well do it for you.

Ask your neighbours in for an *apero* (aperitif). The first time they will leave politely in time for you to eat. After that it will difficult to get anyone to leave before midnight. This is especially so in country areas, so it is just as well to make sure you, like the French, eat well at lunchtime.

In our first house, the hamlet's indigenous population was no more than 11 in number, but it grew in summer with visitors like ourselves including some Parisians, we were told, although we had never seen them until one evening. We were in the kitchen on the first floor, windows open, and became aware of laughter and music somewhere in the distance. Suddenly the voices drew nearer, below the window in fact. Someone cried, 'Hello, English – please come to party'. And that was the beginning of a really good friendship between four couples and their children. We stayed with them in Paris, and they with us in the UK. Almost every evening somebody would have some sort of social gathering. We were all, French and English alike, building our maisons secondaires. The villagers loved the summer when we all descended. The older ones would recount hair-raising stories of the Resistance, Nazi reprisals, Gestapo atrocities. Their friends and families had heard it all before but we were new and eager to know about a living history that could never be found in books.

Those summers gave us all a new lease of life.

Although town life does not have the bonding community feel of a village, we were lucky because again we found delightful ex-pat residents who were a constant source of inspiration, when everything was falling about our ears. There you'd be, knee deep in debris, when a friendly voice would bid you down-tools, bundle you in a car and take you home to lunch. That is when good neighbours are most appreciated. Through community life you will find the short cuts to problems, bureaucratic and social, which only the locals know.

Always leave your house keys with someone, a neighbour, friend or builder, and ask them to look in from time to time.

Fortunately we did that the first time we left our first house, doing it out of courtesy rather than necessity. It so happened we had left all the shutters open for, being unused to them, we felt they were decorative rather than essential. However within days of our departure a howling mistral tore across the terrain and caused the hamlet sleepless nights, our shutters banging and clattering. Enough was enough, fosse or no, the neighbours entered the house, braved the terrible assault on nostrils and were able to restore nocturnal peace to the village.

The trap that many Brits fall into whilst making modest improvements to their *maison secondaire*, is trying to keep up with the Joneses. There is often a subtle jockeying for best house, an unpleasant sensation that can strike the moment they have left some ex-pat's stunning conversion and returned to their own half done shambles. It can be depressing and disheartening. Have no part in it! Be strong! Others will have more to spend, enough to have everything done for them, while you are up to the armpits in debris. They may have employed a full blown architect. So what? Don't be downhearted when that stockbroker's wife from Sussex shows you their pool. Who wants one anyway with all that cleaning out? You can always buy a family-sized plastic version. Don't be drawn into pecking order.

Whenever a house is going through the birth pangs of restoration, guests are taken on a conducted tour. You will do it, we all do it because it is constructive, as well as satisfying curiosity, and we all need approval. You will hear plenty of 'Ooh! We must get one of those darling'.

Always remember your budget. There's no hurry, so take your time. Some families take 10–15 years to make their second home. If it is going to be your permanent home you will have more money to spend to make changes more quickly. Most of the real stunners are permanent homes anyway.

Of course there are Brits who manage to convert even *maison secondaires* into palaces, like friends I once had in the village, and who really were called Jones.

They had a pool and a house of beautifully-designed minimalism in cream and white. I used to feel the undeniable pangs of dissatisfaction each time I returned from their eloquent statement to my French *brocante* maximalism. Their house certainly gave inspiration.

I have always made a point of having at least one social gathering for friends and neighbours every year, and there seems to be no difference in the generosity of guests whether in village, town or city; a generosity which is embarrassing at times. In the country where the population mainly works on the land, don't expect to be invited back to dinner. Dinner parties are more of an Anglo-Saxon habit. In the town, French professionals are more likely to invite you to dinner in a local restaurant than back to their home. But wherever you are – and particularly in the country – provided you make the effort to make friends, you will find seasonal gifts of grapes, asparagus, and assorted baskets of herbs placed outside your door.

French children are like their parents, very polite to strangers, and they have certain endearing habits which I encouraged my own children to adopt, like for example always shaking hands with either a *'comment allez-vous?'*, or *'tres bien merci madame/monsieur'*. Small children always proffer a mouth to kiss you on the cheek. So try never to appear surprised. I once saw an overbearing, loud Anglo Saxon male, laugh uproariously when a delectable little five-year-old tilted her head to kiss him. He made an embarrassing spectacle of what, to that little girl, was a completely natural and polite thing to do.

The kindness and generosity of the France I have known for over 25 years is overwhelming. They remain features of a life reminiscent of the good neighbour stories my mother used to relate about our small town in South Wales. Perhaps it is that essential ingredient of community which we may have already lost or be in danger of losing, and it is the pressing need to recapture some of those old values that sends us scurrying to France in our thousands. To thank a neighbour for some kindly act is usually received with a smile, a shrug and *'C'est normal'*.

No doubt about it, life in France is different. *Vive la différence.*

USEFUL FRENCH

Avoir du culot	To be cheeky
Une histoire gauloise	A dirty story

10
A WALK ON THE
CULTURAL SIDE

France has always been a magnet for the Arts.

Paris, in the north, Nice in the south, to say nothing of the cities in between, have drawn painters, writers, giants of literature (*belles lettres*), dancers, and musicians for the past few hundred years and, even today, France could claim to be the centre of European culture.

Their education system embraces all forms of the Arts, and philosophy is on the teaching curriculum of Lycées, the French being rightly proud of their historical tradition of philosophers. Maybe this is why most French are natural and frequently lengthy talkers. This ability to launch into discursive conversation is as much part of French life as *croissants*. You have only to watch certain television programmes, not all (some are quite as banal as ours), but stations like Arte, to see a theme, hammered out and analysed for two or even three hours, which says a great deal about the viewers' span of concentration.

I have noticed, even on a town bus, perfect strangers will talk, particularly if there is a cuddly baby or dog to focus attention. After four stops they are swapping life stories, after six, half the bus is joining in the conversation. This is a great example of natural communication, which is surely what art is all about.

Of course you are going to find examples of cultural pursuits at their most refined in all large cities, that is, culture as we understand it, concerts, opera, art exhibitions, ballet, lectures and readings from well-known writers.

But what of the smaller townships, and large villages?

Whilst they cannot afford to bring in the big shows (*spectacles*), there is throughout the country a well defined pattern of indigenous regional culture, festivals and *fêtes* that often go back to the Middle Ages. Rustic certainly, but culture nonetheless, in a solid earthy form, from the Celtic festivals of Brittany, to the cowboys who run the young bulls through the town (*abrivado*) in the south-west and the battle of the flowers and Carnival in Nice.

But there is another very potent culture in France, one which the French invented and developed, and which today has worldwide resonance: film. The film industry in France receives government support and funding, and film buffs may be happy to know that there are festivals in towns large and small, throughout the country and throughout the year.

For anyone contemplating making a film in France and wanting full financial support, certain criteria have to be met relating to author, script, director, cameraman, performers and technicians. Each of these categories is awarded points based on artistic and technical requirements, and the total number of points relate to the percentage of funding. But the overriding demand is that the film may be classified as 'French original expression'.

The Cannes Film Festival started in 1946 as a rather impolite hand-gesture to the Venice Festival. It was also a deliberate attempt to revive the country's tourism, and its wilting film industry after World War Two.

Back in Venice in 1939 a French film entry had been tipped for the prize, but as the fascist regimes were gathering momentum and influence, not surprisingly a German and Italian film tied for first place. The French, British and American judges resigned forthwith. Fortunately the winners of that festival were themselves obliged to resign six years later.

According to backroom intelligence, there is an annual Porn Film Festival that carries on alongside the parent festival, in Cannes basements. However, judging by the publicity stunts organised for every moment of the day there seems to be an ample selection of salacious cavorting amongst so called starlets, running hither and thither on the beach, both topless and bottomless, and of both sexes. But curb the excitement, there may not be government funding for this category!

FILM FESTIVALS

France holds more than 150 annual Film Festivals with an astounding diversity of theme guaranteed to captivate the most pernickety.

This could be another aid in regional selection.

TOWN	TITLE	TELEPHONE	DATE	THEME
ABBEVILLE	Festival du film de l'oiseau et de la vie sauvage	22.24.02.02	April 13–24	Environment
AIX-EN-PROVENCE	Rencontres aixoises du cinéma court	42.27.08.64	Dec 10–14	Short films
ALBI	Festival International du film	63.77.60.28	July 24–29	Amateur
ALÉS	Festival du Cinéma d'Alés	66.30.24.26	March 19–26	International
AMIENS	International Festival	22.91.01.44	Nov 8–27	Unknown films
AMIENS	Biennale Internationale du film medical	22.80.05.80	Sept 19–29	Scientific

AMIENS	Film d'archeologie	22.97.33.44	Jan 24–28	History
ANGERS	Festival Premiers plans	40.17.07.74	Jan 21–30	Young writers
ANNECY	Fest International du film d'animation	50.57.41.72	June	Animation
ANNECY	14èmes Rencontres du cinéma italien	50.33.44.00	Dec 3–8	Italy
ANNONAY	Fest Int du ler film et de la jeunesse	75.33.11.77	Feb 9–19	Childhood/ Youth
ANTIBES	Fest mondial de l'image sous marine	93.61.45.45	Oct 30–Nov 3	Environment
ARCACHON	Fest du cinémas des monde latins	59.24.80.50	Sept 2–7	Latin- American
ARGENTEUIL	Les cinglés du cinéma	39.61.78.03	Jan 26–28	'Crazy'
AUBAGNE	Fest des passions	91.57.50.57	Nov 29–Dec 2	Unknown films
AUBERVILLIERS	Fest des films pour eveillierles regards 6–13 ans	48.33.52.52	Oct 7–16	Childhood/ Youth
AUTRANS	Fest Int du film – neige, glace. aventure	76.95.30.70	Dec 4–8	Environment
AVIGNON	French-American	90.25.93.23	June 26–30	American workshop
AVORIAZ	Fest du film français	47.53.95.80	Jan 15–19	French
BAILLARGUES	Fest du cinéma d'animation	67.10.14.54	Nov 6–16	Animation
BASTIA	Fest du film et des culture Mediterranéenes	95.32.08.32	Nov 20–26	Mediter- ranean
BEAUNE	Rencontres cinématographiques	53.42.40.00	Oct 25–27	Europe
BEAUVAIS	Cinémalia	44.45.90.00	March 23–30	Environment
BELFORT	Fest du film Entrevues	84.54.24.43	Nov 23–Dec 1	Young Writers
BIARRITZ	Écrans sonores rencontres int des musiques a l'image	40.39.03.39	Nov 14–20	Music
BIARRITZ	Fest national de l'audiovisuel et de la communication Fest Audiovisual europeen de l'image de t'entreprise	47.20.22.10	June 11–15	a/v company films
BLOIS	Fest du cinéma quebecois	42.52.90.92	Oct 16–20	French speaking Canada
BOBIGNY	Theatres au Cinéma	48.30.32.87	March 20 –Apr 5	Arts/ Entertainment

BREST	Fest du film court	98.44.03.94	Dec 5–11	Shorts
CABESTANY	Rencontres d'hiver de video-photo	68.66.36.07	March 30–31	Audiovisual
CANNES	Rencontres cinématographiques	93.99.04.04	Dec 9–16	Int production
CANNES	Cinémas en France	45.63.80.70	May 17–28	French
CANNES	Fest International du film	45.61.66.00	May 9–20	Int production
CANNES	FIPA Fest Int de programmes audiovisuel	45.61.01.66	Jan 7–12	Audiovisual
CANNES	Quinzaine des realisateurs	45.61.01.66	May 9–20	Int production
CHAMROUSSE	Fest Int du film d'humour	76.84.11.56	March 19–24	Humour
CHÂTEAUROUX	Fest du cinéma independant	54.34.80.04	Dec 12–15	Amateur
CHAUMONT	Rendezvous du cinéma français	25.30.39.90	Nov	French
CHERBOURG	Fest du cinéma britannique	33.93.38.94	Oct 15–22	British
CLERMONT-FERRAND	Festival du court metrage	73.91.65.73	Feb 2–10	Shorts
COGNAC	Fest Int du film policier	46.40.55.00	April 6–9	Crime
CRÉTEIL	Fest Int de films des Femmes	49.80.38.98	March 22 –Apr 30	Women
CRÉTEIL	Semaine des films Europeen sur la famille	45.69.01.30	Nov 13–23	Environment
DEAUVILLE	20ème fest du Cinéma americain	46.40.55.00	Sept 6–8	American
DIGNE-LES- BAINS	Memoire du cinéma	92,32.29.33	Nov 8–22	Heritage
DIGNE-LES-BAINS	7ème cine d'été	92,32.29.33	July	Int production
DINARD	Fest du film brittanique	99.88.19.04	Sept 26–29	British
DOMPIERRE SUR BESBRE	Rencontres		March 22–24	Environment
DONZY-LE-NATIONAL	Cine-pause	85.59.20.80	Aug 1–4	Environment
DOUARNENEZ	Fest du cinéma	98.92.09.21	Aug 18–25	Unknown films

DUNKERQUE	Rencontres cinématographiques	28.66.47.89	Oct 2–22	Int production
ÉVREUX	Ciné-Scenes	32.78.85.25	Feb 9–17	Int production
GERARDMER	Fantastica - carrefour des fantastiques	46.40.55.00	Jan 31 –Feb 4	Fantasy
GINDOU	Rencontres de cinéma	53.66.86.45	Aug 27 –Sept2	Unknown films
LA BAULE	Fest du film europeen	45.25.83.28	Oct 6–11	General
LA BIOLLE	Fest du film rural	79·54.76.06	Nov 15–17	Environment
LAMOTTE BEUVRON	Fest Int du film chasse-natur	54.88.21.75	Nov 15–17	Environment
LAON	Fest Int du cinéma jeune public	23.20.38.61	March 25 –Apr 4	Childhood/ Youth
LA ROCHELLE	Fest Int du film	48.06.16.66	June 28–July 8	Unknown films
LE MANS	Fest de l'image	43.28.16.47	Nov 23–Dec 8	Audiovisual
LE MESNIL LE ROI	Fest Int cinéma non-profesionel	39.62.85.89	Oct 4–6	Amateur
LILLE	Fest de film court	20.15·48.25	Apr 28 –May 3	Shorts
LORQUIN	Fest de Lorquin	87.23.15.90	June 10–14	Scientific
LUSSAS	États generaux du documentaire	75.94.28.06	Aug 19–25	Documentary
LYON	Fest Int cinéma, television et monde urbain	72·43·90·59	October	urban cinema/tv
MANOSQUE	Rencontres cinématographiques du réel a l'imaginaire	92.70.34.19	Jan 23–28	Int production
MARCIGNY	Rencontres cinéma	77.25.83.65	Oct 29–Nov 3	Int production
MARSEILLES	Atelier cinéma	91.81.77·39	July 15–31	Cinema techniques
MARSEILLES	Vues sur les docs	91.84.40.17	June 18–24	Documentary
MAURIAC	Fest Int du film medical et de santé	71.67.37.37	March	Scientific
METZ	Fest Int du film de création super 8	87.75.17.63	Nov 23–24	Amateur
MEUDON	Fest du court métrage d'humour	41.14.80.00	Oct 11–13	Humour shorts
MONTE CARLO	Imagina	49·8).26·93	Feb 21–23	Audiovisual
MONTPELLIER	Festival du film chinois	67.34.73.78	Feb 23 –March 3	China

MONTPELLIER	Fest Int du cinéma mediterranéen	67.66.36.36	Oct 25–Nov 3	Mediterranean
MONTREUIL	Fest Int du film lesbien	48.70.77.11	Oct 26–30	Lesbian
NANTES	Fest des trois continents	40.69.09.73	Nov 19–26	Unknown films
NANTES	Tout feu ... tout flammes. Fest des films des femmes	51.82.31.09	March	Women
NEVERS	De Nevers a l'aube	86.21.48·93	Dec 11–14	Experimental
NEXON	Films du cirque	55.58.34.71	July 15–Aug 7	Arts/Entertainment
NÎMES	Fest Int du film et des réalisateurs des écoles de cinéma	72.02.20.36	1997	Film schools
OBERNAI	Chimeres	88.95.68.19	March 13–17	Journey in time
ORLÉANS	Biennale du cinéma japonais	38.62.96.90	Jan 27– Feb 5	Japan
PALAISEAU	Fest Int du film scientifique	60.14.22.22	Nov 13–20	Scientific
PANTIN	Fest court métrage	48·91.24·91	June 7–16	Shorts
PARIS	Biennale des cinémas arabes	40.51.38.78	June	Mediterranean
PARIS	Biennale Int du film sur l'art	44.78.47.22	Oct 16–21	Arts/Entertainment
PARIS	Bilan du film ethnographique	47.04.38.20	March 18–22	Documentary
PARIS	Cinéma du réel	44.78.44.30	March 10–17	Documentary
PARIS	Cinémemoir	42·56.87.76	Nov 22–Dec 30	Heritage
PARIS	Festival d'automne	42.96.12.27	Sept 15–Feb 28	Autumn
PARIS	Fest du film de Paris (cinéma et jeunesse)	45.72.96.44	June 19–25	Childhood/Youth
PARIS	Fest Int du film d'art et pedagogique	42.65.08.88	Nov 22–Dec 3	Arts/Entertainment
PARIS	Fest Int du film d'environnement	53.68.88·93	Nov 23–27	Environment
PARIS	Rencontres Int de l'audiovisuel scientifique-images et sciences	49.60.41.38	Sept 28–Oct 6	Scientific
PERPIGNAN	Confrontation 30	68.66.30.33	Apr 3–21	History

11

SO WHERE?

Having read thus far of the delights, the pitfalls, the cautionary tales, some of which could accompany you in your bid for a place in the sun, the problem of 'Where?' may still be present. Before we start on the regions, and to further help you make up your mind, here is recent information gathered by the French institute of national statistics. They took 100 towns/cities and under section headings relating to various aspects of living, sent each town/city detailed questionnaires. When the results were analysed in each separate section using a points system, they were able to list the towns in order of merit. Some of the results were quite surprising.

TOP TWENTIES

The most active towns with a dynamic growing economy

1	LYON	11	STRASBOURG
2	PARIS	12	MULHOUSE
3	MARSEILLE	13	TOURS
4	TOULOUSE	14	NICE

5	GRENOBLE	15	REIMS
6	LILLE	16	AVIGNON
7	BORDEAUX	17	METZ
8	NANCY	18	CAEN
9	NANTES	19	RENNES
10	ROUEN	20	DIJON

The best places to find employment

1	LYON	11	LE MANS
2	NIORT	12	RODEZ
3	AURILLAC	13	QUIMPER
4	TOULOUSE	14	ORLÉANS
5	DIJON	15	COLMAR
6	PARIS	16	BOURG-EN-BRESSE
7	LAVAL	17	AJACCIO
8	GAP	18	THONON-LES-BAINS
9	LA ROCHE-SUR-YON	19	NANTES
10	ÉVREUX	20	MONTAUBAN

The top twenty for housing to buy or to rent

1	CHOLET	11	CARCASSONNE
2	SAINT-NAZAIRE	12	LAVAL
3	LA ROCHE-SUR-YON	13	ALENÇON
4	CHÂTEAUROUX	14	MONTAUBAN
5	CASTRES	15	LORIENT
6	SAINT-BRIEUC	16	SAINT-MALO
7	LE MANS	17	NARBONNE
8	ALBI	18	VANNES
9	QUIMPER	19	BREST
10	NIORT	20	BOURGES

CRIME

Most towns and cities in France have seen crime levels drop in the past few years, but there are still black spots, notably Paris and the Mediterranean.

These are the top twenty with the lowest level of crime

1	CHOLET	11	VANNES
2	RODEZ	12	PAU
3	LIMOGES	13	CLERMONT-FERRAND
4	CASTRES	14	BREST
5	AURILLAC	15	MONTLUCON
6	CHERBOURG	16	PÉRIGUEUX
7	GAP	17	LAVAL
8	LA ROCHE-SUR-YON	18	DIJON
9	CHÂTEAUROUX	19	BASTIA
10	NIORT	20	ÉPINAL

The safest roads, i.e. lowest accident rate

1	COMPIÈGNE	11	NARBONNE
2	CARCASSONNE	12	CHAMBERY
3	BEAUVAIS	13	LAVAL
4	QUIMPER	14	CAEN
5	PAU	15	RODEZ
6	ALBI	16	ST-ÉTIENNE
7	BOULOGNE-SUR-MER	17	CHOLET
8	ARLES	18	NIORT
9	CHARLEVILLE-MÉZIÈRES	19	VALENCIENNES
10	PERPIGNAN	20	VALENCE

EDUCATION

Where you will find the best education in terms of schools, and higher education, and where the best academic results are achieved.

1	AIX-EN-PROVENCE	11	ARRAS
2	VANNES	12	CAEN
3	BAYONNE	13	TROYES
4	ANNECY	14	NANCY
5	BREST	15	LA ROCHELLE
6	ANGERS	16	CHOLET
7	RENNES	17	BORDEAUX
8	TOURS	18	LYON
9	METZ	19	NIORT
10	LA ROCHE-SUR-YON	20	ÉPINAL

ENVIRONMENT

How much is spent per capita on making the town more attractive and pleasant to live in?

Here they are in order of local authority input.

1	CANNES	11	DUNKERQUE
2	VICHY	12	CHAMBERY
3	BLOIS	13	BOURGES
4	BORDEAUX	14	CAEN
5	BAYONNE	15	PÉRIGUEUX
6	LA ROCHELLE	16	CARCASSONNE
7	BELFORT	17	TOULON
8	ORLÉANS	18	AVIGNON
9	LIMOGES	19	ANNECY
10	PAU	20	TOURS

LEISURE AND CULTURAL ACTIVITIES

These are the towns/cities where you will find the best variety of *divertissements*.

1	PARIS	11	AIX-EN-PROVENCE
2	LYON	12	ROUEN
3	BORDEAUX	13	METZ
4	MONTPELLIER	14	GRENOBLE
5	NANTES	15	TOURS
6	TOULOUSE	16	AVIGNON
7	STRASBOURG	17	NICE
8	NANCY	18	CLERMONT-FERRAND
9	CAEN	19	MARSEILLE
10	LILLE	20	NÎMES

QUALITY OF LIFE

In this section points are awarded for factors such as proximity to sea and ski, public transport, sightseeing, urban density, parks and gardens. To many of the towns listed the title *Ville Fleuri* is applied.

1	CANNES	11	TOULON
2	FRÉJUS	12	NARBONNE
3	SÈTE	13	ST-ÉTIENNE
4	NICE	14	TOULOUSE
5	MARSEILLE	15	AVIGNON
6	VALENCE	16	NÎMES
7	BÉZIERS	17	ARLES
8	PERPIGNAN	18	LYON
9	MONTPELLIER	19	GRENOBLE
10	ANTIBES	20	AIX-EN-PROVENCE

There is no town that has it all, but according to the statisticians the top twenty prizes for the best all-round French towns/cities are awarded to the following.

1	LYON	11	DIJON
2	TOULOUSE	12	NIORT
3	BORDEAUX	13	ANGERS
4	NANTES	14	STRASBOURG
5	TOURS	15	PARIS
6	GRENOBLE	16	ROUEN
7	RENNES	17	NANCY
8	METZ	18	CAEN
9	ORLÉANS	19	VANNES
10	CHAMBÉRY	20	NICE

Maybe the statisticians have steered you towards a choice. If not, perhaps the next chapter will.

The regional section to follow is not meant as a travel guide nor tourist handbook. It is merely intended to point you in general directions, any one of which may appeal – so please be understanding should I omit to mention a town or a special place of interest that you happen to know. I shall give you the broad outline, it is up to you to fill in the details according to your personal preferences.

When finally you do choose a place to put down a few if not all of your roots, 50% is logic, and the other 50% is your own gut reaction.

12

THE DEPARTMENTS

France is divided approximately into 22 ancient provinces, but to simplify administration and postal services, there are now 95 departments, each one with a *préfet* and a general council of administration. Napoleon had much to answer for when he devised the system, now so over-complicated that it drives thousands of civil servants (*fonctionaires*) into manic despair and worse.

The last two digits of a car registration correspond to the department where it was first registered. If you change departments you could waste half a day at the *préfecture* to have the number and number plate changed. This is to be addressed and a change of number plate will soon be unnecessary.

The first two digits of the postal code correspond to the number of the department, so if you write to someone in the Gironde the post code will begin with 33.

Departments

1	AIN	33	GIRONDE	65	PYRÉNÉES (HAUTES)
2	AISNE	34	HÉRAULT	66	PYRÉNÉES-ORIENTALES
3	ALLIER	35	ILLE-ET-VILAINE	67	BAS RHIN
4	ALPES-DE-HAUTE-PROVENCE	36	INDRE	68	HAUT RHIN
5	HAUTES-ALPES	37	INDRE-ET-LOIRE	69	RHÔNE
6	ALPES MARITIMES	38	ISÈRE	70	SAÔNE (HAUTE)
7	ARDÈCHE	39	JURA	71	SAÔNE-ET-LOIRE
8	ARDENNES	40	LANDES	72	SARTHE
9	ARIÈGE	41	LOIR-ET-CHER	73	SAVOIE
10	AUBE	42	LOIRE	74	SAVOIE (HAUTE)
11	AUDE	43	LOIRE (HAUTE)	75	PARIS
12	AVEYRON	44	LOIRE ATLANTIQUE	76	SEINE-MARITIME
13	BOUCHES-DE-RHÔNE	45	LOIRET	77	SEINE-ET-MARN
14	CALVADOS	46	LOT	78	YVELINES
15	CANTAL	47	LOT ET GARONNE	79	DEUX-SÈVRES
16	CHARENTE	48	LOZÈRE	80	SOMME
17	CHARENTE-MARITIME	49	MAINE ET LOIRE	81	TARN
18	CHER	50	MANCHE	82	TARN ET GARONNE
19	CORRÈZE	51	MARNE	83	VAR
20	CORSE SUD/HAUTE	52	MARNE (HAUTE)	84	VAUCLUSE
21	CÔTE-D'OR	53	MAYENNE	85	VENDÉE
22	CÔTES-D'ARMOR	54	MEURTHE-ET-MOSELLE	86	VIENNE
23	CREUSE	55	MEUSE	87	VIENNE (HAUTE)
24	DORDOGNE	56	MORBIHAN	88	VOSGES
25	DOUBS	57	MOSELLE	89	YONNE
26	DRÔME	58	NIÈVRE	90	TERRITOIRE DE BELFORT
27	EURE	59	NORD	91	ESSONNE
28	EURE-ET-LOIRE	60	OISE	92	HAUTS-DE-SEINE
29	FINISTÈRE	61	ORNE	93	SEINE-ST-DENIS
30	GARD	62	NORD-PAS-DE-CALAIS	94	VAL-DE-MARNE
31	GARONNE (HAUTE)	63	PUY-DE-DÔME	95	VAL-D'OISE
32	GERS	64	PYRÉNÉES ATLANTIQUES		

As a further guide to location, here is a chart of average daily maximum centigrade temperatures. Obviously there will be degrees of variation depending on global warming and heatwaves.

	J	F	M	A	M	J	J	A	S	O	N	D
PARIS	7.5	7	10.2	15.7	16.6	23.4	25	25.6	21	16.5	11.7	7.8
STRASBOURG	5.5	5.3	9.3	13.7	15.8	23	24	26.3	21	14.9	7.6	4.7
ST. MALO	9	8.6	11	17	16	22.7	25	24	21.2	16.5	12	9.3
TOURS	7.6	6.8	10.3	16	16.4	23.6	25.8	24.5	21	16.2	11.2	7
LYON	7.4	6.7	10.8	15.8	17.3	25.6	27.6	27.6	23.5	16.5	10.4	7.8
BORDEAUX	10	9.4	12.2	19.5	18	23.7	27	25.7	24	19.7	15.4	11
TOULOUSE	12.4	11.5	12.5	17.6	20	26.5	28.4	28	26	21	15.8	13.5
AVIGNON	12	12	14	18.5	20.8	26.6	28	28.4	25.2	22.2	16.8	14
NICE	13	14	15	18.5	21.8	26	28	28.4	25.2	22.2	16.8	14

13
REGION 1
BRITTANY, NORMANDY, PICARDIE,
NORD-PAS-DE-CALAIS

Fifty years ago, when the Brits who could afford it sallied forth abroad after the restrictions of war, the first stop was Northern France. It was near, a short channel crossing, and a perfect place to experience the delights of a foreign country. The language, the money and the food were so completely different, and comedians made jokes about French loos, plumbing and garlic: those who are scraping the barrel for material still do.

In any case Northern France is firmly in Anglo-Saxon blood having been invaded and conquered by William the Bastard, as he was known to the locals, who were probably only too happy to get rid of him. For the next couple of hundred years we managed to get our own back by appropriating various chunks of the country through our conqueror's progeny, and finally murder their own Joan of Arc. And, despite the possible collusion of the French religious elite, the responsibility for her death, was ours.

BRITTANY

Although we were finally thrown out of France, there may be something in that historical sub-conscious that has urged us back to Normandy and the north. If you are Welsh there is a natural and palpable affinity with the Bretons, its language, people and folk-lore. In fact one of the Professors of Celtic studies at Rennes University is a Welshman. There are many identical words in Welsh and Breton; for example a mouth of a river is an '*aber*' in both languages, as is *du* (black), *ty* (house), and many similar words like *armor* (sea) in Breton and *mor* in Welsh. I remember as a child in Wales, seeing the Breton onion sellers converse quite happily in Breton with my Welsh speaking family. Hardly surprising that Nantes which used to be the capital of Brittany is twinned with Cardiff.

Although there are now flight connections to Rennes and Dinard, and Deauville airport will soon become international, most Brits regard Northern France as a relatively easy drive, despite increasingly costly sea crossings (at least from Portsmouth). Therefore if it is the proximity of a weekend/holiday/part-time bolt-hole, you want, Northern France could be a good choice. Proximity is in the distance from the UK, not in time, because door to door, it could well take longer to drive into Brittany than fly to Nice.

The climate in Brittany is surprisingly warm and temperate because of the Gulf Stream which it shares with western Normandy and has therefore always been popular with British home seekers and holiday makers.

Culturally it may well be the most interesting province of France. It has a marked Celtic identity, through its music, poetry and dance. Each year in June/July the *Quinzaine Celtique*, a Celtic festival, is held in Nantes, followed in August by the spectacular Inter-Celtic Festival at Lorient, possibly the largest gathering of Celts in Europe. I have known of fellow Celts who were so seduced by the *bonhomie* of this event, that they disappeared for several weeks thereafter. Roads are closed, traffic stops and the streets are given over to poetry recitals, harps and songs.

Then there are the megaliths and dolmens dating from 5000–2000BC. At Carnac alone there are about 2,000 megaliths that pre-date the Pyramids, standing in three rows of alignments sited parallel to the sea. As if that were not enough to make your spine tingle, there is the legend of King Arthur and his Knights of the Round Table. The forest of Paimpon is said to be the location of Brocéliande, the home of King Arthur. Nearby is Merlin's seat where he would look out to sea and contemplate, although Carmarthen in South Wales also claims him. And despite the fairy tale doubts, the forest is said to be a magical place, and few people wander through it. Those who have, tell of strange sounds and noises, of footsteps rustling in the grass, of twigs snapping suddenly overhead and – most spooky of all – the sound of horsemen when none are there.

Brittany's coast is renowned for miles of smooth white sand, and is ideal for families. There are plenty of sea sports on offer and, of course, excellent sea food.

Rennes is a lively city with a medieval quarter, museums, galleries and an excellent university. St Malo, with its citadel, is a tourist attraction while Dinan, another beautifully preserved medieval citadel, attracts fewer visitors. And for those with more down-to-earth interests there is an annual winkle spitting competition held annually in Moguériec, near Roscoff: current champion managing 10.40m. Start practising.

From Brittany's towns there is a good public transport system, with trains running frequently to all major French cities and efficient local bus services.

I spoke to Madame Yvette Folliard the mayor of Meneac. She remarked on the different types of Britons who were now coming to Brittany, not as tourists but buying homes either for holidays or for more permanent domiciles. Twenty years ago they came in couples searching for an escape, *la vie bohème,* to live in their caravans and campers, and did not bother to be part of the community. The British who bought holiday homes during this period caused problems with the religious proclivities of Breton communities that were staunchly Roman Catholic. This is not so any more. Yvette Folliard has observed during the last three to four years the Brits are really coming to find a new all-round life and are more willing to integrate by beginning to learn French. Some still work in the UK from Monday to Friday and come 'home' at the weekends. Some, of course, invade the province with a military determination to do what they want to do irrespective of local planning regulations. They soon find out, the hard way. There are a few British enterprises in the town; one builds swimming pools. Ten percent of children in primary schools are British, so even if their parents cannot speak French, the children do. Learning the Breton language is not obligatory, unless it is a special Breton school.

She says there were problems in the past when the local 'paysans' would allow a tumbledown cottage to fall into disrepair, and it would remain like that until a Brit did the renovation and sold it for a handsome profit. She used to explain to her aggrieved compatriots that they could do the same thing if they wished. Apparently the locals are now 'wising up' and having their share of market goodies. This has meant inevitably that property prices have risen.

According to Mlle Carine Morice, assistant director of Immobilière des Phares (*phare* – lighthouse) with offices in Penmarch and Le Guilvinec specialising in coastal properties (00 33 2 98 58 45 84), more and more people are buying their principal home in Brittany, but families tend to go further inland into the more rural areas while holiday homers stay on the coast. Carine's email; *contact@immobilieredesphares.com.*

Examples of property for sale

Nr Vannes. House 105 sq.m. Land 520 sq.m. 6 rooms (4 beds): 196,800€

Côtes-d'Armor. St Laurent 2 beds 95 sq.m.: 87,000€

Côtes-d'Armor. Prat. House 1,100 sq.m. Land 2000 sq.m.: 288,000€

There seems to be a strong community spirit in these Breton townships and integration is the key word.

These agencies are nationwide covering any region you choose: *www.immofrance.com*; *www.avendrealouer.fr*; *www.seloger.com*.

I interviewed Shirley Cooklin, a senior citizen, feisty as a forty year old and far from retired. She is a writer and painter who spends six months of the year in her large cottage in Brittany, and her French is excellent. She found her 'fairy-tale' home advertised in a *notaire's* window for only £2000, 15 years ago, whilst staying with an English friend nearby. It was a total ruin apart from a good roof. For the next five years while she accumulated enough spare cash to put it right, she stayed with her friend and could only gaze longingly at her idyll. For ten years now she has been installed and in some style, in her beautiful cottage, surrounded by lawns and shrubs. The nearest towns are Meneac and La Trinité Porhoet. Dinard with its small airport is about one hour's drive away. During her annual six months in France she lets her flat on the SE coast of England, the rental keeping her solvent. It takes five minutes in the car from Shirley's hamlet to the nearest mini-market, and she assures me it would be impossible to live there without a car. Her social life is quite lively for she has both British and French friends all within half an hour's drive. I asked her about the suitability of the area for a young family.

'They should be very careful, and think it through – perhaps rent something before buying. It's difficult to make a living now. The *gîte* market seems to be dead, because there has been such an increase in cross channel fares. And in any case you have to be near the sea. I have friends living in Mid-Brittany who just can't sell their house and *gîtes* and probably that's why.'

Are there lots of Brits relocating to Brittany?

'Far too many! They're not Francophiles, and seem to forget that they are the foreigners. Francophiles like us try to become absorbed in the community, but they don't mix, and stay closeted together. They have pushed up house prices for the locals and are consequently very unpopular. Some communities here are bursting at the seams.' She smiled, 'You should hear them in the supermarket, they're so rude some of them'.

And the cost of living?

'Still cheaper than the UK, although everything went up with the euro.'

With hindsight would you change anything?

'Yes. As I get older driving long distances becomes more of a chore. I'd like to be nearer Dinan.'

Shirley's *taxe foncière* for 2004 was €216.00 as was the *taxe d'habitation*.

Water cost €169.00, and the local commune's *ordures menageres* (household refuse), €125.00.

NORMANDY, NORD-PAS-DE-CALAIS AND PICARDIE

Further east, the regions of Normandy, Nord-Pas-de-Calais, and Picardie have seen more than their fair share of horrific warfare. There is barely a single soul in the UK who does not have some emotional reaction to their very names. The poppies of Picardy, the battlefields of the Somme, the landing beaches of World War II are all part of living memory, but the historical significance of the region goes back centuries.

It is the part of France that lies closest to the UK with, at one point, a mere 22 miles of Channel separating the two countries. Over the past ten or so years the Channel tunnel has revolutionised travel particularly to the north of Europe. It is now feasible to work as far north as London and commute back to Normandy each evening with Eurostar, and many do.

There are three particularly chic coastal towns in Normandy: Trouville, Deauville and Honfleur – the Norman Riviera. Deauville was always a favourite with well-to-do English and French in the 19th century with race-track, casino and elegant houses to match. Each September there is the American Film Festival, encouraging the town to style itself the Cannes of the North. It may well become as busy as its southern sister when the airport becomes international. Property in this area is expensive, but you could find good value for money a little further inland around Lisieux.

The Cotentin Peninsula is slightly cut off from the rest of Normandy and despite having the industrial port of Cherbourg at its tip, where I believe you can still buy the famous Cherbourg Umbrella, there are some lovely seaside townlets like Barfleur and St Vaast la Hougue close by. The superb beaches of the peninsula are a far cry from the carnage of WWII, but there are several war museums to remind us.

At Ste Mère Église for example, a small inland town that was vital to the Allies, a paratrooper dangled for hours during the battle with his parachute caught in the steeple. Today, as a commemorative gesture, a model paratrooper hangs from the church spire.

For anyone thinking of a B&B or *chambres d'hôte*, this piece of France attracts a wider public than the average tourist. Apart from historical value this whole area is a walker's paradise.

If you are searching for an 'away from it all' location, the west coast of the Cotentin Peninsula is surprisingly wild and empty, but it does house a large nuclear recycling plant and power station, so perhaps you should have a re-think.

Further north is Dieppe, on the *Côte d'Albatre* (the alabaster coast), so called because of the ice white cliffs. Today it is a small port but with an impressive visitors' list. Renoir, Sickert Pissaro, Monet and Whistler came here, as did our own exiled Oscar Wilde.

Etretat is another pretty town easily accessible with a spectacular coast-line, and one of many similar townships that could offer an interesting life style for any house-seeking Brit.

Train services, as one would expect, are excellent, as are the local bus services. After all, southern Picardy is close to the Parisian commuter belt.

House prices in Normandy vary enormously, inland being cheaper than the coast and smaller resorts cheaper than the smart ones.

I spoke to Madame Fillatre who runs her own agency in Honfleur: tel 0033 2 31 89 34 12.

She says more people are buying second homes in the region and this will grow when the new international airport at Deauville is finished. But the three towns have historically provided second homes for Parisians as much as the British. I asked her about new urban developments or building projects. She very sweetly reminded me that in France they were more interested in preserving their heritage *patrimoine* and renovating than in new-builds.

Examples of properties for sale

Cherbourg. House. 120 sq.m. Land 200 sq.m. 5 rooms, balcony: 180,000€

Cherbourg. House. 130 sq.m. on 3 floors. 4 beds, 2 kitchens, terrace, cellar: 172,800€

Deauville. Apartment. 65 sq.m. 3 rooms: 222,600€

Trouville. House. 110 sq m. 8 rooms: 340,000€

Dieppe. House. 4 beds, big loft to convert. Veranda + terrace overlooking garden: 185,000€

Étretat. Authentic fisherman's house. 3 beds, large sitting rm: 166,000€

Nr Fécamp. Partly restored barn to finish. 2400 sq.m. land with pond: 97,000€

www.fillatre-immobilier.com
www.normandie-immobilier.com
www. immobilier-edouarddenis.com
www.argenton-immoServices.com

If French websites are difficult to find, try *www.google.fr* first.

I spoke to Chris and Gareth Davies, two people who upped sticks from South West England, to settle permanently in Normandy where they have been residents for four years, although they have known the area for about 30 years. Their nearest large town is Cherbourg which is about 20 km distant.

It was the tragic loss of one of their sons that was the deciding factor. They are both retired from very active lives in the theatre. Gareth was a television director and Chris a busy working actress. They had already bought their rundown cottage, little more than a ruin, and Gareth. a fantastic bricoleur, had already begun work on it. The intention was to use it as a holiday home. But after the family tragedy their lives changed. They sold their lovely house in Bath and Gareth threw himself into restoring the cottage almost single–handed; a therapy, he says, in retrospect.

After four years in their beautiful home would they recommend their life style?

'Well, for a young family, no we wouldn't. It's ten minutes to the nearest shopping centre, and while we are bang in the middle of a rural farming area, with utter tranquility always on offer, we are at the point where frankly we need more than that.

Life hasn't changed very much here. You could call it 'old-fashioned' when compared with 21st century Britain. Heart-warming. The government puts money into sustaining the quality and continuity of farming life, and families have been working and living in the same farms for generations, and that's wonderful.'

Would they consider moving house and why?

'Yes. Sometime within the next year or two, and for several reasons.

'We'd like easy access to an urban area, where we wouldn't have to use the car constantly. Also we'd like a little more 'buzz' from a social point of view. Meeting some ex-pats with a similar background would be great. I love political discussions, but that's difficult here unless your French flows. That's it really, finding like minds. And then of course there's the weather. Too much like Britain. We want somewhere warmer now.'

Gareth has transferred his accounts to France, to an English speaking accountant, and in one year he will be free of *plus-value*, (capital gains tax), when he sells the house.

Where would they go?

'Depends what we can buy for the money available.'

Would they ever return to the UK?

'Definitely not. Food is better quality and the general cost of living 25% cheaper here in France.

'And that includes our private health insurance. That's cheaper than we'd get in the UK.'

ooOOoo

Further east, five miles away from Crécy, and sixty miles from Calais, Roy and Jane, semi retired, live for a few months of the year in a small hamlet of 120 inhabitants.

When they bought their cottage in 1991, they found exactly what they wanted, an 'away from it all' location, with the barest minimum of mod cons. They bought near Calais (60 miles) because, according to Jane, Roy never took a holiday, so this would be convenient for weekend breaks. They rented it for two years before buying. The cottage had been modernised in 1960, and they have added no further modernisation. They have a piano, a radio, a fridge and an oven, but no television, no

132

washing machine and no microwave. They wanted a simple life, one where they made their own entertainment, which is indeed what their daughter and her friends did during holidays and half-terms. Their village is about two hours' drive from Paris, shorter now since the completion of the A16, and although there are many French second homes, there are three Dutch families, and four English. There are no shops, but bread, meat and grocery vans deliver regularly. They have made friends with many locals, Jane's French is excellent, and they are regularly invited out to drinks and supper. The mayor has become a good friend and they wouldn't dream of missing the *quatorze juillet* (14th July Bastille Day) celebrations. They love the communal village lunches and the dances; nothing seems to irritate them and they were both in total agreement that the cost of living is far less than in the UK. They are not sure about relocating but they are debating about living in France permanently, and, with retirement looming, Roy thinks they may well look now for a bigger house. They are particularly pleased that Speedferries, a new cross channel company has started up and challenged the higher-priced operators. Booking in advance on this catamaran (Dover-Boulogne) reduces fares to about £25 or less each way. As they love the sea and dislike the tunnel this suits very well.

And advice to newcomers?

'Try to learn some of the language. It's impolite not to.'

14
REGION 2
PARIS AND THE
ÎLE-DE-FRANCE

PARIS

Anyone who thinks of France thinks of Paris. Many would paraphrase Dr Johnson's words, 'He who is tired of Paris, is tired of life'.

For this city has always been, and still is, the Mecca of the Arts, of literature, of painting and of philosophy, where men and women from all nationalities have come in their quest for a *'vie bohème'*, to breathe in the very atmosphere of the city and to share the romance of literary *soirées*, where great names gathered to talk, and make music.

Paris has given, and continues to give the world's artists and intellectuals more freedom and respect than they would ever have at home.

Henry Miller would never have been published in America, neither would Frank Harris have been published in England. It provided Edward

VII with a highly salacious romping ground, where he knew his obscenities would be kept secret. I have often wondered whether the signing of the *'Entente Cordiale'* in Paris in 1904, was not another way to silence royal gossip.

Paris, despite wars and occupation, has remained a truly beautiful city with its broad vistas and avenues, since Baron Haussman tore down the airless streets of rat-infested slums.

Adolf Hitler called Paris his 'City of Light', refused to have it bombed, and charged his architect Speer with the task of making Berlin as beautiful.

There are restaurants and cafés, like *Les Deux Magots* and the *Café Flore* where latter-day artists and intellectuals still meet to talk and to drink, as did Jean Paul Sartre and Simone de Beauvoir.

I remember, as a girl of sixteen, visiting Paris for the first time, and falling in love with the city – didn't we all? There was certain smell in the Metro – a mixture of *Gaulloise* cigarettes and heavy perfume that I can still recall; a heady smell which for an adolescent was synonymous with romantic love, moonlight on the Seine, *les bateaux mouches*, L'Opera, and the romance of intellectual pursuit.

Just before the suburban riots in 2005, Paris had been voted one of the best cities of the world in which to live. In a survey of 127 world cities, carried out by the Economist Intelligence Unit (EIU) it came fifth while London was forty-seventh.

Property in Paris over the last five years has seen a 60% increase in prices, driven partly by low mortgage rates. One newspaper reported that artists' garrets were being turned into luxury lofts. Although the boom is now beginning to slow down, rents are rising by about 3–4% a year and, according to a recent survey, one in five property buyers in Paris is foreign, the average cost of a piece of the city beyond the reach of many French.

Paris is more compact than London, easier to get about and, according to a friend, the *quartiers* have a distinct village life of their own.

According to Monsieur Bouhout (*www.standingimmobilier.fr*) who sells apartments in Paris as well as very grand *hotels particulier*, there are dozens of Brits packed into *arrondissment* (district) number 7. He also sells larger country houses *châteaux*, found predominantly in central France.

Jo Webb, a retired and full-of-life lady, is a widow now.

She and her husband had a boat many years ago when their girls were growing up, which they kept moored in the South of France, but decided to change it for a house in Normandy.

On the edge of a village it had four bedrooms and a garden, but finally with her husband's health deteriorating, he suggested they looked for an apartment in Paris. They found the Norman winters too cold and with the fast boats stopping in October, visiting outside the summer period was limited. They wanted to be somewhere where the car was unnecessary; where a *baguette* was within walking distance.

It took them 18 months to sell the house, and four days to find their apartment in Paris. It is on the ground floor of a *bourgeois* block in the seventh *arrondissement*. It has two rooms, and a *cave* (cellar), was fully furnished with immense style, and cost them 206,000€ in 2002 and has increased by €100,000 since then. The yearly charge for the apartment, which covers her *taxe foncière* and hot water, is €800.

Jo loves her quartier. It is full of elegant government and embassy buildings, and her great joy is being able to walk to the Louvre, Les Invalides and the Eiffel Tower. At the moment she visits Paris a few days every month.

Would she like to live there permanently?

She has been tempted, but the family is in the UK.

The apartment is near Rue Clare, which she considers to be a microcosm of French life with many small shops and a market. 'Paris has a village life', she says. 'My quartier is a village and they go to such lengths to look after it. You should see it at Christmas time.'

As a woman alone in Paris Jo feels absolutely secure in her apartment block. She goes out more in Paris, than she does in her native Brighton, but puts it down to the never-ending voyages of discovery in her adopted city.

She freely admits Paris has a far greater 'buzz' for her than London these days.

Would she ever think of re-locating in France?

'Never,' she laughed. 'Paris is great.'

And words of advice to a Brit newcomer?

'Keep an open mind, and try to learn some of the language.'

ooOOoo

Another very happy Parisienne is Ann Queensberry who has an apartment.

She loves France and has spent a great deal of her life here. Her French is so good she translates plays into English. And why plays? Because when she isn't in Paris she is a working actress in the UK; many will remember Ann in the long running television serial 'Tenko'.

I asked her if she had thought of relocating to another part of France.

'No. I enjoy visiting the country, but cities are where I like to live.'

Would she like to live permanently in Paris?

'Not really, because of family and work in the UK.'

And what does she enjoy most about her French life style?

137

'Feeling free to do exactly what I like. I love the cinema, theatre, and wandering about the streets.'

Does it differ from her British life style?

She paused, 'Well, in England I never seem to catch up with all the things I should be doing. In Paris I find it easier to pace myself, or say no!'

Any irritations?

'None! Even the buses wait if they see you running,' she laughed. 'They don't in London.'

And her social life?

'Most of my friends are French, obviously not all, and I'm often invited to people's houses for dinner or to stay. But restaurants are good and affordable, so it's easier for working couples to entertain friends, outside.'

What advice would she give a newcomer?

'Learn as much French as possible! When French people see you have made an effort to learn their language, it is much appreciated.'

ÎLE-DE-FRANCE

It would appear that not many of us Brits choose to have holiday homes around the metropolis, not even in such choice areas as Versailles or Fontainebleau.

Fountainbleau

The *mairie* at the latter enumerated the business schools and the *école superieur* attended by foreign students and that there were a number of weekend cottages owned by Parisians. It takes only an hour by car to get to Paris on the A6 and by train about 40 minutes and is very much a commuter township, rather like Tunbridge Wells is to London.

Here's a place that has easy access to Paris, is extremely beautiful and could provide horse-mad daughters with any amount of holiday fun. Not only has Fontainebleau the glorious château, where the King's mistress Madame de Montespan lived, but it has 280,000 hectares of forest. Apart from its history, the town has an amazing number of sporting activities for its citizens, old and young, from swimming classes for six-month-old babes to senior Tai Chi, rambling and cycling. In between, there are lots of activities for children including circus, dance, fencing and archery, while adults have Alpine sports, karate, judo and the usual field sports.

But Fontainebleau is most renowned for its multitude of equestrian activities including a Pony Club, which is only what one would expect, having been the epicentre of Royal horsemen and hunters for centuries. The forest itself caters for mountain bikers, climbers, ramblers, runners, and more. A nature lover's paradise, here is an astounding variety of protected flora and fauna, and explorers are warned not to go into the forest in bad weather when there is a real danger of falling rocks, and to keep to the known pathways.

Three- to four-bedroomed properties are quite reasonably priced and this area, with all it has to offer, particularly access to the metropolis, would seem to be a wise choice for a B&B, as the château and forest attract visitors all the year round.

Examples of property for sale

All the following are in **Fontainebleau**.

House. 1 bedroom: 146,000€

House. 2 beds, few metres from centre and gardens: 211,000€

Town house. 2 beds. Large sitting rm: 234,000€

Period house. 2 beds plus outbuilding. Garden: 256,000€

House. 4 beds with lovely garden: 340,000€

House. Quiet sector. Period house 2 apartments or renovate into 4 bed house: 284,000€

Around Fontainebleau are small rural villages, like Avon, which is very close to the town. Samureau, Ury, Chailly-en-Bière, Chartrettes, Hericy, Bois-le-roi, and Barbizon are all within a few kilometres.

The choice for Megalie, who works at the tourist office would be Chailly-en-Bière because it is a typical French rural village close to the A6, a 45 minute drive to Paris, (35 minutes by train) and outside the village is a very large commercial centre. The big plus is the Forest of Fontainebleau on the doorstep. Art historians may be interested to know that the painters Millet and Rousseau are buried in Chailly.

Don't forget when attempting to contact estate agents (*immobiliers*) it is sometimes easier to try *www.google.fr* first. Typing in the town and/or region will link you to a number of local *immobiliers* and also to Orpi, Century 21, Logic-immo, and Seloger, all nationwide chains.

Here is a selection of village property.

Chailly-en-Biere

Village house. 4 beds. Garden 617 sq.m. Pool: 429,000€

Traditional house near A6. Paris 45 mins. 4 beds: 320,000€

House. 3 beds, 2 recep. Loft to develop, heart of village: 190,000€

Avon

House. 4 beds, garage: 345,000€

House. 4 beds, v large sitting rm: 350,000€

House. Near Fontainebleau, medieval village, 17th century, 7 beds, garden 700 sq.m.: 450,000€

Hericy

Village house. 4 bed, calm, possible extension: 240,000€

Bois-le-Roi

Village house. 4 beds, possible extension: 239,000€

Barbizon

House. 4 beds. Garden 1,500 sq.m. laid to lawn and trees: 370,000€

Now to make your mouth water…

Château. 1 hr 50 from Paris, 15 rooms. 16 hectare park. Ewardian period, 700 sq.m. Excellent condition: 1,605,000€

And a cool 3,000,000€ will buy your very own forest!

orpi-chailly immobilier. Tel. 00 33 1 60 66 49 46

www.lesiteimmobilier.com

www.agencemercure.fr

www.immofrance.com

www.acheter-louer.fr

Fontainebleau Immobilier. Tel. 00 33 1 60 72 07 20. They have dozens of properties, easy to navigate. Find the site through *www.google.fr*.

Versailles

Versailles began life as a modest few houses around King Louis XIII's hunting lodge, surrounded by a moat, but his son Louis XIV was so jealous of the size of a palace belonging to one of his ministers he set about forthwith making the modest hunting lodge a hundred times bigger. And so Versailles village grew alongside the ever expanding palace, into a new town.

Conceived by King Louis XIV, one could call it a chic Welwyn Garden City of its time, and not surprisingly it influenced the designs of St Petersburg and Washington DC.

King Louis XIV, the Sun King, as he liked to be known, believed fervently in his own divine right, and being second only to God, spared no money building his palace, this obscene monument of sheer self indulgence. The fact it was not his money to use deterred him not one iota. With that credo, such squandering could be completely justified.

Louis was very close to his exiled English cousin and brother-in-law, Charles with whom he had been brought up. When Charles finally returned to England to take up the new job as restored king, Louis' parting gift, so they say, was the British national anthem, music by Lully, and in my opinion the worst national anthem ever heard on a football pitch.

Louis XV, like his father, continued spending on the palace and even had the *Petit Trianon*, a small mansion in the grounds, built for his mistress Madame Pompadour, and after her Madame Dubarry. Even then the royals made sumptuous houses for their lovers.

His son Louis XVI embellished the castle still further, and added a farm to the *Petit Trianon* for his wife, Queen Marie Antoinette, complete with farm animals, where she could play milkmaids and discover peasant life, as she fondly believed.

Alas for them, the *sans culottes* had by now lost patience with the arrogant profligacy of their royals in the midst of such abject poverty, and the King and Queen duly lost their heads.

After the Revolution the French preserved the King's palace as they had paid for it in the first place, and it is now one of the most visited monuments in France. Michel Gaudo, the writer, has described it as an 'enormous royal *patisserie*, which was literally built on the bodies of the workers who constructed it'.

So much for the palace, but of Versailles city, opinions are conflicting. It has been described both as 'cold and bourgeois', and as a 'great city which saw the rise and fall of the monarchy and became the cradle of the Revolution. It remains the historic capital to which elected Presidents of the Republic come.'

As a young girl visiting Marie Antoinette's farm, I was told the story of two English schoolteachers to whom something remarkable had happened when they stopped to take in the vista. In the clearing in front of the farm a group of young women had appeared dressed as 18th century milkmaids and frolicked around the pond, laughing and talking. One seemed to be in charge as they played with the animals, one even milked a cow. The teachers were mesmerised.

Then the pageant disappeared. They recounted the idyll to their French hosts, assuming it had been a show organised by the city. But they had been the only spectators, and in fact no such event had been organised. Somehow the two women had slipped back into the mysterious cycle of time. I sat staring at the very spot for an hour willing the same apparition. I gave up, but who knows, it could happen again.

The city's population today is about 87,000, and it takes pride in the many higher educational establishments like the *Ecole Superieur* for Architecture, the Academy of *Beaux Arts* and, not least, the university with advanced science departments. It is served by three motorways and by five train stations, to Paris and the rest of Europe. By train to the Eiffel Tower, takes about 30 minutes. Property in the city is expensive especially if it is near the palace, the top location, and because the King's ministers and indeed subsequent ministers built themselves very substantial establishments, you will find a few of these *'hotel particulier'* listed in estate agents offerings.

A three-room apartment in Versailles is unlikely to cost less than 315,000€.

Houses centrally located, of average size are rarely less than 615,000€.

Examples of properties for sale

Versailles

House. 3 beds: 625,000€
Bergerie. 18th century, 4 beds, loft to renovate: 499,000€
Centre ville. Immense 6 bed house, 230 sq.m.: 1,570,000€

143

House. Newly renovated. 3 beds, garage: 625,000€

House. 4 beds: 580,000€

Maison de ville (town house). 120 sq.m. near the palace: 640,000 (not a large house for the money)

But what about this?

Apartment. 280 sq.m. Ground floor of a 19th century *Hotel particulier*. Private park and orangerie, plus caretaker's house: 5,000,000€

St-Germain-en-Laye is an elegant little town near Versailles, choc full of its own history and beautiful *châteaux*. Several kings and Claude Debussy lived here. The population today is 41,000, and according to the *mairie*, there are numbers of British and American resident families in the town. Currently it is not a holiday home location. St Germain is the French centre for Ford cars, and as one might expect it has an International *Lycée*. Property prices are possibly a little cheaper than Versailles, but not much.

St-Germain-en-Laye

Apartment. 3/4 p.: 272,000€

Centre ville. Duplex, 4 beds: 590,000€

Town house near *château*: 680,000€

House. Period 1930. Close to station for Paris: 2,200,000€

www.explorimmo.com

www.lesiteimmobilier.com

www.fontainebleau-immobilier.com

www.explorimmo.lefigaro.fr

www.agencemercure.fr

15
REGION 3
THE LOIRE VALLEY,
LOIRE-ATLANTIQUE

To those of us who have ever visited the area, it is synonymous with breathtakingly grand *châteaux*, each surrounded by a village or town. The truth is, not many of us seem to stay there either on a permanent or even semi-permanent basis. Obviously I speak in general terms, having had long conversations with the various *mairies*.

Nantes, for example, is a lovely city, twinned with Cardiff, but a somewhat lugubrious gentleman from the *mairie* implied that the Atlantic coast was uninviting and the weather generally too treacherous for any holiday home enthusiasts. Looking at the map he was probably right. Having had two never-to-be-forgotten experiences crossing the Bay of Biscay, whatever they say about this horrendous crossing, I can confirm it is absolutely true.

Following a drive through the Loire valley, Nantes could be the last stop.

In the autumn of 2007 it will be hosting a few World Rugby matches, and access by ferry and train would be the simplest route. Historically the Château des Ducs in Nantes' medieval quarter has had an impressive guest list – Machiavelli, John Knox, Bonnie Prince Charlie; and Gilles de Rais (Bluebeard) was executed here. Rather like Bristol, in the late 18th century, Nantes grew fat on slaves and sugar, and inevitably its riches have dwindled.

Chartres, at the region's northern edge, is a pretty market town with a famous cathedral which was built on a Pagan centre of worship. The town is only 80 km south-west of Paris and trains run every hour from Paris Montparnasse.

This is a town with an impressive history, old and recent. Jean Moulin, the courageous leader of the French Resistance was *préfet* of Chartres at the beginning of World War II. There is an industrial zone outside the town where a number of rather genteel light enterprises (as opposed to heavy industry) have been established; perfumery in all its stages, cosmetics, and fabric. Tourism is also an industry, the cathedral bringing in sightseers throughout the year. It is close to Paris, yet it may not be as good for a *chambres d'hôte* or a B&B as its neighbours further south in the Loire.

Orléans a bustling city on the river Loire and was once an important port taking goods and passengers to and from the capital. Although the city's fortunes all but disappeared in the last century, fast transport links have revitalised it bringing in a plethora of cosmetics factories. Even the old industrial area of quaint narrow streets leading down to the riverside quays is being renewed.

It is very much St Joan of Arc's city; she is everywhere. May 8th is Joan of Arc day with processions through the streets, a medieval fair and fireworks. Orléans is only 100 km from Paris, and when I spoke to the *mairie* they did not seem to think any Brits lived there at all! So be it.

In Blois, however, the panoply of the glorious river and magnificent *châteaux* really opens up. This has to be one of the most beautiful regions of France. The climate is gentle, the soil rich and fertile.

Between Blois, Tours, and Angers there are countless delightful villages and small towns like Beauregency and Gien restored to their 15th century charm, after massive bombing in World War II. Sully sur Loire has a fairytale *château* with pointed towers. The home of Tintin's friend Captain Haddock was modelled on the *château* of Cheverny. Loches, quiet and peaceful, has a stunning medieval citadel surrounded by clusters of 15th century houses.

Blois is a particularly impressive small town with its own Château de Blois, and is within 20 km of a group of other *châteaux*. The town has a light industrial area producing chocolate for Cadbury and Schweppes, health and beauty products, automobiles, financial services, and a Christian Dior factory.

Tourism is big business in Blois.

The other big tourist attraction in Blois is proximity to the superb *Golf des Bords* – reputedly the best course in Europe. Golfing holidays are becoming very popular with both sexes, which gives the region an extra point.

For anyone thinking of completely relocating or part-time living, Blois would be a good choice largely because of tourism. Of course with a good command of language, an enterprising Brit could find a job in one of the town's outlets, but until that time, what better way to earn a crust than providing bed and breakfast? Always remember a UK property sale will generally give you a far bigger purchasing budget in France, so you can think big, or at least bigger than you would in the UK.

The Sologne is a vast, often bleak rural area which anyone with agoraphobic tendencies should avoid. It is given to hunting, particularly between October and March, when it is advisable to give the area a wide berth as many people have been shot in error. Obviously one should not wear a furry hat with floppy ears when strolling through the undergrowth. Some parts of the Sologne are out of bounds, belonging to a number of 19th century *châteaux* built by well-to-do industrialists, presumably so that they could hunt and shoot to their heart's content.

Tours is the largest town in the Loire Valley, proud of its history and architecture. Until recently it was considered somewhat bourgeois and a little stuffy but, since the TGV arrived making Paris only an hour away, it is now a haven for commuters, bringing with them a needed breath of fresh air. There is a lively night life here, Irish pubs, *bistrots*, night clubs and, during the warm summer evenings, the sounds of classical music float across the river frequently accompanying *son et lumière* performances.

There are daily, weekly and bi-annual street markets; the average midday temperature from June to August 22–24°C, and in January 8°C. Here the commercial side of tourism is catered for with attractive shopping centres.

Tours sees itself not only as a crossroad in the centre of France, but as a latter-day Technopolis with a well-developed and expanding centre for medical and pharmaceutical research surrounded by schools and university faculties providing a strong complementary scientific input.

The Loire, and particularly Touraine, is synonymous not only with *châteaux* but also with wine and gastronomy; its vineyards producing the white wines of the Sauvignon grape, like Vouvray, Chenin blanc, Azay le Rideau, Sancerre, and more. Chinon, and Bourgeuil are just two of the red wines produced from the Loire's Cabernet grape. As for gastronomic delights, think of game in all its varieties, mushrooms likewise and goats' cheeses.

They also say the Loire Valley has the best French accent in France. Can't be bad!

Examples of properties for sale

Tours

Town house *(maison de ville)*. 4 beds: 399,000€

Restored house, perfect con. Private courtyard, nr station. 2 beds: 215,000€

House. 19th century, nr town, 4 beds, garden: 306,000€.

House. West sector. 160 sq.m. Land 2,350 sq.m. 5 beds: 262,000€

Chinon

(This the most mouth watering bargain I have seen in years.) Mansion. 19th century 8p. 4 bed, 4 reception. Original fireplace. Land 1,650 sq.m. Ideal guest house/small hotel. (A stunning period piece): 193,000€

Blois

House. 3 beds. Study. Land 1,500 sq.m.: 182,000€

House. 240 sq.m. 6 beds. Study. Recep rooms. Land 2,700 sq.m. Pool, garage: 440,000€

House. 15 km north. Smallholding to restore + outbuildings. Land 2,500 sq.m.: 195,000€

House. 1 km Between Blois and Vendome, in village with shops. 4 beds. Office. Mezzanine. 2 garages + studio. Gas CH. Land 3,600 sq.m.: 243,800€

House. Left bank. 3 beds, private enclosed garden. Garage: 201,160€

Loches

Town house. Walled garden, 3 beds. Outbuildings: 161,000€

House. 2 km. Character. 8 rooms, 2 garages, 2 studios, 80 sq.m. Outbuildings: 258,600€

Despite thinking that the Loire Valley is generally better than the Chartres area for tourist catering, I came across these two superb houses, which are in the mansion/small *château* category.

If the intention is gracious living plus an income, this type of investment, for my money, scores handsomely.

Near Chartres

Mansion, Bourgeoise 350 sq.m. Land 1,184 sq.m. 5 beds. Games room. Superbly equipped kitchen: 529,000€

Mansion/small *château*. 19th century *(maison de maitre)* 450 sq.m. Park land 4,500 sq.m. Numerous annexes, paved courtyard, tennis court: 620,000€.

If you wish to have more similar mouth watering temptations, just look up any of the websites.

Agence MC Rochou. Tel. 02 47 61 42 94

City A Planchon Immobilier. Tel Chinon 02 47 93 23 00 or *www.CityA.com*

Laforet Immobilier. Tel. 02 54 90 90 90
www.abonim.com

Hardouin Transactions. Tel. 02 47 60 90 71

www.lesiteimmobilier.com

www.likhom.com

www.standingimmobilier.fr

www.agencemercure.fr

Please note: for any telephone numbers given without the country's prefix – 00 33 – remember to drop the first zero of the telephone number when adding them. Thus 02 47 60 90 71 becomes 00 33 2 47 60 90 71.

A Dordogne village street.

1

Nord-pas-de-Calais: often overlooked, but very beautiful.

A street in Aigues-Mortes in Languedoc.

Semur in Auxois, Burgundy.

Lake facing Mont Blanc, Alpes.

The old port at Dinan, Brittany.

The château at Chenonceau, Pays de la Loire.

Abrivado in the Camargue.

The square at Montpellier, Hérault.

On the banks of the Rhône, Lyon.

Lavender fields in Provence.

16
REGION 4
POITOU, CHARENTES, DORDOGNE, LIMOUSIN, CHER

The centre of the area is agricultural with hectares of rolling wheat fields, maize, sunflowers and, nearer the coast to the west, the *bocages*. This is the name given to small fields enclosed by hedges and trees, intended to prevent top soil from being eroded by scourging Atlantic winds.

Poitiers is the capital of this region, a delightful town with a lively pavement café-life, weekly markets, and the centre given to pedestrian precincts. There is plenty of street music and night life which in term time is university driven. The centre of the old town has narrow streets and buildings of great architectural beauty. Whilst Poitiers may no longer have the national influence it once had when it was the seat of the Dukes of Aquitaine, the modern Futuroscope just outside is a great attraction and certainly draws visitors to its court. This high-tech theme park is set in acres of greenery. Huge screens, like the Geodome in Paris, show films, for example, of dizzy ski runs that draw the spectator into perilous situations with frightening reality. Surrounded by fountains linked to evening fireworks and music, Futurama has put Poitiers back on the commercial map without touching the town's historic charm.

Montmorillon, population 7,500, near Poitiers is also known as the *Cité d'écrit* – the city of writing. It has an ancient tradition of books and bookmaking and at one time had a substantial printing press. Now it specialises in old manuscripts and rare books. The library is a magnet for book collectors and historians. The *mairie* tells me there are lots of English here. And do they work? Yes, from home on the Internet. They have also opened up two English teashops (*Salon de Thé*), so you would know where to go for a chat or a moan. There are evening classes to teach French to the incoming Britons, while the children go to school and learn it the easy way. Montmorillon, being a riverside town, offers an abundance of water sport activities, particularly canoeing and kayaking.

I spoke to Monsieur Xavier Robelin of the prestigious Agence Mercure which has a particularly wide catchment area all over central and southern France through its many agency offices. This agency goes for houses with character, town houses, bourgeois houses, manors and *châteaux* and the prices could well surprise you. In his view, properties around Poitiers and in Poitou Charente are considerably cheaper than a few kilometres south in the Dordogne. Consequently there are lots of Britons here, the town of Civray being the local epicentre – a pretty market town with attractive fairy-tale towers and sculptured façades on the banks of the River Charente.

Examples of properties for sale

Poitiers and surrounds

House. A town house, tall windows, creeper on walls. 6 beds, 2 storeys. Garden 300 sq.m.: 220,000€

House. Fantastic: 370 sq.m. Land 5,242 sq.m. Huge recep, sitting rm, dining rm. 4 large beds plus 185 sq.m. of loft. €489,000

Civray

House. 19th century. *Bourgeois*. 250 sq.m. Divided into two independent parts. Panelled walls. Grounds 3,000 sq.m.: 460,857€

House. Character. 11 rooms 380 sq.m. Grounds 3,375 sq.m.: 399,000€

House. Character. 5 rooms 200 sq.m. Grounds 1,400 sq.m.: 248,000€

Agence Mercure. Tel. 05 49 60 27 00

Agence Bleu Soleil. Tel. 05 49 36 19 00

www.agencemercure.fr

www.bleu-soleil.com

oooOooo

Most French towns preserved their medieval citadels while the growing towns spread outside the ramparts. So it is with Chauvigny, a busy market centre on the banks of the Vienne, 20 km from Poitiers but with a difference; this *vieille ville* has five medieval *châteaux* within its walls. Apart from tourism, there is a lumber mill and a couple of porcelain factories.

Between Poitiers and La Rochelle is a curious fen-like landscape, the Marais Poitevin, marshy as its name suggests, and crisscrossed by canals. Called *La Venise Vert* (Green Venice) visitors can punt along the canals, in true British style. The best access to the Marais is through Coulon, a whitewashed village on the banks of the Sèvre and, as a point of possible interest, accommodation here is relatively sparse, but remains in demand.

La Rochelle is a delightful, unspoilt coastal town with a stormy religious history.

Through the remarkable foresight of a mayor the whole of the 17th and 18th century centre and waterfront has been pedestrianised, which would surely have pleased Eleanor of Aquitaine who gave the town a charter in 1199.

In 1627 La Rochelle was besieged by Richelieu. The town finally had to give in despite the fact that the Duke of Buckingham had been sent there by the UK to help. The trouble was the old Duke treated the whole exercise more like a jolly than a battle to save hundreds of Huguenot Protestants from Richelieu's persecution. The story goes that he drank too much and ate too much and consequently slept through the worst of the battle when he was most needed. Not a great day for British history, but in the end we benefited because hundreds of persecuted Huguenots and their skills settled in Britain.

Public transport is very efficient so you do not need a car for La Rochelle.

Just off the coast is the lovely Île-de-Ré, with glorious sandy beaches and inland, vines, asparagus and wheat. The law says all the houses cannot be more than two storeys, and all must be painted white with green shutters. St Martin, the island's capital has had a military history apart from the Duke of Buckingham's snooze. It was an embarkation point for prisoners bound for the French penal colonies, French Guiana and New Caledonia. 'Papillon' was one of them, but finally he escaped and wrote a book about it. For any amateur historian who wants a holiday of interest and lazy beaches, La Rochelle/Île-de-Ré would be an interesting choice. And a fact worthy of note; tourists are advised to book up early as accommodation goes quickly So, if you are thinking of buying a holiday home with a few B&Bs, why not think of this area? Or even a holiday home you could rent out when you are not *in situ*. A superb toll bridge, 3 km long, connects the island to the town at the point in the harbour that housed a repair workshop for German submarines during the war.

Examples of properties for sale

There are dozens of small villages near La Rochelle, where you will find 3–4 bed houses with land for under 200,000€. In the town they cost more.

House. Very pretty 2 bed + office + sep. studio in garden: 212,000€

House. 4 beds + sep s/c garden studio, gas CH: 315,000€

Frankly I was staggered at the price of property on the Île-de-Ré. *Recherché* it may be, obviously Buckingham and Papillon must give it an edge and, of course, it is very picturesque with all the white and green, but there is quite a difference in land values.

Rivedoux

Bungalow. 3 beds, edge of pinewoods superb views: 370,000€

Bungalow. Stunning. De Luxe 2 beds: 457,000€

House. 150 sq.m. Village centre. 3 beds, possibly make 5. Huge salon: 727,500€

St Martin

House. *Maison du village* (village house). 3 beds. 2 bathrooms: 529,000€

House. Over port, comprising nine 2 and 3 room apartments with large garden, trees and shrubs: 1,900,000€

www.immobilier-rochelais.com. Tel. 05 46 41 68 80

www.bordemer.com

ooOoo

In the town of Cognac with its medieval half-timbered houses of the old quarter, the smell of maturing brandy assails the nostrils. It is hard to imagine a more pleasurable combination: medieval architecture combined with a perfume, sometimes so pungent a deep breath could induce unseemly behaviour.

This is the home of the Hennessy Cognac family. The first Hennessy was an Irish officer serving in the French army, who gave up the army to start the business along with an Englishman from Jersey, so the story goes. And didn't the lad do well? A wise choice.

Examples of properties for sale

Reparsac (nearby village)

House. 3 beds: 64,600€

Cognac

House. 130 sq.m. 7 rooms (4 beds), 3 bath: 135,000€

House. Elegant period town house, circa 1900. Walled courtyard and garden. 4 beds. 2 baths + office. Very large outbuilding + 2 garages: 256,000€

www.orpi.com:80/leonard.cognac. Tel. 05 45 82 14 19
www.avendrealouer.fr
www.logic-immo.fr
www.focusfrance.com

ooOOoo

Whilst hitch-hiking in France as a penniless student, I remember being dropped off in Angoulême.

In those days it seemed to be a very small town, rural to the point of rustic. We had read there was an *Auberge de la Jeunesse* (Youth Hostel), and eventually we found it. The hostel was no more than an isolated little farmhouse at the end of a narrow road leading into what seemed an open mountainside. The jolly *madame* in charge must have taken pity on these two rather down at heel hungry girls, for she immediately sat us at a huge oak table in the big kitchen, the only downstairs room, and served up large plates of hot beef stew straight from the pot on the hob, with a huge loaf of fresh bread and home-made butter and cheese. I can honestly say I have never to this day enjoyed a meal so much. We must have been eating with considerable relish because her two sons came in from the farmyard to watch.

It was our first experience of hole-in-the-ground loos and, although there was no bathroom, we could use the pump and bucket in the yard – it was summer, after all. Being well brought-up gels we took turns at holding our large towels around each other for discreet sluicing to take place, which caused a few Gallic sniggers in the neighbouring cowsheds, possibly waiting for a gust of wind.

The beds made up with spotlessly clean sheets, were very hard and we had small roly-poly pillows – another new experience – but we were young and sleep was easy. The next morning kindly *madame* set out big bowls of steaming coffee, hot milk and fresh bread rolls on the oak table and I fell in love with France all over again.

Angoulême was always a cathedral city, but I must have missed the edifice all those years ago. Its prosperity used to depend on a huge paper mill, but in the 1980s the mill was obliged to close. Since then Angoulême has turned to tourism to retrieve its fortunes. The charming old quarter criss-crossed with tiny streets is pedestrianised now, full of restaurants and bars and no doubt a spanking new *Auberge de la Jeunesse*.

Examples of properties for sale

Angoulême

Farmhouse. 140 sq.m. Land 2,000 sq.m. Courtyard. Barn. Outbuildings. Gardens, woodland: 360,000€ . Contact. *www.focus-france.com*

Colin and Yvonne Moorfoot, originally wanted a holiday home, but now they are spending over half the year in their house in the Charente about 18 km from Angoulême.

They decided to find somewhere south of the Loire, because it is Colin's belief, and no doubt quite justified after many years of observation, that the weather is noticeably warmer and more settled. First of all they rented a house from friends living in Châteauneuf and drove around the region before pin-pointing exactly where they wanted to be.

Their property is set in rolling countryside, vineyards and arable farming: 'very rural and does not have hordes of British as one tends to find in the Dordogne'.

I asked them what were the main differences in quality between their French life style and British.

'A slower pace of life, a definite plus; everything stops at lunchtime, and hardly anything is open on Sundays. There is no class system, and no great material envy. A large number of people still live off the land, and there is copious local produce in the supermarkets for bottling, pickling or freezing. In England we live in a tiny hamlet in Devon but our French life style is even slower. It's like England 30 years ago. Children are brought up to be polite to adults, and in Angoulême – which is large city – you never feel threatened as you do in England, even if you walk about at midnight.'

What did they enjoy most?

'Being able to eat outside, to have an inexpensive coffee or glass of wine outside a café, and we enjoy the challenge and stimulation of speaking French with the locals.'

Their nearest shops are one kilometre away, but they would never re-locate.

When the last offspring left the nest they downsized in England in order to buy in France, and although they do not have many French friends, they are invited to various aperitif sessions and an occasional meal, and they have always been made to feel very welcomed.

Colin and Yvonne find the 'mix of British friends and acquaintances and

French friends, interspersed with regular visitors from England, is quite enough'.

And advice?

'You must have reasonable French. France is a large country – when you have decided on your region take time to really look around before homing in on a particular location.'

Their son would like to live in France full time, and one of their daughters is about to start a job in Normandy. If they decide to settle in France, 'things could change. Who knows?!'

ooOOoo

The Dordogne for the French means a large river that bisects the old province of Dordogne. To us Brits, however, the Dordogne means an area encompassing the territories of the Périgord, Limousin and the Lot (see Region 5).

The Dordogne is where, for some time now, Brits seem to go first on holiday, then holiday home followed by retirement, or rather non-retirement, for so many set up *chambres d'hôtes* to augment UK pensions.

The Périgord has four areas in all:

Périgord Noir, so called because of the dark oaks that forest the region. Here you will find *châteaux* and the cave paintings at Lascaux. The capital is Sarlat which is beautiful, but property is expensive.

Périgord Vert is green and lush, a little like the UK in that it has a higher annual rainfall than its neighbours. It has a stunning river landscape and I well remember the first time I drove through the Dordogne being struck by the lushness of the vegetation. I had no idea of the name of the area, but immediately thought 'rainfall'. Maybe, but nothing like the rainy season in Swansea, so don't worry.

The capital is Brantôme and it seems we Brits love it.

159

Périgord Blanc, so called because of the limestone rock. The capital is Périgueux, which is also the capital of the whole area. Périgueux is a provincial market town with a beautiful cathedral, but otherwise unremarkable.

Périgord Pourpre (purple), so-named because that's the colour vine leaves turn in the autumn and this area's capital is Bergerac. Now this beautiful riverside town with the statue of Cyrano prominently placed used to be an active port for wine from surrounding vineyards, maize and tobacco from the region's farms. In the *vieille ville* amidst medieval houses are the museums of tobacco and wine.

The whole region is stunning, with breathtaking vistas; reason in itself, you would think, for attracting so many Brits to live there *en permanence*, but I have another theory. It may be in the blood.

The landscape is littered with picture-postcard *bastides*. I remember not being able to drive on until I had explored, and finally stayed the night, in a *bastide* that was not of this world, it was unreal. Perched quaintly on a green hillside, compact, solitary, defiant and impregnable, for ten minutes I just stared. It could have come straight out of a fairy tale in its beauty. A *bastide* is a hillside village enclosed by a fortified wall; arches with substantial gates are the only way in or out. They were fortresses defending the inhabitants from attack, and it all started with one Eleanor of Aquitaine who was married off to the King of England, Henry II, bringing with her a dowry that was the whole of south-west France. Quite a dowry. But more of this unusual lady in the next chapter.

The French, quite rightly, did not wish to have their nationality forcibly changed overnight, so spats with the English occupying forces were inevitable. Eleanor's second son who became Richard I (Coeur de Lion) of England, spent nearly all his time in France and some of that time at the Château Beynac – that is when he wasn't crusading with his friend Blondel. An English king who barely knew England and had to deal with bellicose barons in the Périgord, did not bode well, although he was probably good to his mother. After his untimely death, the area soon became consumed in the Hundred Years War, when England and France growled and fought, each side building more protective fortress *bastides* to keep the other side out – even farmhouses were fortified. Alas, the countryside suffered with this constant warring and after only a brief spell of peace, the repeal of the Treaty of Lyons kick-started the Wars of Religion, for another hundred years.

Perhaps you can now see why this theory about the Dordogne being in the blood may not be quite so far-fetched.

Within the last 30 years the area has started to revive, largely through tourism, and the apparent targeting of the area by us Brits once again. And not just holiday homes. We are more permanent fixtures. We even have our own cricket teams, C of E church choirs and clubs for everything. One community has an English mayor. This may not be your idea of living in France but, on the other hand, it could be quite a comfort to know there is someone who speaks the same language in an emergency, but of course your children could be more French than English.

The total population of the Dordogne is around 400,000, although in summer, villages of 7,000 can swell to 20,000. Gastronomically, it is celebrated for the wines of Bergerac and Montbazillac, its truffles, *foie gras* and variations on duck and goose. With such magnificent rivers, water sports are high on the list, but the primary sporting activity in the region is golf, the gentle slopes of the terrain being perfect for superb courses.

Périgueux is the home of 'French News' the very successful monthly anglophone newspaper and its editor, Miranda Neame, is a busy enterprising woman who has raised her family in the region.

Although Miranda herself spent her early years in a 'rambling old house in the south-east of England', she knew France as a child as her grandfather had a property near St Tropez. Armed with an inheritance of £3,000 she came to France as a young adult with partner and baby girl. At this point she had not entered the world of journalism. Her French life started in Corsica, and finally to the Lot et Garonne where Miranda's parents had a holiday home.

I asked her why she came to Périgueux.

After the break up of her marriage, she needed to find work because 'there aren't many job opportunities in rural Lot et Garonne'.

What made her stay?

'I found work teaching English which I did for 13 years. I taught everyone from primary school children to the retired, lorry drivers, executives, the unemployed – I met a lot of people.'

And what about re-location if there were ever an opportunity?

'I love the Basque country, but there are many other regions that tempt, like the Massif Central and the Cévennes, parts of Brittany, the Charente-Maritime.'

Miranda listed the aspects of her French life style she most enjoys.

'It gives me the freedom and anonymity of being a foreigner; the space, scenery, ancient architecture, quality food, and wine, a good climate generally, gardening, the gallantry and social flirtation. French people are very welcoming on the whole, but their culture and institutions are an endless source of amusement, bafflement, frustration and admiration.'

She was glad she was able to bring up her children in France. 'I believe the environment is much healthier, although both have had to return to the UK to find jobs.'

I asked about the social scene, were her friends more French than English?

'Far more French, although the locals in the Périgord have known each other since school, and live in a very closed circuit together. But,' she added, 'there are signs of breaking with the weekend tradition of

Sundays with the in-laws, led by the young.'

And what advice would she offer to incoming Brits?

'Learn French. Don't come unless you are sure you can afford it or have a ready-made business/job, or are used to sleeping rough. Don't expect anything to be the same as in the UK.'

Miranda explained that in areas where there was a concentration of new arrivals, there are more and more organisations being set up to help them.

And how were local schools dealing with the influx of English children?

'They are gearing up to it with special catch-up classes.'

So do the French accept the Brits with equanimity?

'Yes, provided they make an effort to integrate. Holiday-home owners who leave houses empty most of the year, lager louts and those who employ and buy British, may not get the warm reception extended to other Europeans.'

I suppose the $64,000, had to be asked; would she ever return to the UK?

'I hope I never have to! I enjoy the odd visit, especially to my daughter in Walthamstow. But that is increasingly a culture shock!'

Examples of properties for sale

Bergerac

House. 2 beds, nr schools/shops: 86,400€

House. 125 sq.m. 8 rooms (4 beds) nr. centre, cultivated gdn. 2 offices. New kitchen: 183,500€

House. 316 sq.m. Land 5,000 sq.m. 7 rooms, good con. Studio 1,000 sq.m.: 225,400€

House. Bergeracois style. 190 sq.m. Land 2,000 sq.m. 8 rms: 246,100€

Périgueux

House. Over Périgueux valley. 5 beds. Playroom. Terraces. Land 13,500 sq.m.: 395,000€

House. Town centre. 4 beds: 113.327€

House. 150 sq.m. Town centre 6 rms (4 beds): 173,600€

House. Périgueux 25 mins. 140 sq.m. Land 4,500 sq.m. 7 rms. Sauna. Pool: 382,000€

House. Nr Montignac. Totally renovated. 4 large beds. 3 recep, terrace + garage, workshop. Land 3,600 sq.m. Patio, lawns, orchard: 243,000€

House. Nr Le Bugue. 2 large beds + loft to convert. CH. Separate apartment: kit/diner, garden access. 2 beds. CH. Land 8,000 sq.m. Lawn, meadow, woodland: 212,000€

www.windsorandpartners.com. Tel. 05 53 06 11 57

www.orpi-dordogne.com. Tel. 05 53 57 83 22

Michel Hayart. Tel. 06 77 12 89 49

www.orpi-perigueux-immobilier.com

Thomas Lherm. Tel. 06 70 01 17 79

ooOoo

Limoges, north-east of Périgueux is best known for its porcelain, its cathedral and the surrounding fertile countryside for the Limousin cattle. And who would have thought the all-embracing shepherd's cape the *limousine*, would have given its name to the city-swish, ultra-sophisticated automobile. The population in this part of France is sparse and the region agricultural, with dozens of small villages. One is Aubusson, famous for its beautiful pale woven tapestry carpets. Another is Oradour sur Glane, site of one of worst atrocities perpetrated by Hitler's SS in 1944. There had been rumours of Resistance activity in the village which, as it happened, were ill-founded. Nevertheless reprisals had to be taken. The troops therefore marched in on June 10th rounded up the men in the village square and the women and children were put in the church. They shot all the men, and set fire to the church shooting most of the women in the legs first so they could not run out. They put the village baker and his family into the hot ovens and set fire to the village. It stands today a charred ruin. The crypt has been turned into a small, pitiful museum where you can still see half burnt out children's toys and prams. Outside they have erected a memorial with photographs of many who died so senselessly. The only ones who escaped the massacre were a few young lads who were working in the fields when the regiment marched in.

A new village has been built beside the burnt skeleton of the original.

Walking through the burnt-out shell it is impossible to speak; a cloak of reflective silence falls, as each tourist becomes a pilgrim.

I have known Susan Turner and Mark Cleal for many years, and about four years ago they found a cottage to renovate near Limoges. They are both in the police force with grown up children – one, a newly qualified doctor. When the time comes they intend to retire to France. Apart from school trips when young, Susan and Mark have since made several in-depth motoring holidays together in France.

I asked them why not a home in Spain or Italy?

'Well we don't much like Brits abroad – you know the endless 'Happy Hours' and lager louts in Spain, and waiters who think they are being funny when they imitate current UK soap opera phrases. Of course there are Brits here too, but they tend to barbecue in their own back gardens!'

And other regions of France?

'We had travelled through various parts of the country but Limousin appealed to us because it was so green, similar to rural Wales. Also we had limited resources and time, and as the Limousin had not been invaded by Brits like the popular regions, house prices had not been pushed up.'

I asked them about the major differences in life style.

'Without being political, society is changing in the UK and there's recently been a massive increase in crime. In France there is a respect for family life and values that is sadly missing from the younger generation in the UK. They are polite and courteous even to strangers. Our locals in Lubersac always say 'Bonjour' whenever they enter a restaurant, and their laid-back attitude is so appealing.

It's wonderful to relax in a safe environment with courteous people. We always have a sense of being at home whenever we are there.'

Would they ever relocate?

'No! Not to another country, but perhaps further south, the Dordogne – somewhere near a river or the sea. Next time I would look into the area more carefully.'

And irritation?

'Yes! Artisans and red tape. It took so long to get our shower and central heating put in the cottage I had to make a scene in the plumber's office. Work was then completed pretty swiftly!'

I asked them how they would manage financially when they retired in five years.

'Well we'll have our two pensions,' said Mark. 'However I may do odd jobs for local people, or renovate a house to sell on as a project.'

And advice?

'It's very important to at least have the basics in French,' said Susan who is becoming a proficient speaker. 'How on earth can you expect to be accepted into a community when you cannot converse with anyone?'

'Yes,' Mark added, 'and make sure you are really in love with France, and not just the idea of living in France. And don't take England to France either. They won't appreciate that. When in Rome do as the Romans, and you'll be accepted.'

Susan's last words of advice were 'Take your time to find an area you love first, then see what's available in the *immobiliers*'.

ooOOoo

At the north edge of Region 4 is one of France's most beautiful cities, Bourges.

Although it could have been included in the Loire valley section it is pivotal to the wide agricultural areas of central France.

Bourges has seen a long and sometimes terrible history. There was a fire in the 15th century that destroyed a third of the city, but the rebuilding has left a rich legacy of wood-framed houses, the sort that have intricate patterns of wooden beams decorating the façades, stunning *hotels particuliers* and majestic municipal buildings. As a town it is vibrant with something going on all the time. There are markets almost every day including a big covered market. There are museums, concerts playing everything from Dixieland to classical, exhibitions, theatre, dance, poetry classes and cinema.

Industry concentrated in the industrial zone outside, is chiefly concerned with aerospace and associated military projects. The university is particularly strong in science and law with the addition of two top status colleges, *École National Superieur d'Ingénieurs* and the *École National des Beaux Arts*.

I have had long conversations with Monsieur Jacques Chassigny, director of the easy-to-navigate Agence Mercure, specialising in houses of character, bourgeois houses, manors and *châteaux*.

According to this experienced house agent there are lots of Britons coming to settle in the Berry/Cher area around Bourges. Apart from the city's attractions it is a gateway town to the Loire *châteaux*, which immediately has B&B potential. It was a surprise to know there are a number of British farmers who are now buying into the rich farmlands of the region. And why not? According to a recent UK report there is no money to be made out of British farming these days, and our farmers have the highest suicide rate. Will France offer them a better livelihood? I'm sure they will have done their research, and joining the French system means they will benefit from all farming subsidies.

Houses in this area can be sumptuous and grand but, for all that, in British terms, reasonably priced.

Examples of properties for sale

Bourges

House. 300 sq.m. 12 rooms (7 beds). Land 2000 sq.m.: 342,400€

House. Nr centre 265 sq.m. 19th century elegant *bourgeoise*. 9 rooms (6 beds). Office. Library. Small outbuilding. Land 802 sq.m.: 392,200€

*Pavilion (*Lodge*)*. 15 km Bourges. 100 sq.m. in hamlet, edge of forest. 3 beds + office. Land 2,950 sq.m. Well kept, lawned gardens: 182.250€

www.agencemercure.fr or *www.agencemercure.co.uk*

17
REGION 5
AQUITAINE, MIDI-PYRÉNÉES, PYRÉNÉES-ALANTIQUES, HAUT-PYRÉNÉES

This region covers a very diverse set of living conditions, of climate and of land values, from the province of Aquitaine, on the west, down to ski country in the Pyrénées, up to Toulouse and the very rural and stunningly beautiful Aveyron.

Parts of this sector may well be some of the most exciting in the Hexagon from the 'discovery' point of view, and as it's always good to be in on the ground floor, would be worth making a special journey for the short list.

Bordeaux is a major coastal city with one million inhabitants. It is the capital of Aquitaine (the land of water from the Latin *aqua*), its region, as well the administrative capital of Gironde.

The city stands on the river Garonne, wide enough for ocean liners, and has been a producer of wine since the eighth century. First it was a Celtic settlement then Roman. In the 12th century, a lady already mentioned, Eleanor Duchess of Aquitaine (she had previously divorced the King of France saying she wanted a man, not a monk), married the French speaking Prince Henry of England who within weeks became Henry II, the French speaking king of England, and she became queen. If Eleanor's dad hadn't played so fast and loose with the indigenous French in south-west France, and given them away as a package with her dowry when he married her off, they could well have avoided ravaging spats and battles. But to be positive, during that difficult three hundred years it was the British and their love of Bordeaux's red wine which they called claret that encouraged those medieval vineyards to produce *(rien ça change)* and gave the region its first economic boost.

It wasn't until the 18th century that Bordeaux began to rebuild and flourish and had its second economic boom. Baron Haussman, Bordeaux's *préfet* used the city's new urban development as a model when asked to re-plan Paris. The city's beauty impressed Victor Hugo so much that he said, 'Take Versailles, add Antwerp, and you have Bordeaux'. Because of its very large 18th century architectural urban area, Bordeaux is sought after by film-makers and of course tourists. Tourism is an important industry, as much for the beauties of surrounding Aquitaine as the city's architectural gems and museums.

There are large companies, with space-age and aeronautic establishments in the majority, and major campuses. The university has four separate faculties and several advanced study colleges for engineering. Education in France for younger students and children is generally of a very high standard.

The city has a mixed population of Spaniards, Italians, Germans and North Africans along with native French, and it is growing into an urban sprawl, nevertheless it attracts more than three million tourists a year, and the night life is very active.

With the flourishing city went the burgeoning wine trade. In fact the wine took its name from the city, and became the world's wine capital. In terms of area the Bordeaux region is not the largest wine-producing region in France, but it generates high quality and prestigious appellations as well as ordinary table wines. There are over 9,000 wine-producing *châteaux*, with names that run like a page in Debrett: Château Lafite Rothschild, Château Margaux, Château Latour, Château Haut Brion, Château Mouton Rothschild. The vineyards and villages of St Emilion, Entre Deux Mers, Les Landes, Côte d'Argent, Medoc and Sauternes are all in the department of the Gironde and form a semi circle around the city.

This truly is wine country that attracts something more than your average tourist. These are the afficionados of grape, crop and vintage who will visit right through the year from all over the world. You could do what a number of Britons have already done and buy a vineyard, or maybe it is easier to live near enough to house the guests.

Examples of properties for sale

Lamothe

House. 60 km east of Bordeaux. Renovated with tower. Land 7,000 sq.m. Spacious living + kit + study. 1st floor newly built for conversion to 4 beds. 2 baths: 294,990€

House. Large, plus watermill. 2 sep living areas: 1 with Recep. Kit. Office. 1 bed. Other with recep, etc. + 4 beds. Large garden. Bamboo grove. Pool. Stream nearby Dordogne river. Surrounded by vineyards: 530,000€

Monpazier

Hamlet for sale: 16 rooms. 4 houses, one complete apartment. Total 500 sq.m. Land 4,590 sq.m. with pool: 508,000€

Lalinde

House. 10 rooms, middle of town. To renovate: make 3 domiciles: 321,000€

St Savin

House. Truly stunning *Bourgeoise* 18th century, 160 sq.m. Land 2 hectares plus grange 280 sq.m. ready for *gîtes*: 29,800€

www.frenchestateagents.com

Leggett Immobilier, St Emilion. Tel. 05 57 55 06 06

www.seloger.com/immobilier/aquitaine.htm

www.guy-hoquet.com. Tel. 05 56 33 23 23

If you cannot find these websites easily go to *google.co.uk* or *google.fr*, and type in either Aquitaine estate agents or Aquitaine *immobiliers*.

ooOOoo

Agen is between Bordeaux and Toulouse. Although its roots are in antiquity, it did not have real regeneration until the fifties. Around the town it is still wine country but, according to the *mairie*, there are no sizeable numbers of Britons living there; some Belgian and Dutch maybe.

I have a particular interest in this town, because it happens to be twinned with my home town in Wales, Llanelli. I couldn't fathom why this rural French crossroads town should be twinned with a small ex-industrial town in South Wales. Then the penny dropped, just like a goal – it was rugby! That was the reason. Agen has a super stadium and has been the national rugby championship winner eight times, a fitting twin therefore to the well known Scarlets. The person I spoke to in Agen's *mairie* had already visited the twin town and I was full of admiration because she pronounced it correctly.

The town's industries concentrate on pharmaceuticals, food production and agricultural research.

The housing market is always a good indicator of a town's prosperity. There is property in and around Agen ready for renovation from 140 sq.m. town houses to 100 sq.m. houses that can be bought for 50,000–75,000€. There is more for renovation here than I have seen for years, so if you feel inclined it could be worth a visit.

Toulouse is France's fourth city and is called *la ville rose* because of the rose coloured brick of its buildings. It is a city with the advantage of a wide river, and is an extremely good centre for south-west France with TGV, autoroute, and air links: Easyjet flies daily from Gatwick.

The city has the largest university outside Paris and is very well endowed with cultural pursuits. The Toulouse Chamber Orchestra has an international reputation, a highly respected *conservatoire* of music and plenty of museums. A city may not be the place for a holiday home, nor even for a permanent home unless you have work, but there are dozens of attractive rural areas around Toulouse. I have friends living in the Tarn and Garonne and their monthly expeditions into the city, seem to assuage any lust for city bustle.

The climate of the town and *environs* is relatively temperate, mild autumn and spring, hot dry summers and a few freezing days in winter.

South of Toulouse is the Midi Pyrénées.

One October a few years back I drove into the most beautiful little town called Mirepoix, near Foix. Although this is not Pays Basque country which, strictly speaking consists of three provinces further west along the Spanish border to the coast, the Basque influences were already quite evident.

The terrain was flat and, I felt, rather disappointing, but the spectacular backdrop of the mountains made up for it. The architecture in Mirepoix could have been another version of Stratford upon Avon. I remember walking along the tiny streets and through the town square, flanked by a neat town hall and central fountain, in amazement at its sheer perfection. It reminded me of the toy villages that were packed in large boxes at Christmas time. We had dinner in a medieval inn before a blazing fire, the walls festooned with hunting trophies staring down with glazed eyes. The owner said he was looking forward to December and January when the skiers came.

We drove around Andorra and further into the hinterland. I was looking for a house, but at the time there were no economy airlines, making accessibility too difficult; also the houses I was shown were far too expensive, and the estate agents too glib. I have learnt since that during that period many agents were just trying it on and asking ridiculous prices.

It is a different story today, largely because we have 'wised up', but property prices in the midi Pyrénées are high, although in the department of Gers you could find better value. Further west into Landes you can still find old mansions and farmhouses to renovate at reasonable prices.

My favourite is the real Basque and Béarn country – the Pyrénées Atlantique, a department of Aquitaine. Here you have it all; towering mountains, rolling hills, river valleys and the sea.

Salies has salty thermal spas, Orthez is a charming market town, and Pau, the department's capital, has an airport to which Ryanair makes daily trips from the UK and Ireland. In fact the *mairie* told me a number of Irish had bought houses in the area as a result. This area has never had the attraction of Normandy or the Dordogne for the majority of Brits until only recently, when the arrival of low cost airlines began to change the economic picture.

Pau itself has been nicknamed the 'English City', probably dating from the time the Duke of Wellington defeated Marshall Soult at Orthez in 1814. It's an easy, elegant little town and, thanks to two Scottish officers in Wellington's army, the game of golf was introduced outside Pau in 1814, although the first golf course in Europe – the Pau Golf club – was not founded until 1856. Again thanks to a Scottish doctor in

Wellington's army who loved the climate and was convinced of its curative powers, the English came down to Pau in droves, bringing with them horse racing, hunting, cricket and croquet. That is why there are so many English tearooms in the town. Many French writers arrived with the first railway line, Victor Hugo, Stendhal and Lamartine. Then came the first French rugby club in 1902. Nowadays Pau is not only a great golfing centre; a vintage car grand prix is held every May, and no prize for guessing which country has the highest representation for that. Outside the town are stud farms and stables and the big attraction, yet again, for Brits is the Grand Steeple Chase held every January. There are lots of Britons in villages around Orthez, and, according to estate agents, they seem to go for those that need renovation, thus boosting local economy.

Six kilometres from the coast is Bayonne, the capital of France's Pays Basque. It is an old Roman town, but it reached its prosperity peak in the 18th century with a flourishing armament industry, giving its name to that lethal weapon the bayonet. Gastronomically, Bayonne has left its mark with cured ham, chocolate made for Lindt, and possibly sauce Béarnaise, although Pau could also put in that claim. The town is surrounded by excellent golf courses.

A few kilometres away on the coast is Biarritz. Napoleon III turned it into a rich playground for gambling crown heads and wealthy wasters. The town was truly a rival to Monte Carlo.

In the sixties however the Côte d'Azur began the rapid climb to popularity, again bringing about its rival's decline. But Biarritz is a beautiful town, in my view quite as beautiful as Monte Carlo, with elegant Belle Epoque buildings, fabulous beaches, an impressive Casino and a spectacular shoreline. It seems to have become popular again with young Parisians and, for any house hunters, this neck of the woods is certainly a place to visit and think about, with sea, surf, ski, golf, horses and not forgetting vintage cars!

A reminder, that the nearer the sea, the more you pay, but tourism is being developed here about 50 minutes' drive inland in many of the lovely villages.

Examples of properties for sale

Iholdy Villa. Village 40 mins Bayonne, 5 rms. Land 1,238sq.m.: 325,000€

Biarritz Apart. Centre. 1 bed. Nr beach: 240,000€

Béarn Region

House. Beautiful character hse 170 sq.m. 7 rms. Land 2,728 sq.m.: 340,000€

Villa. 164 sq.m. Land 1.26 ha. 6 rms: 290,000€

House. 8 rms 220 sq.m. Land 1,288 sq.m.: 300,000€

Pays Basque

House. Character hse. 12 rms. 400 sq.m. Land 307 sq m.: 330,500€

House. 170 sq.m. Land 664 sq.m. 7 rms: 200,000€

www.agencemercure.fr, email: *mercure.biarritz@wanadoo.fr*.
Tel. 05 59 22 76 48

www.maisonsetappartements.fr

Social association for English speakers: Anglophones Pau Pyrénées.
http://pau.anglophones.com (don't use www).

AVEYRON

It was always the objective for us driving south so often and for so many years to find different routes and new places. One year it was the turn of Clermont-Ferrand to St Flours route and I decided to stop over in Millau. It was a warm evening in early summer, there were a few visitors but not too many. It is a lovely town of pale stone and somewhere near the centre I saw this wonderful old building set in rolling lawns. It could have been a town *château*, or a *préfet*'s house. It was neither. It had been a 14th century monastery, the monk's cells turned into bedrooms, but beautifully renovated complete with *en suites*. At night there was a slightly eerie silence, but what a great place to stay, and the monks' refectory made a delightfully atmospheric restaurant. Millau in the Aveyron is well placed and not far from Montpellier. That year we had decided to return the same way but, alas, we were dogged by mammoth diversions. There had been a great surge forward in construction of the new autoroute to Béziers from Clermont Ferrand, and on that particular day a new bridge was being manoeuvred into place. All traffic was obliged to drive through the tiny villages with their narrow streets that lay to the side of the new artery. It was our great good fortune that we had been diverted.

Driving through this rustic hidden fairyland was a total joy. I have never seen such beautiful architecture, not as in a Haussman boulevard but as in a breathtaking stage set.

Surrounded by quirky shapes, designs and colour it proved so difficult to leave this fairy tale other world we had to stop and explore. No surprise that the region boasts ten villages in the category *Les plus beau villages de France*; villages like Belcastel, Conques, Estaing, Sauveterre and Peyre. Access across the Aveyron is a little tricky, and even a train – no TGV here – from Paris to Rodez, the region's capital, takes seven hours, but there is an airport. The great joy is the relatively newly-completed A75 – the cause of our diversion – running between Clermont-Ferrand to Béziers, and the even greater joy is only one *péage* which confronts you after the bridge. And this bridge is no ordinary bridge. It is as magical as the rest of the Aveyron. It spans 2.5 kilometres, is 250 metres high, and looks as though it is has been dropped from the heavens by silver threads. So spectacular is the design it collected half a million tourists during the summer of 2005.

Rodez is a very attractive city with a population of around 49,000. The buildings in the old town are mostly 15th and 16th century topped with round, pointed fairy tale towers. Industry seems to be based on its historical agrarian economy, along with smaller light industries like Bosch. Like all French towns it has flourishing markets and it also has a particularly splendid medieval fair in July.

Smaller than Rodez is Najac, another lovely village, where you will find an interesting collection of foreigners including a number of Britons.

Examples of properties for sale

Rodez and environs

House. Period. Rodez centre. 100 sq.m. 3 floors to renovate completely: 47,870€

House. Village, totally habitable, 2 beds: 50,000€

House. Beautiful village. 5 rms, entirely renovated: 58,000€

House. Stone. Village nr lakes. 30 min Rodez and airport. To renovate. 2 beds: 80,000€

House. Delightful. Renovated. 2 beds. 5 mins lakes: 82,000€

Belcastel village and environs

House. Village Belcastel, 130 sq.m. Land 300 sq.m. 4 rooms CH: 320,000€

House. Village. 5 beds 170 sq.m. Covered terrace 30 sq.m. 30 mins Toulouse: 275,000€

House. Village. To renovate. 2 beds: 110,000€

House. Village. Rodez 15 km. 100 sq.m. Land 600 sq.m. 3 floors. Outbuilding 70 sq.m. For renovation. Planning and building permits supplied: 131,150€

House. Salmiech village. Period hse. 110 sq.m. Land 300 sq.m. CH. 3 beds. Fully restored with garden. Extension possible in attic: 170,000€

Fernand Ratier. Tel. 05 65 73 71 00

Selection Habitat. Tel. 05 65 70 10 49

Philippe Daunay. Secteur Rodez/nord Aveyron. Tel. 05 65 42 98 44

www.seloger.com

Agence Hurlevant. Tel. 05 65 71 40 6

www.seloger.com

18
REGION 6
CHAMPAGNE, ARDENNES,
LORRAINE, ALSACE

Anyone who has driven from Calais heading south will know this particular stretch of motorway very well. Just before Reims it divides, one branch of the motorway going off to Paris, the other heading south towards the city of Reims, the first major city in Champagne and its capital. Here the motorway becomes the *péripherique* and skirts around the city, hardly giving time to glance at the cathedral's gothic pinnacles. Reims may give the first impression of an industrial city which, of course, is partly true, but the city's real treasure lies in its vast network of cellars. The department is not called Champagne without reason, for here are stored thousands of bottles of the bubbly stuff. There are some hair-raising World War II stories relating to the champagne *châteaux's* desperate need to keep their best vintages out of Nazi hands. As the invaders approached, so new cellar walls went up. One veteran remembers, as a young lad, placing a couple of spiders on the newly constructed barricade to make it look as old as the rest. Never have walls sprouted greenery so quickly.

Outside Reims the motorway winds through hectares and hectares of flat wheat-fields, the occasional silo providing the only feature of interest in the otherwise monotonous terrain.

Épernay, 26 km south of Reims, is quite a different story. This is the perfect centre for the big champagne houses. In fact one of the main central streets, avenue de Champagne, is lined not only with impressive 18th and 19th century houses but also the big champagne houses. You can start by tasting Moët et Chandon and progress through to Mercier, by which time your taste buds will be comatosed. Winston Churchill called it 'the most drinkable street in the world', so you would be in good company. All around Épernay are the vineyards providing a never-ending mecca for bubbly lovers throughout the year. So too are the numerous delightful villages, Verus, Hartvilliers, Montigny sous Châtillon intrinsically part of the landscape and each of them a potential holiday centre, where champers-tasting and vineyard tours are as easy as taking a nap in the sun.

It must have been about 15 years ago that I first discovered, quite by chance, the Lac du Der Chantecoq or simply the Lac du Der as it is called today. I had driven through charming Vitry-le-François to St Dizier, seen a road marked Giffaumont and as it was getting towards six o'clock, decided to go there just for the night. To say I was shocked would be an understatement. I found an isolated, tumbledown, spit and sawdust bar-cum-hotel, a French hicks-ville, but it was the tourist season, no time to cut and run. The young couple who seemed to be in charge courteously showed me to a sparse but clean room, and I could have dinner in an hour.

The *auberge* lay in a small hollow and I clambered quickly to the top of an easy slope, and that's when I saw the lake. I was stunned, having no idea of its existence. For a moment I thought I had completely missed the route and ended up back at the coast for I could see no opposite bank.

A middle-aged French couple were also standing staring with the same kind of awe at the vast expanse of water. There were a few sailing boats and in the nearest cove was a diverse assortment of birds. Further away was a lone fisherman. It was blissfully tranquil, the only sound was the water lapping on the shore.

'We never knew there was such a place,' the French woman whispered. It would have seemed a blasphemy to shout. That was then.

Today the Lac du Der has changed, but not out of recognition. There is an acute awareness of its beauty and as is general in France, the need to preserve *la patrimoine* (heritage) goes beyond the coarser demands of Mammon. The village of Giffaumont is now a little bigger and many of the houses, almost all in the *champenoise* style – rather like our Tudor architecture – have been restored. Those that have been are festooned with hanging baskets of flowers. Sand has been imported to make a fine beach and there are restaurants and hotels around or near the lake at Montier en Der, St Dizier and Vitry-le-François. There are activities for children and Giffaumont now has a promenade, a modest yacht harbour, a *station nautique* where you can hire small boats, explore the waters in a catamaran, jet ski, or spend the day fishing. There are *fêtes*, traditional markets and, in Montier en Der – a delightful little town with arches and horse-drawn carriages – there are regular concerts in the floodlit abbey. Despite all this activity the Lac du Der has a quiet zone, and a nature reserve; each year in October it becomes home to 24,000 cranes. The lake is 10 kilometres long and has 77 kilometres of shoreline.

This is an area well worth exploring from the point of view of setting up home. It is not a great distance from the Normandy coast and, as you will see, there are houses to be restored which I am sure would pay off handsomely in the future. This area has taken a long time to arrive on the tourist agenda, and as one *immobilier* said, the area is becoming '*plus en plus coté*' – more and more rated/desirable.

Troyes is a large town, I remember driving around the main drag for an hour just trying to get out and, although it used to be the capital of

Champagne, today it is far better known as a clothes centre spawning dozens of factory outlets, where designer labels can be bought for a third of the normal price. Throughout the summer there is a series of outdoor *Ville en Lumière* concerts as well as a very good selection of eating establishments. However, in terms of a holiday home this town may be better as somewhere to visit rather than to live in.

Gastronomically its speciality is the *andouillette* – a sausage made from intestines packed with more intestines. Is this France's answer to the haggis one wonders? Whatever it is, in my opinion the *andouillette* has a quite repulsive smell – even the French admit it is an acquired taste. Nevertheless in Troyes there is a society to preserve the excellence of the sausage, so if you eat one make sure it has AAAA stamped on it – the Association of Amateurs of the Authentic Andouillette.

And good luck!

Colombey-les-Deux-Églises is an inauspicious village/town for the most part strung along the Route National, but it can become oversubscribed by tourists, anxious to see General de Gaulle's home. For me the great tourist attraction is the massive pink granite cross of Lorraine perched on the hill; a moving tribute to the men and women of the French Resistance and the man who inspired them.

Langres is a town nearby which is frequently overlooked, and I cannot think why. Just outside at the bottom of the hill approaching the arches of the *centre ville* are four beautiful lakes, a favourite for sailing enthusiasts. To have breakfast on a private balcony sitting in the hot morning sun, overlooking one of the lakes with glorious vistas all around was certainly my good fortune. Later I visited the town and saw a number of properties for sale in a *notaire's* window whose asking prices were lower than the current market value.

According to Madame Sonia Gouessan of the *Pays de Langres* office which deals with the economy and *patrimoine* of the region, there are few Brits if any, but a number of Dutch and Belgian families with second homes in the area. The Dutch particularly like taking ruins and restoring them. The only trouble, she says, with second-home people – and this applies equally to Parisians – is that their support of the local economy is only seasonal. Yes, the foreigners have pushed up house prices a little, but then house prices generally have risen.

Langres is certainly worth a visit and perhaps even short-listing.

The old province of Lorraine is not an immediate holiday destination. As border country it has provided the perfect corridor of war for centuries. Joan of Arc was born in Domremy la Pucelle and, in fact, it is the very name Shakespeare gives the girl soldier in Henry VI Part One, La Pucelle, literally a maid/virgin.

The region has seen two World Wars at close quarters and none so devastating as the killing fields of Verdun in the First World War. Today Verdun is just another French town containing nothing remarkable except the Rodin War memorial, but it is outside the town that gives its very name a special place in history. One balmy silent day in September I visited the depressingly large cemetery and Ossuaire de Douaument. I was quite alone. Walking through endless crosses, reading the names and the ages of the youngsters who died in the savagery of that battle alone, when France lost the flower of her youth, one gets a French perspective on this brutal war fought within metres of their homes. The relief for so many came when the hero of that battle, Philippe Pétain, as an old man brought the second slaughter to a swift end in 1940. The fact the Vichy Government developed into a regime as fascist as the invader is another page of history, but at the time Marshal Pétain was loved because he had closed the gate on another killing field.

Nancy is renowned for its lovely 18th century classical urban development, and Metz, a frontier town, has a magnificent cathedral. But moving eastwards into Alsace it is Strasbourg, the capital, with its swings and roundabouts history, plus its shared European Union status, that sparks interest. Its German name means the City of Roads or if you are French *'le Carrefour de l'Europe'*: the crossroads of Europe.

From the 17th century until the Franco Prussian War it was French; from 1872 until 1918 it was German; from 1940-44 it was again German. It is a beautiful, prosperous city that has had its full share of tragedy, epitomised by the striking war memorial, of a woman – the city – supporting the bodies of her two 'sons', presumably one French one German, although neither wears a uniform. There are dozens of families that not only had to change their names from French into German, but whose sons were obliged to join the German army during WWII. There was little option as their families were under threat if they refused to comply with the Führer. After the war those who had fought in the Wehrmacht were treated rather shabbily, and the old veterans are still fighting for their army pensions from the French government. I suppose they could hardly claim it from the Third Reich.

Strasbourg has dozens of museums, a renowned university and a famously lovely cathedral. Much of the city has a quaint Germanic orderliness about it, with architecture that comes straight out of Hansel and Gretel. But there is a medieval French quarter too, La Petite France, where the millers, tanners and fishermen used to live and which is full of 16th and 17th century houses, wood framed and covered with hanging baskets of flowers.

Around Strasbourg are dozens of delightful villages which are well worth exploring. For anyone who needs access to northern and central Europe this region has a prime position.

Between Strasbourg and Colmar is Riquewihr, one of the most beautifully preserved fairy-tale wine villages in France, and the most visited by tourists. It has a population of only 1,200, and parking is kept outside the ramparts. During the final year of WWII there was street fighting and some indiscriminate bombing on the part of the Allies. It was difficult to bring in the grapes as the vineyards had been sown with land mines by retreating Germans.

Riquewihr is full of 16th and 17th century houses, some gabled and some balconied with cascading flowers. The village, surrounded by vineyards of Reisling and Muscat, has a wine museum housed in a 13th century gateway. The climate of the region is apparently semi-continental, with cold winters and very hot summers. There is a heart-warming story from Riquewihr, renamed Richenweier during the German occupation: Georges the eldest son of a wine-making family had escaped draft into the German army and, after the fall of France, joined the French Resistance. Johnny, the second son, was not so fortunate: he was forcibly drafted into the German army. When the Allied troops were once again on the march in 1944, Georges rejoined the French army. At this point Johnny was fighting with a German unit around Lake Constance in Austria, but when he saw a column of French tanks approaching he managed to slide into a nearby farmhouse, exchanged his German uniform for some old clothes belonging to the farmer, and ran out to join his French compatriots. A few weeks later in Riquewihr when the brothers were reunited, they found they had both been fighting in the same battle around Lake Constance. For the next three days they went from cellar to cellar and became unashamedly, totally plastered.

Colmar, a few kilometres away and about an hour's drive from Strasbourg, claims to be the driest spot in France – rain not grape. Colmar, with its topsy-turvy, pointed, multi-coloured buildings, like Riquewihr could have come out of a book of fairy tales. The houses are half-timbered and it would be hard to find a straight line anywhere. Colmar's old town is known as La Petite Venise because of the river, and is very touristy. In fact, Alsace has a burgeoning tourist industry amiably supported by the Route de Vin that stretches from the west of Strasbourg to Mulhouse.

There are not many resident Britons in this region, apart from those involved in the European Parliament but, if it feels like your sort of place and the temperatures suit, you could start a trend.

There are at the moment no Easyjet or Ryanair flights to Alsace, although there are plenty of regular airlines going in and out of

Strasbourg. For Champagne it is a relatively easy drive from the coast or there is a flight to Paris option.

Examples of properties for sale

Langres

House. 4 beds. 180 sq.m. Land 1,600sq.m. 5 mins from town: 214,000€

Pavilion (Lodge). 6 beds, 280 sq.m. Land 2,500 sq.m. 30 mins Reims: 320,000€

House. Old village farm. 3 beds, 170 sq.m. 2 hrs Paris, 1 hr Luxembourg. Edge Ardennes forest. Large garden. Stables and barn: 179,280€

House. Historic centre. Town house. 3 floors 200 sq.m. Attics, outbuildings, interior courtyard. Would make 5 apartments: 122 000€

House. Lac de Langres. Villa 5p, 170 sq.m. View over lake: 154,000€

Near Langres

Farmhouse. Renovated. 8 rooms. 250 sq.m. heated pool. Orchard and garden. Land 5,700 sq.m. Quiet village: 153,990€

Vitry-le-François

Bungalow. 134 sq.m. 5 rooms + barn. Interior courtyard 100 sq.m. Some work: 139,000€

House. 20 km Vitry. 155 sq.m. Land 2,026 sq.m.: 149,000€

Lac du Der

House. Period. 100 sq.m. Well restored. Land 1,500 sq.m. Minutes from lake. Outbuildings and barn. CH: 128,000€

Montier en Der

House. *Champenoise* to renovate, 5 rooms. 100 sq.m. Land 6,000 sq.m. Stable block, small lakes for fishing. Enclosed garden. Panoramic view: 106,000€

Strasbourg

Apartment. City Centre. 4p. Ex condition. View over canal: 260,000€

Villa. 4p. 90 sq.m. Garden 590 sq.m.: 347,000€

Villa. 7p. 170 sq.m. Terrace, small garden: 340,000€

Villa. Koenigshoffen district. 6p 170 sq.m. Land 450 sq.m.: 399,000€

COLMAR AND SURROUNDING VILLAGES

Molsheim

House. 165 sq.m.: 330 000€

Heiteren

House. 167 sq.m. 5 rooms: 312,000€

Riquewihr

House. Centre. 4p, 100 sq.m. Beamed ceilings + 40 sq.m. attic: 205,640€

Here is something that could be of interest to perhaps two couples wanting a business project in the centre of Riquewihr. A couple alone would have a very large living area and, in any case, there would be immediate income from the *gîtes*.

House/Restaurant. 380 sq.m. 13 rms. 9 beds. 4 bath. Restaurant 30 places + 16 places terrace + 2 apartments, each 100 sq.m. + 2 *gîtes* 45 sq.m. and 35 sq.m.: 770,000€

Agence Immobilier Zen. Tel. 03 80 36 89 35

www.seloger.com

Guy Hoquet Immobilier. Tel. 03 29 33 03 23

http.//immo.dna.fr

Agency ONP. Tel. 03 29 33 03 03

Laforet Immobilier du Nau. Tel. 03 26 72 28 28

IDIMMO. M Dion. Tel. 06 60 63 06 80

www.logic-immo.fr

www.openmedia.fr

www.colmar-immobilier.com. Tel. 03 89 41 11 99

www.arkadia.com/fra

19
REGION 7
BURGUNDY,
FRANCHE-COMTÉ

Burgundy remains as popular with us Brits as when we owned it, or at least when the Dukes were our best friends. Perhaps it's the lure of the grape rather than history, but it seems a number of us live there – *en permanence* – according to the *mairie* in Auxerre, although in the outlying villages, not in the towns.

Those of us who have spent hours driving down the A7, or even the old N7, which used to be called '*La Veuve*' (the widow) because there were so many accidents, will know the route and town names off by heart. The first time you meet them it is like reading a mobile wine list and, if you avoid the autoroute, you meet them face to face from Chablis in the northwest to the magic Côte d'Or south of Dijon. Villages and towns like Gevrey-Chambertin, Vougeot, Nuits-St-Georges, Volnay, Meursault, Beaune, Mâcon and the Beaujolais villages combining to make the 'route de Beaujolais'. The romance of these villages is in the wine, for as villages go they straggle along the N74 with not very much hinterland except perhaps for Nuits-St-Georges and the Beaujolais villages. Finding a lodging without pre-booking is tricky because the place is teeming not only with ordinary tourists, but also with dedicated and serious wine buffs. I once stopped off in Gevrey-Chambertin and, after a long, almost desperate search, finally found a charming small hotel on the main road. Fortunately all the sleeping accommodation was in a separate annexe at the back. These places are rich, and anyone who buys a patch of land here should never be lacking a crust or two. The trouble is not many patches come up for sale, which is an indication of their profitability.

During the last stages of WWII when the Allies were pushing through France towards Germany, Wynford Vaughan Thomas, a well-known war correspondent, was with the forces in Burgundy and was approached by an American officer. 'Thomas,' he said, 'I hear you are going back to see the Frogs this afternoon, and there's a little problem that's got us kinda worried. I've got a feeling they're doing a bit of a go-slow on us. I've a hunch our friends are staying a bit too long in this Chalon something or other.'

The town referred to was Chalon-sur-Saône, the very portal of Burgundy's Côte d'Or. The American was right – the French were doing a go-slow to avoid turning the vineyards into battlefields. Later that day a French Intelligence officer confided to Wynford V.T. 'I need hardly tell you of the terrible consequences of such a decision. It would mean war, mechanised war among the '*grands crus*' (great wines/vintages). Would France forgive us if we allowed such a thing to happen? We must not forget 1870!' He was referring to one of the last battles of the Franco Prussian War when the vineyards all around Nuit-St-Georges were turned into battlefields. 'It must never happen again.'

A moment later a young officer burst into the room wreathed in smiles. Saluting, he said 'Great news *mon colonel*, we have found a weak point in the German defences. Every one is on a vineyard of inferior quality!'

This confirms – as if we needed confirmation – that wine is not only a vital commodity in the nation's economy, but it is integral to the life force that embodies the spirit of France, and is of extraordinary importance in her emotional well-being. Soldiers in the army have a generous daily ration, as do all patients in French NHS hospitals (at least at the time of writing, but don't count on it continuing!). It is only recently that I have appreciated and understood the terrible dilemmas during WWII when French troops at the outbreak of war were faced with the possible destruction of their vineyards – an act tantamount to the desecration of holy shrines.

Auxerre and Avallon are attractive towns, the latter with medieval fortifications, great markets and great restaurants. I spoke to the tourist office in Auxerre who assured me there were lots of Brits living in Burgundy. Further south in Dijon, Mme. Sophie Herrent of Agence Mercure assured me there were fewer Brits looking for homes than in previous years, and those that were seemed to want something very inexpensive. I suggested they were perhaps looking for houses to renovate. Unfortunately this particular agency does not take on anything needing restoration, but there are others that do.

Dijon is the old historic capital of Burgundy, where the dukes lived: their ancestral home. Today the stunning Palais des Ducs is now the town hall. The city was the centre of government in Burgundy for hundreds of years and the fact that iron and coal were found in nearby Le Creusot added to the wealth of the province.

And the reason why the famous mustard has such a culinary status is the soil. It is the high content of calcium that gives the grains their particular strength. But Dijon's gastronomic contribution is not confined to mustard. Blackcurrant bushes flourish in the region, thus the blackcurrant liqueur *Crème de Cassis* has its origin there. And, curiously, it was a spirited young local priest during WWII, Felix Kir, who gave his name to that delicious *aperitif*, made with *Crème de Cassis* mixed with white wine. Finally there are two more table favourites from Dijon, *Boeuf Bourgignan,* and *pain d'épices*. Not a bad record.

Dijon is a city with fine architecture, museums, galleries rich town houses and old churches, and twinned with York, incidentally. Its university is one of the most prestigious in France and the city has become one of France's main conference centres. It has been classified as a city of Art and History, and was liberated by French troops at the end of WWII – no doubt, very carefully! No surprise!

Going south there are three major wine towns, Beaune, Chalons and Mâcon. Beaune still manages to preserve some of its antiquity despite being a magnet for wine tourism, and most of the shops stay open at lunchtime, something to please us Brits. It is full of narrow, cobbled streets with plenty of pavement cafés. The old town is enclosed in ramparts and pretty tightly packed. A delight for real wine aficionados, a three-day wine festival is held each year on the third Saturday of November, 'Les Trois Glorieuses', when wine is auctioned. The prices fetched apparently indicate the pattern for the season. You could have some real influence here.

Chalon-sur-Saône is a busy industrial town with a thriving, navigable river at this point thus giving the town status commercially. It may not be the location for a holiday home, but it's worth looking at as a convenient stepping-off point to the vineyards.

Despite its busy prosperity with its central position in the national wine industry, Mâcon still has the old town, plus a delightful waterfront on the river bustling with cafés and restaurants; it could almost be the Riviera. Of the major towns in Burgundy for my money, if I wanted such a location, it would be Mâcon, but the surrounding region is seductively packed with stunning little villages, timbered houses with their pitched roofs and quirky round towers. Vistas from the top of the gentle hills are without exception breathtakingly lovely. In the Mâconnais a major tourist attraction is the abbey of Cluny, worth visiting for the delightful village, as little remains of the once powerful seat of spiritual control.

Jan and Jon Rollason have lived between Mâcon and Cluny for about twenty years. It all started with a holiday with Jon's daughter in Paris. They decided to explore Burgundy, loved the area, looked at houses, fell in love with a village and a particular house, instructed a *notaire* and that was that.

As Jan says, 'We were self-employed and could work from a computer with email anywhere in the world. We'd reached a time when we wanted to give our lives a twist and a new dimension.'

I asked her about relocating in France. 'We do like the area south of Lyon, the winters are not so harsh and we think the area is even more amenable than Burgundy.'

However, they have made lots of French friends, mostly neighbours and their friends and, although there is an English community, Jan was happy to point out, 'It's not "Little England". Acquaintances and friends we have made are spread about in homes of all shapes and sizes: small, large, new and old, in hamlets or in the middle of nowhere to a magnificent *château*.'

And the essential differences between their British life style and French?

'Obviously not having to contend with British weather, which means outdoor living is such a norm that we take it for granted. And we do seem to mix with a very broad spectrum of terrific people, whom we might never come across in Britain. We agree when friends say their social life is much more hectic than in Britain!'

I asked them about the most attractive aspect of their French life.

'When we first arrived and we were DIY-ing ourselves to death, we always stopped work on Sundays to go and explore. Every new place was either stunning, interesting or charming, and we were always surprised that people were so friendly. We'd drive around for miles on country roads and not pass another car. And the delightful custom when a French person enters a shop, café or bar in town or country, they automatically say 'Bonjour tout le monde'.

And did they think more Brits were moving to France now than when they first arrived?

'Well, we hear of new families arriving, but they tend to keep to themselves at first – they 'play house' like we all do. Although in Burgundy there are many Swiss and German incomers.'

Why was this?

'Probably the whole ethos of French life. It is so attractive, neat clean towns, respect for others, polite manners and customs.'

A few years back Jon was diagnosed with prostate cancer. How did they find French medical services?

'French medicine was absolutely faultless and second to none. Jon had chemotherapy treatment for his cancer, and a year later had a replacement hip operation. The waiting list for a replacement hip is two weeks. All treatment, care and nursing were faultless. The hospitals were like the private sector in the UK, and it was ordinary French National Health.'

Finally I asked them both what advice they would give to novice Brits wanting to buy a home in France.

'Learn some of the language before you go, or at least make your very best effort to be able to ask for things in shops, and be polite when meeting French people. It will reward you no end, will be much appreciated, and will help you make friends. And always keep something back in the UK to return to if things don't turn out – you never know!'

FRANCHE-COMTÉ

Further east is Franche-Comté a less well known and far less touristy area of the Hexagon, maybe because it is too far over on the left as we hurtle down to the southern sun, for it is nearer Geneva than Paris. Its history is inevitably mixed with that of Burgundy, but it became part of

France in 1793. At the north-eastern edge of Franche-Comté is the city of Belfort, in the Territory of Belfort, a great winter sport centre. The town was the site of an heroic siege by the citizens against the Germans in the Franco Prussian war of 1870. They held out against fearful odds. Finally, through their sheer fortitude, the siege was broken and the Territory of Belfort remained part of France while their neighbour Alsace-Moselle suffered the ignominy of being annexed to Germany. The commanding officer of the time was Colonel Denfert-Rochereau, a name instantly recognisable if you have ever used the Paris Metro, and the most famous town monument is the eleven metre high red sandstone lion carved by Bartholdi out of the rock face to commemorate the siege.

The inhabitants of Franche-Comté, which is made up of three departments, are called Francs-Comtois. The region has stunning scenery, the Jura mountains a mecca for nature and winter sports lovers. More than half the land is covered by lakes, rivers and waterfalls and there are plenty of opportunities to swim, kayak, canoe or raft in utter tranquillity. It really is a terrain where you can get away from it all and be alone – a far cry from the overcrowded beaches of the south. Through the forests surrounding the lakes are innumerable paths for biking and hiking. Hardly surprising the Jura mountains provided a perfect location for the French Resistance in WWII. In Besançon, the capital and an old university town, amongst its many museums is one commemorating the courageous exploits of the men and women who fought in it. Besançon is also the birthplace of Victor Hugo and the Lumière brothers. The *mairie* is understandably proud of the city's reputation as a multi sport centre. Cross country (*ski du fond*), mountain ski (*ski alpin*), raquettes and dog sleighs are just an hour away from Besançon in the Juras, and in summer all the water sports imaginable are available, plus hot air ballooning. *Bateaux mouches* make regular tours on the river Doubs surrounding the town. At Malsaucy is a water sport lake, and Ornans, on the river Loue, birthplace of Gustave Courbet, with its ancient houses overhanging the river is thought to be the archetypal Franche-Comté village and has consequently become a tourist centre. Dole, the birthplace of Louis Pasteur, is a quiet, elegant little town with an Aquapark and, further south, is the spa town of Lons le Saunier – more famous as the birthplace of Rouget de l'Isle composer of the *Marseillaise*.

Gastronomically it has an interesting mixture of French delicacy with the solid no nonsense 'keep out the cold' food of Southern Germany and Switzerland. Specialities include chunky soups of cabbage and potatoes, creamy soups made from frogs' legs and white wine, and a baffling variety of *charcuterie*, whilst pork features in numerous guises. There is a type of veal schnitzel stuffed deliciously with cheese and ham – not in the slightest like the UK supermarket versions – a fine variety of cheeses. Comté is probably the one we know best and to my taste buds very like Gruyére, but cheaper. There are desserts galore, but the most mouth-watering has to be *Mont Blanc*, a meringue covered in chestnut purée and whipped cream.

A village, near Besançon in Franche-Compté is home to Joe West, his French wife Hedwige, their two sons Clement and Felix, aged 8 and 10, and the latest family member, baby Mathilda.

Joe and Hedwige met whilst at University in Manchester, and after some post-grad research decided to move to Cornwall and try a 'Good Life' existence, putting into practice some of their personal and well-considered ideas about food, environment and quality of life. Meanwhile, between growing all their own produce and rearing livestock while being acutely eco-conscious, Joe began teaching in a local primary school with computer training for adults as an extra. Though loving Cornwall they both felt like outsiders in the community and, said Joe, 'When it rained for 101 days we both felt we had had enough of this liquid sunshine'.

Hedwige's parents lived in the Jura, where she had been brought up, with dozens of family living nearby, Joe's French was excellent, so it was a perfectly natural next step, to move to France. But there were two people who were not quite so happy to see their young grandchildren moving abroad; Joe's parents Prunella Scales and Timothy West.

'I've come to accept it now', says Pru, 'more than Tim really. He finds it harder. But really we get to see them quite as often as we did in Cornwall. We can never make long-term plans because we don't know what we'll be doing, so we go when we're free. We are there whenever it's possible. In fact I'm going down next week on my own because Tim's working. The journey's not too bad – about six hours by train.'

It didn't take Joe and Hedwige long to settle into French life, in fact Hedwige has just taken another diploma at Dijon University so she is now a *professeur* in secondary education. Joe cannot teach in the French system because he hasn't French qualifications, so he teaches English and IT privately through the local Chamber of Commerce. 'Not like ours with dust on the door handle! More like a business school.'

Through both working part time, and sharing family responsibilities, living in France means that one parent is always there for the children, and at the same time they are able to maintain a high standard of healthy 'green' living.

However it hasn't all been plain sailing. At first one of the boys refused to speak French but gradually teething problems have been eased away by eminently sensible parenting.

Because Joe was not happy with the very strict and, he felt, unimaginative approach to education in the local primary school, he and Hedwige decided to educate the boys at home. They have been doing this since September and so far it is going well. The boys have a good social life with their French peer group, while parents ensure standards of spoken and written English do not suffer. Their 'home' school has to be inspected by the local education authorities, because at the next level the boys will probably slot back into the system. He thinks they may eventually attend UK universities after having gone through the rigorous grounding of the French Baccalaureate examinations.

Joe, feels 'the country appreciates you for what you are', but knows the difficulty in transferring skills, and 'self-employment is very expensive'.

The social scene?

'Mosty French.'

Would they ever think of going back to the UK?

He laughed, 'Not particularly.'

And advice to newcomers?

'Learn the language. Learn the language of bread and wine. And you have to love the country.'

Franche-Comté is well worth a visit, even just for the *Mont Blanc* but, alas, the airport at Dole is for internal flights only. By road from Calais takes about six hours, and by TGV from Paris to Besançon, two and a half hours. The nearest international airports are Geneva in the south and Basel-Mulhouse further north.

In my opinion Franche-Comté would be a perfect location either for a sport-driven family, or people who just want to get away from it all.

Examples of properties for sale

Here are some house prices and it may be a surprise to see the difference between Burgundy and Franche-Comté.

Pouilly-en-Auxois

House. 56 sq.m. Major renovation. Walls and roof good. Main drain: 37,000€

Nièvre

Village house. 41 sq.m. Habitable 7 rooms. Land 1,347 sq.m.: 85,000€

Nevers

Château. 14th, 17th and 19th century. 500 sq.m. Land 120,000 sq.m. 12 rooms: 900,000€

Sancerre-Nevers

House. 19th century *bourgeois*. 375 sq.m. 12 rooms. Land 300 sq.m.:
385,200€

Autun

House. Centre ville. 350 sq.m. 3 levels. 12 rooms, large walled garden:
470,000€

Chalon

Château. Period. 13 rooms. 400 sq.m. Land 1,700 sq.m. Statuary in
garden: 495,000€

Côte d'O

House. Village. 6 rooms 80 sq.m. 3 boxes + outbuildings + barns.
Land 11 hectares: 300,000€

Mâcon

Barn. Renovation. 150 sq.m. Land 400 sq.m.: 50,500€

House: 19th century village. Magnificent views. 3 beds 76 sq.m. Land
400 sq.m.: 98,500€

House. Old stone village hse. 100 sq.m. Access to autoroute. 3 beds,
bath, new roof. V good condition. Land 1,600 sq.m.: 165,000€

nr Cluny

House. Old village pharmacy. 19th century. 128 sq.m. Land 335 sq.m.
5 rooms: 160,000€

Beaune

House. 120 sq.m. Land 700 sq.m. With pool, 3 beds. CH: 256,000€

House. Character. 250 sq.m. Land 600 sq.m. Orchard and enclosed
garden: 315,000€

House. Character. Close to historic town centre. 150 sq.m. Renovated annexes suitable for family or professional purposes. Land 1,100 sq.m.: 470,000€

Dijon

House. Period. 3 beds + office, quiet area: 399,000€

House. Period. 3 floors. 3 beds, terraces: 420,000€

Belfort region

House. 207 sq.m. 5 beds. Land 7.5 hectares: 235,000€

Apartment. Belfort centre. 90 sq.m. 5 rooms. Garden 2 hectares: 134,000€

JURA

Grigny

House. Mountain village. House circa 1703. 120 sq.m. 6 rooms: 59,000€

Vesoul

House. 15 mins Vesoul, 2 apts. 250 sq.m. 9 rooms. Land 2,500 sq.m. Plus large barn and building planning permission: 96,300€

Montbozon

House. In village. 180 sq.m. 7 rooms + outbuildings. Land 1,300 sq.m.: 107,000€

Vauvilliers

House. Period. 180 sq.m. Land 2,500 sq.m. 7 rooms: 136,500€

Faverney (nr Vesoul)

House: In village 250 sq.m. Land 2,000 sq.m. Pool: 320,000€

www.lesiteimmo.com

www.agencemercure.fr. Tel. 02 48 24 88 39

www.seloger.com

Immogroup. Tel. 03 85 39 14 14

Espace immobilier. Tel. 03 85 29 28 47

www.immofrance.com

Immobilier Patrick Echinard à Beaune

www.echinard.com

www.avendrealouer.fr

www.vivastreet.fr

www.immofrance.com

20
REGION 8
AUVERGNE,
RHÔNE-ALPES

AUVERGNE

The Auvergne is made up of four Departments and, apart from its capital Clermont-Ferrand and some smaller, though spectacular townships, it is the most sparsely populated region of France. The isolation of its mountain regions has created an enclave of exclusivity that persists today despite the fact that so many autoroutes converge on Clermont-Ferrand and that it is now only three hours from Paris by train. The stretches of mountain plateau in the centre offer majestic and awesome vistas. It's like being on top of the world, flying with eagles, bleak and barren, while looking down on steep, verdant slopes packed with foliage, geological reminders that this has been active volcano country, albeit 8,000 years ago. I remember once driving along these empty mountain roads in May, passing banks of snow and later seeing a large sign that told me I was now in the Centre of France. There were more signs driving into villages warning of the danger of being cut off by snow in winter. The fact I had rather a dodgy car at the time made the journey not a little unnerving and knowing the centre of the Auvergne is called *la diagonale du vide* (the empty/barren diagonal) didn't help. I stopped at a wayside restaurant/inn standing solitary on the steep slope into another valley, anticipating some regional gastronomic delight to match the stupendous vistas all around.

I entered, in utter silence. The place, sparse and cold was empty of other clients. Eventually a woman shuffled in from the back, a French Mrs Danvers no less. I was clearly disturbing her afternoon. Food? What food? No salad either. I settled for an omelette, which turned out to be the worst omelette ever, as was the coffee. Salmonella was on my mind for a couple of days, but the panoramas were so spiritually uplifting, even Madame Danvers was forgotten.

Industry here is centred on Clermont-Ferrand with Michelin tyres principally, and at Montlucan with Dunlop. There are thermal spa centres like Vichy, La Bourboule and Volvic that produces the famous mineral water. Tourism has had an extra boost since the big leisure park 'Vulcania' devoted to the region's volcanoes, opened in 2002. Winter sports are hugely popular and are not as expensive as in the more sophisticated centres of France. There are a number of mountain ski stations at Super-Besse, Le Mont-Dore, and Le Liorcan as well as many solely dedicated to cross country.

The Auvergne preserves its own language, *Occitan*, but even that takes on its own form – *Auvergnac* – and is different from the *Occitan* spoken from time to time in the Languedoc. Of course they speak French too, but in a form of dialect. Their music and traditional songs are beautiful and Canteloupe's arrangements of Auvergnais folk songs are more familiar to many British households, than probably the region itself.

The mountain pastures are given to dairy farming producing cheeses that are familiar: Bleu d'Auvergne, Cantal Entre-Deux, Cantal Jeune, Fourme d'Ambert, Roquefort, and Bleu des Causses. There are very attractive farmsteads with *chambres d'hôtes* that are excellent value for money.

Years after the awful omelette I stayed in a glorious farmhouse about an hour south of Clermont-Ferrand up on the plateau. The scenery was magnificent, the woman who ran it delightful and, being so far away from anywhere else, she was obliged to serve an evening meal for her B&Bs which was excellent. Next morning the husband farmer, obviously very proud of his Limousin cattle offered to take me on an inspection tour of the very large cowshed. Although not of a dairy farming disposition it would have been churlish to refuse such an enthusiastic invitation.

He wanted me to see his prize possession, the bull. He told me this when we were well and truly inside the hangar else I should have turned on my heels. Passing dozens of cows dozing in their stalls I was led to a massive recumbent cream animal, tethered too loosely for safety, I thought, lying in regal splendour in a suitably king-sized half enclosure. He looked every square metre, a prize winner. 'He is magnificent,' said the farmer, 'and he serves them all'. He made a sweeping gesture to encompass the bull's harem of doe eyed blondes in adjacent bed-sits.

'He is the best bull I have ever had, strong and virile. D'you know we use him for artificial insemination too. Look I'll show you.'

At this point I wasn't quite sure what the farmer had in mind. However he patted the bull's rump and began coaxing the sleepy creature to its feet. Slowly the cream mass heaved itself up and although it looked pretty harmless there was an unmistakeable glint in the black eyes, and a suggestive flare of a nostril. He towered over us. Perhaps he was used to this, being a prize-winner and a regular on the bovine cat-walk. The farmer smiled proudly and beckoned me round the side, to the huge animal's flank.

'You see madame, why he is so fertile?'

Nonplussed I shook my head. Obviously amazed at my stupidity, he cried, 'Madame look!', and pointed underneath the bull.

'Have you ever seen such enormous, such magnificent testicles?'

I hadn't. And they were.

There are many attractive villages here; Ambert is one. I'm told Ambert is in a Middle Ages time warp and quite enchanting, with the best markets in France. So is Pleaux, but here the buildings are medieval too.

The first time we drove into the centre of Le Puy it was like pure science fiction. This charming little town is surrounded by astonishing pinnacles of lava rock thrown up by successive volcanic eruptions. Atop one of these volcanic needles is Notre Dame de France and, on another, a colossal statue of the Virgin Mary. Le Puy isn't taking any chances obviously.

Puy-de-Dome is the highest peak in the volcanic range of mountains. Nearby Riom, the old regional capital, built on a Roman site, has unusual Renaissance houses fashioned out of the surrounding black volcanic rock. The town's claim to recent historical status relates to the trial of Leon Blum (France's Jewish Prime Minister) in 1942 by Petain. Blum argued so brilliantly, running rings around Petain, he avoided being labelled a traitor, and instead was taken to a concentration camp, survived, and returned to France after the war to give evidence against Petain.

Vichy, despite its associations with the WWII collaborationist government, is an attractive spa town with sulphur springs attracting numbers of tourists both ailing and fit. It has a genteel feel to it, as most of the inhabitants are quite well heeled. I once found a small hotel with restaurant for the night. It was out-of-season Vichy, and *Madame* was as genteel as the ambience. As she looked me up and down I began to have doubts as to the suitability of my dress, which was certainly by now the crumpled-car look. After dinner I went to my attractive room overlooking the river. Suddenly I was aware of something in the room with me. There was a growl and scrabbling. And there it was, in the bathroom, a very large angry looking Persian cat. *Madame* was mortified and ushered her adored pet away, but she was even more mortified when later I found a collection of feline calling cards, placed with lavish abandon. Next morning *Madame* could not do enough. I had a very good breakfast and she sent me off with a couple of croissants to eat *en route*. A night to remember, indeed!

Jill Wilmott, a semi-retired director of dubbing and lip synch at World Wide Films in London has had a house near Ambert for about twelve years. She bought it, she said, as an escape from London. She had always wanted her own small piece of France, and had gone about the search slowly, ending up in the Auvergne mainly because the price was right. She bought her rather elegant, four-bedroom house – which is more like a *Maison de Maître* than a rustic farmhouse – through a Dutch *immobilier* in Clermont-Ferrand. It has 2000 sq.m. of land and no pool because, as she says, not many homes have one in the Auvergne. Jill is a good cross-country skier, but she still finds the winters long and bitterly cold, running well into spring. The temperature can drop to –15°C, while the summers are baking. There are very few English, although she has noticed an increase in holiday home buyers during the last couple of years and, of course, the region comes alive in the summer. She has lots of French friends, mostly those like herself who are holiday-homers. She loves Ambert and its markets, and is full of praise for the local services. In winter roads are cleared every day with snow ploughs, and there is even a local library with a computer.

I asked Jill about ever relocating in France.

'That is exactly what I want to do,' she said.

She does not intend to give up her Auvergne home, but is looking for something else in France, possibly a flat with a friend somewhere for the winter. 'You need a car here,' she said, 'that's why we always drive down. Unfortunately there are no UK flights to St Etienne any more.'

Despite feeling the need to search out somewhere else, she added.

'Quite honestly if you love nature, and I'm so close to the nature reserve, there's everything here. Fantastic mushrooms, fish in the lake; take your pickaxe into the forest and you find amethysts, but I'm feeling the need for some cultural activity, because I spend about half the year in France now.'

Where would she think of going?

'Maybe down to the south but, although my friend loves the country, we have to be sensible and find a place where the car is not an absolute essential, and where there is some public transport.'

Finally I asked her what was the essential difference between her French life style and her UK life.

'Well – I suppose it's all the things we love about France: the way of life; the great standard of life; the sociability; the people.'

And advice to Brits thinking of a home in France?

'Research, research, research! Don't do anything in a hurry.'

Examples of properties for sale

AMBERT REGION

Auzelles

House. 130 sq.m. 5 beds. Land 500 sq.m.: 125,000€

Farm. To renovate. 214 sq.m. Land 2000 sq.m. 5 beds. Outbuildings: 172,000€

Chazelles-sur-Lavieu

Farmhouse. 103 sq.m. Land 1,250 sq.m. 7 rooms + studio, cellar: 200,000€

Riom

House. 100 sq.m. Land 1,140 sq.m. 6 rooms. Pool: 235,000€

Vichy

House. 80 sq.m. Land 224 sq.m.: 168,000€

Vendat

House. Vichy 10 mins. 170 sq.m. Land 4,000 sq.m. 6 rooms. Nr shops: 23,000€

Manor. Vichy 20 mins. 200 sq.m. Land 10,000 sq.m. 8 rooms: 328,600€

Randan

House. 150 sq.m. Land 1,300 sq.m. Outbuildings: 160,000€

Pleaux

House. Stone house and shop in med village (Cantal). 3 floors. 5 rooms: 64,000€.

Clemenceau Immobilier. Tel. 04 73 93 27 61

Guegan Immobilier. Tel. 02 96 33 29 30

Avis immo. Tel. 04 77 96 90 00

www.photoimmo-puydedome.fr

Capi. Tel. 04 67 92 46 77

Rhône-Alpes

This region encompasses no fewer than eight departments, is the second most populated region of France, having over 6 million inhabitants, and has a very broad climate range. Its capital is Lyon, although Grenoble does lay claim to the title Capital of the Alps. There is an astounding difference in property prices; for example, around Annecy, that chic little town with antiquity, a lake, and proximity to the Alps and Lake Geneva, property is about the same price as the Riviera, while in the Lyonnais hinterland there are some bargains needing total or partial renovation.

The route of the A7 is probably the one that those of us who have spent years driving in France, know best. It is not the cheapest route to the south as autoroute tolls are regularly on the increase, but certainly the most convenient.

There's no doubt the weather changes south of Lyon.

There is a perceptible difference even as one approaches the city, especially if, on a baking summer day, you're in a car without air conditioning. Shallower roofs and russet Roman roof tiles are the immediate promises of the southern sun, and it is fair to assume that almost anywhere in the region could be a tourist trap.

My first experience of Lyon was standing on a bridge somewhere in the *centre ville* with a student chum, in the pouring rain thumbing a lift. It was the days when hitch-hiking was pretty much the student norm, and the French autoroutes were just beginning. The city today, France's second biggest, has a reputation as a gastronomic centre with some of the best restaurants and, I presume chefs, in France. Up to about the middle 1930s it had been a thriving centre of the silk industry, as the textile museum documents, and where a constant series of remarkable exhibitions are housed.

The old town is an absolute paradise with narrow winding streets and labyrinthine secret passages called *traboules*. Its more recent history is nothing less than dramatic. During WWII the Gestapo chief Barbie, known as the Butcher of Lyon exercised his own fiendish brutality upon anyone suspected of resistance. From a tip-off still cloaked in mystery, Jean Moulin, the leader of the French Resistance and de Gaulle's second in command was captured by Gestapo agents in a doctor's surgery in Lyon.

Recently one of my daughters spent a working fortnight in the city, and came back brimming with enthusiasm for the atmospheric old town, the superb food even in the lowliest restaurant, the Roman ruins, the basilica just above the city, and the highly efficient and cheap Metro transport.

She vows if ever she bought a home in France she would buy somewhere near Lyon.

Around the city are forested hill slopes offering peace and tranquillity, and dotted with picturesque little villages. Certainly an area worth exploring.

Look at it this way. Lyon's International Airport is busy in winter because of its proximity to ski-centres and in summer because the southern sun starts right there. A great city.

We once had a breakdown on the motorway outside Lyon in a clapped out camper van, packed to the gunnels with children, mattresses, bedding and all types of kitchen utensils for our *ruine*, three hours away, that was about to become our first French home. We were all very excited, although at the time we had no idea we would be sharing it with so many species of French wild life.

Alas, no one could repair the old van until the following day, so we were led to a small hotel called 'Les Trois Canards' (The Three Ducks) in Belville, a little village nearby on the Saône. It was a haven of peace and calm. The summer restaurant under a pergola of vines was so close to the river, lapping water accompanied the sounds of the diners. We loved it. Our misfortune had become instead, our good fortune, and this delightful small hotel remained one of our family landmarks to which we always returned whenever we could. Naturally being so close to Lyon, the food was fantastic.

Alas the van was going to cost more to repair than the cost of our little house, so two afternoons later, we had to be rather ignominiously towed by a truck with lights flashing like a fairground into the hamlet and our new home, arriving well after dark. The tow I remember cleared me down to my last franc. We left the dead van on the patch of land that went with house, and at the end of the holiday returned to the UK by train.

It had to be the broken down van that was responsible, because two years later a couple of customs officers were seen inspecting it. By this time it had become a stately home for a colony of mice. What exactly the customs men read into this mice-ridden van is hard to tell, but a year later my husband received his call up papers for the French army. We were baffled. Did they think a deserter was living with the mice – my husband? His feet were too flat even for the Korean War and would certainly have been hopeless kicking up sand in the Foreign Legion. Obviously French Intelligence knew nothing about the shape of his feet. Perhaps British Intelligence had actually donated him, ostensibly as a generous gesture, but in fact as a dastardly weapon to disrupt and debilitate the French Army. Those feet were potent. Anyway in the event we decided to do nothing and say nothing even when the second summons arrived. We received no further communication.

But it could happen to anyone. Be prepared!

After Lyon, charming old towns Vienne and Valence, one Roman – the other medieval in origin – skirt the river as it runs parallel with the autoroute pushing southwards, traversing wide bridges on the route to Orange, through the beginning of dry *garrigue,* escarpments of scrub and rock typical of a Mediterranean climate. But turn off the autoroute and you will find villages and small towns like Tournus, Annonay and Privas and they are all worth exploring.

Still further southwards is the glorious Ardèche.

The huge natural bridge of rock at Vallon Pont d'Arc is a tourist magnet and the best departure point for a tour of the Ardèche gorges and spectacular grottoes. Seven kilometres away is the old fortified town of Ruoms with a number of 14th and 15th century houses, and the magical 16th century Château of Vogüé backed by cliffs of marble. There's much to see in the Ardèche.

To the east, however, in the Haute Savoie, the tip of France that touches Switzerland, the terrain is green and alpine. Here are the thermal bath towns, and winter ski centres: Thonon-les-Bains, Evian-les-Bains, Megève, Megevette, Chambery. I have friends who have decided to invest in a couple of inexpensive small ski chalets that sleep two, intending to let them throughout the year to skiers and hikers. They happen to be keen skiers so I suppose that lessens the financial risk as they can always use one of the chalets. I have read of companies that will become your letting agents if you buy through them. However if you and the family like winter sports there are opportunities to buy near ski stations, and as the area is always popular the property could generate income in your absence.

Grenoble is an old elegant town, the birthplace of Stendhal, with a 14th century university. It was one of the first French cities to re-introduce the tramway. There are elegant town houses for sale although not in abundance. Grenoble is very much a student city with the university attracting students from around the world. There are always dozens of post-graduate courses on offer and heavily over-subscribed. It follows that apartments rather than houses feature prominently in estate agents' windows. I'm not sure that investment in an apartment would necessarily be the answer to a holiday home search, but if it is look up *www.google.fr* for Grenoble.

Like Lyon it has an international airport that will be open to Easyjet in 2007. Ryanair flies to Grenoble-Lyon airport, and flights seem to be at a premium in the winter. No surprise.

Examples of properties for sale

LYON

St-Rambert-d'Albon. 50 km Lyon.

Farmhouse. 360 sq.m. Land 2,000 sq.m.: 380,000€

MONTS DU LYONNAIS

St Catherine

House and watermill. 265 sq.m. renovated, 170 sq.m. further renovation. Garden 250 sq.m. Land 10,000 sq.m. 4+ beds. 1 hectare of river frontage. Ideal horses: 398,000€

Hamlet – part of. 2 houses. 2 long barns + outbuildings. Water + electricity *in situ*. Bread oven, wells etc. Land 5,300 sq.m. For renovation: 99,000€

Annecy

Town house. 67 sq.m. + attic 30 sq.m. Garden 350 sq.m.: 330,000€

Apartment. Old Town. 2 beds: 200,000€

ANNECY REGION

Sillingy

Villa. New. 120 sq.m. Land 690 sq.m. 3 beds: 390,000€

Megevette

House. 100 sq.m. Land 1,200 sq.m.: 295,000€

Chamonix

Studio. Nr ski lifts. Furnished, sleeps 3: 90,000€

Contamines-Montjoie

Chalet. 22 sq.m. 2 beds fully equipped. Parking. Elec. Heating: 74,000€

Evian-les-Bains

House. 125 sq.m. 4 beds. Views Lac Leman and mountains. Land 900 sq.m. Elec. CH: 410,000€

SAVOIE

Domaine-des-Sybolles

Studio. Furnished for 2. Middle of 6 good ski stations. 310 km of pistes: 27,000€

Les-Arcs Paradiski

Studio. 17 sq.m. with balcony: 44,690€

Aix-les-Bains

Apartment. 1 bed: 55,000€

DROME

Beaumont-en-Diois

House + bergerie. To restore. 100 sq.m. Land 200 sq.m. Mountain village, alt. 1000 m. 4 rooms.: 60,000€

ISÈRE

Les-deux-Alpes ski station

Studio-Cabine. 24 sq.m. Equipped for 4. Furnished: 70,500€

ARDÈCHE

Vallon-Pont-d'Arc

House. Town centre. Stone. 153 sq.m. + building and attics to renovate. Land 300 sq.m.: 278,000€

Alboussière (20 mins west Valence)

Villa. New. 2 individ. apts. 125 sq.m. and 65 sq.m. Land 450 sq.m. In village close shops: 290,000€

Colombier-le-Vieux (20 mins Tournon)

Farm. Habitable, with extensions to restore. Land 11 hectares with woodland. Quiet, not isolated, good condition. Suitable horses: 200,000€

www.pasdagence.com

info@idim-transaction.com

www.immofrance.co.fr

Barjac Immobilier. email: *barjacimmobnilier@wanadoo.fr*. Tel. 04 66 24 58 76

www.france-tourinfo.com

21
REGION 9
LANGUEDOC

The Languedoc is an old southern province of France, and was historically distinct from the rest by the language that used '*oc*' for yes instead of the traditional '*oui*'.

The *langue-d'oc* was called *Occitan* and we have already met it and its variation in the Auvergne. However no need to worry – stick to French and you'll get by. Today's Languedoc covers a number of provinces and spans down to the Spanish border and eastwards to the edge of Provence.

The whole area has had a tormented, troublesome and certainly dramatic history that has left behind architecturally splendid edifices, religious and secular, along with pagan-based festivals disguised as religious romps.

In Limoux for example is the Féchos, the Carnival that runs every weekend from the end of January until the Sunday before Palm Sunday. The place is awash with figures in white baggy pants and lots of masked groups in fantastic costume, accompanied by music and drums parading through streets and pavement cafés.

The whole region is very Spanish-influenced, particularly with the fiestas and paellas cooked by the bucketful, that accompany them. There is, of course, a bull culture, that can be both cruel or benign depending on your point of view. But the strength of this noble creature is admired, almost revered, for the silhouette of the bull is seen everywhere almost like a talisman for luck. This bull culture does not emanate solely from Spain but from the Camargue in the Bouches du Rhône (see next chapter.)

Aigue Mortes – a beautiful, walled town on the border of the Gard, in which every stone has a history – is now inland, but during the reign of Saint Louis it served as his embarkation point for the third Crusade. Nearby are the Listel vineyards, where the vines are grown on reclaimed land and which produces a deceptively good *'brut' champagnoise* wine, a very good *rosé* and a stunning *gris de gris*. There is a story that unless you can see grains of sand at the bottom of a *gris de gris* bottle, it is not a Listel.

Nîmes is a beautiful city with a notably Roman past: it was the capital of Roman Gaul. It has a *'Maison Carré'* (House of Justice), that Augustus built for his grandchildren, an Arena that rivals Rome, the Temple of Diana, and *Tour Magne* at the top of the Fountains Gardens. Originally Roman gardens with an open spacious lay-out, they were restored in the 18th century, with baths, benches and changing rooms preserved on the lower levels. And, of course, the restaurant with tables and umbrellas is a delightful place for rendezvous and cappuccinos.

The statuary, sweeping steps and balustrades are impressive, and lead up to the top of the hill and the prominently-placed *Tour Magne* from which, presumably, the Romans could see anything approaching the garrison by land or sea. The city has wide boulevards of mostly 18th century houses, dotted with small elegant squares with the emphasis on outside eating. The Arena is a great place for concerts, *corridas* and big *spectacles,* seating thousands. But during Whitsun there is nothing to match the Feria. Nîmes becomes almost entirely Spanish, with Spanish dancers in every square, flamenco in the streets, processions, carnival costumes that rival Venice, floats with amazing collections of visual eccentricities and, to cap it all, huge pans of paella at every street corner – with liberal quantities of wine, naturally.

Round about 1870 a certain Monsieur Levi from Nîmes, emigrated to the USA. Hard up, he started to weave the cloth that field workers used for trousers back home in Nîmes. It was *de Nîmes* cloth and that's how denims were born. So Nîmes made its mark on the world, and Monsieur Levi made enough to pay his rent and more.

Between Nîmes and Uzès is the magnificent Pont du Gard built at the cost of hundreds of slaves' lives to bring the water from Uzès to the Roman garrison in Nîmes; an extraordinary feat of architecture. Recently they have revamped the site, but it is still delightful to visit, especially after dark when the floodlights switch on.

Now Uzès, I always feel, should be the Tunbridge Wells of the Gard.

Some years back it received the accolade of being an historical site, richly deserved, resulting in the winding streets of medieval houses that always looked like a stage set, being sandblasted back to cream stone, making them even more beautiful. As a town it has much to offer: buildings, markets, shops, schools, plenty of restaurants, friendly people and a very low-key British colony.

Every July there is a special fortnight of les *'Nuits d'Uzès',* based on the fact that Racine lived in the town for a while; his house is still there. He was so captivated by the place that he wrote to his friends in Paris telling them 'Our nights are better than your days'. Thus resulted the two weeks of largely baroque music with concerts, small ensembles, orchestras, and choirs, in the cathedral, the gardens of the Bishop's palace or in the enchanting large courtyard of the Château d'Uzès. It's quite something listening to Rameau on a silent, warm night, enclosed by the *château's* walls, drenched in moonlight and still glowing from the day's sun.

Surrounded by attractive villages and hectares of vineyards it is a town very much worth visiting, positioned as it is near the airport at Nîmes and near so many places of interest. August sees the week of Uzès' *fête* when the cowboys from the Camargue run baby bulls through the main street from top to bottom, with gleeful spectators waiting for something to go wrong smugly secure behind barricades. The horses run in a delta shape enclosing the bull. This is called an *Abrivado*, and should not be confused with a Pamplona bull running. The *Camarguaise* bulls are smaller with less dragon fire than their Spanish cousins. On several occasions I have watched a bull run off, causing shrieks of laughter, screams and total confusion. Every small town and village has its own *Abrivado* during the summer *fêtes* and, when there are wide open spaces, the bulls are more difficult to control. Once we saw a large bull escape the horses and cowboys twice, as he was run through this very open village street. Cleverly he escaped the horses and cowboys to the nearest vineyards where he could be seen trampling the vines. After half an hour we gave up waiting for the bull to be recaptured and the *Abrivado* to restart and left, as did others, only to find the narrow road leading from the village, blocked by the big van used to transport the bulls. There we saw and spoke to four perspiring men pulling the large bull away from a telegraph pole that he was about to uproot. Finally they managed to tether him and with all of their strength and force they pushed him into the van using really encouraging words of affection like 'good boy', 'come on old chap' and 'that's it Olive'. And who was Olive? That was the big bull's name.

Frank and Liz Greenwood first came to France as holiday homers about 18 years ago when they bought a small apartment in a Riviera tourist trap. After a few years, though, they relocated to a village house just outside Uzès because it was less congested, and because they knew the area through their many friends living nearby. 'It was perfect for holidays and very photogenic.' Frank and Liz have officially retired, he is an architect and she, an interior designer but, after 11 years to-ing and fro-ing to their village holiday home, two years ago they decided make the break and live in France permanently. Although their village house had become perfection, they decided to relocate again to another village further away.

Why?

'Well,' said Frank, 'outside the French holiday season the place was abandoned except for us and a few cats. We had more time available and we were seeking 'France profonde', where people and life functioned throughout the year instead of being full of itinerant semi strangers for three or four months.'

Any other reasons for the relocation?

'Smaller village, prettier countryside, more space and garden.'

Had they made many new friends or were they still part of the Brit colony?

'Still part of a larger international colony with French friends thrown in.'

And the essential difference between life in France and the UK?

'Quality of life.'

And the most attractive element?

'France profonde is much the same as rural England was half a century ago, but with added sunshine!'

And the irritations?

'Adolescent French drivers.'

Anything he missed?

'Pubs.'

I asked them what advice they would give to novice Brits about to do the same thing.

'Travel widely through the country, locate your preferred area and try to spend some time there throughout the year before looking seriously at property.'

In this region every town and village will have some form of fiesta or *fête*, particularly during the summer months, starting as the school year finishes.

Each sizeable village and town also has its own arena, a Roman legacy and again used in the bull *spectacles* of the *fêtes* season, and while large cities like Nîmes, Perpignan, Béziers and others go in for *corridas*, smaller places are content to watch the '*cours camarguaise*', which is far more civilised than watching the slow ritualistic killing of a dignified animal. A piece of ribbon – *la cocarde* – is tied around a horn of either a young bull or a sprightly heifer and each member of a team of about six to eight white-clad, nimble young men has a small sharp comb tied around a wrist. These young men are the *rasateurs*. Animal and humans enter the arena and the contest begins, lasting no more than about 15 minutes. Which of the nimble-footed can get the ribbon off the horn? Many's the time young men receive very sore bottoms from a thrusting horn as they leap up the iron barricade out of the way. However it is good fun, and here the bull is the star. I have seen a young bull receive a standing ovation because no *rasateur* managed to cut his *cocarde*, and he loved the applause so much they couldn't get him out of the arena. The *rasateurs* become local heroes, with a championship at stake for the best team and the most successful *rasateur*. League tables rather like our football ones appear in the local papers. I remember having to drive to see countless *cours camarguaise,* when my 16-year-old daughter developed a crush on that year's championship contender. I should add that if you don't know the music from Carmen before a visit to a *cours camarguaise* you will afterwards.

Béziers, further down the coast, is a great rugby town, the game brought to them by a Welshman. The old town is intersected with small alleyways, and Renaissance buildings. There are attractive open spaces with well laid-out gardens, like the *Plateau des Poètes*, and it is the capital of the Languedoc wine country. Rugby and *corridas* feature strongly here and Béziers' *feria* is in August. The city has had a rough time since 1944, when it was bombed by the Allies during WWII. Later, hundreds of HLM blocks (council flats) had to be built to house repatriated Algerians after independence and, consequently, unemployment rose alarmingly. The University of Montpellier has recently used sites in Béziers for two major extensions, and with the arrival of the new A75 autoroute Clermont-Ferrand to Béziers, the city is set for a renewed period of prosperity. A good time to buy, perhaps?

Pézenas, associated with Molière, was at one time very prosperous when it was the seat of the Languedoc Parliament, and it was set to become a second Versailles. Part of this legacy can be seen today in some of its stunning 14th century to 18th century domestic architecture.

I once attended a hilarious Easter romp in a village outside Pézenas where the men dressed up as women, some as pregnant women and some as priests. It was broad, bawdy, and politically hopelessly incorrect, but side splitting. The priests instead of crosses around their necks wore small rubber penises. They and the crowd made up of plenty of children sang together an obviously well known local song, which involved placing the left hand in the elbow crease of the right arm, and raising the right arm with force several times. The *mairie* addressed the crowd and the celebrations finished with a huge tug-of-war between two teams of 'women'. It was truly basic wholesome bawd without the snigger element of seaside postcards.

I visited Perpignan in bleak mid winter *en route* to Andorra, and it didn't ring any bells for me. Perhaps it's better in summer. It really feels more Spanish than French, perhaps not surprisingly as it took in so many escaping the Spanish Civil War. Friends tell me it has plenty of good restaurants, a lively night-life and of course it's near the ski slopes.

The oldest medical school in Europe, an Oxbridge of French medicine is in Montpellier, a lovely city. Today it has all the latest in medical expertise and is the centre of international medical research. In fact two dear friends of mine, both doctors, after inspecting the huge hospital, decided to buy within easy reach for that very reason. The old quarter housing the university has barely changed since the 17th and 18th century, and the city in general has an abundance of public buildings and private mansions from the same period. It also has a huge, shop-till-you-drop mall: a teenager's paradise.

Just outside Montpellier and *en route* to the city's airport is a stunning long stretch of sandy beach and fantastic dunes at Carnon Plage. We always came here when beaches further along were crowded. Carnon itself has a perfect small marina with mouth-watering restaurants fringing the water. There are also some fabulous shops, not cheap, but very chic. The town has the physical advantages of a Nice or Cannes, but without the pesky crowds. I have been on its long, long beach quite alone during the first week of a September, and maybe that's a norm.

Of course if you want a wild night life better to try it out first!

The other major resorts along the coast are busier. Grau de Roi is a very attractive old fishing village with harbour, and La Grande Motte, has distinctive pagoda shaped condominiums, and an expanding rich marina nearly rivalling Cannes or Antibes. I remember when this expensive little town, with its well-manicured lawns and squeaky clean roads was once a rustic collection of fishermen's cottages and a few shops selling beachwear around a battered harbour, in which there were several hard-working fishing boats. Then the land was drained and architects were invited to send in designs. I know progress has to be made, and we must move on, but those hard-working fishing boats were grounded in reality far more than the cosmetic perfection that has taken their place.

One of the favourite tourist haunts is Carcassonne, the medieval walled citadel perched surreally alone on a hilltop. The city has had a bloody history of savage religious prejudice. Simon de Montfort lodged there when he slaughtered the Cathars, the object of his brutal Albigensian crusade.

The lower town below the citadel was founded by St Louis (Louis IX), the very one who took the Third Crusade out from Aigues Mortes.

The old city has an unreal feel to it, like walking through a film set, possibly because it has been restored to almost too high a degree of perfection. It seems to attract the rather laid-back tourist and traveller. I remember we were desperate to find a lodging, and luckily we found one in the old citadel. Later, in search of food, we found what looked like a converted barn not only with minstrel's gallery but also with minstrels, providing perfect period accompaniment to very good restauration, at an agreeable price. After the performance the minstrels descended to chat to the diners only to continue impromptu musical renditions, which became less restrained as the night went on.

Welsh speakers Anne and Graham Jones, just retired, have both worked in television for years. Grahame was a director and producer with HTV in Cardiff, where they have a home. They first visited France in the seventies and since then have 'almost' bought châteaux near Paris and near Bordeaux. They have continued looking at older properties until last year when they downsized in Cardiff and began the search for a 'new build' in France. After hours of Internet surfing they decided on the Carcassonne area with which they were already familiar. They now regard their village 'new build' outside Carcassonne to be their second home rather than a holiday home. They love the historical associations with the area, the climate, the landscape, and also because the locals still speak *Occitan* which is taught in schools. This strikes a particular chord with Welsh speakers. There are Brits in the area, but searching them out was never a priority. As Anne says, 'we have made friends of all ages in the village and have been invited to their homes and parties. Spending long periods here has made it easier to get to know people. We already leave house keys with the next-door neighbours.'

Did they feel isolated?

'Not at all. Our house stands on the edge of the village bordering on a vineyard, and we are close to international transport. Ryanair flies to

Carcassonne, Perpignon and Toulouse.'

And the difference in life style?

'It's far less stressful. The climate itself allows for a difference.'

Whilst there were no sources of irritation, 'I miss having a daily newspaper,' said Anne. 'It's a day late here, but we do have satellite television to keep up with the news.'

The cost of living?

'Definitely lower,' they both agreed. Also they had not met any unexpected costs with their 'new build' home because they had done their research.

And advice to newly-arrived Brits?

'You must use French as much as possible and it is appreciated. As Welsh speakers we appreciate the efforts made by those who have not been brought up with it. Buy local papers, go to the mairie, find out about local events and do your best to participate.'

'Yes, respect the culture,' Graham added.

And what about living in France permanently?

'There is a very strong possibility that we shall.'

Just north of Uzès is Alès, once a relatively prosperous coal mining town, but the environs are far more interesting than the town itself. The town lies in the foothills of the Cévennes, with the *Parc National* providing a dramatic backdrop. A tortuously winding road climbs higher and higher along the Corniche des Cévennes through spectacular and frequently stomach-turning mountain vistas of sheer cliff face and plunging ravines. Not suitable for vertigo sufferers nor, indeed, for careless drivers. I was warned I could well see an eagle up there flying alongside the car. Hardly surprising that the French Resistance more or less started in the hidden caves of the Cévennes mountainsides and on the rough scrub land (*maquis*) of the lower slopes – the reason why those who were part of the Resistance were called the *maquisards*.

On the descending route you will go through idyllic villages, perfect but isolated. Access could be tricky in winter, although there are good *routes nationales* covering the area. Mende on the northern edge of Languedoc is a pretty little town with stage-set streets and old houses and good rail and bus links to Paris and Nîmes. A 15th century bridge spans the River Lot and the town is close to Mt Lozère, so you can count on breathtaking panoramas, though snow bound in winter. At one time the area was densely forested and the haunt of wolves and lynxes that today are kept in the zoological park at Chastel Nouvel, 6 km away. The last wolf was shot here in 1870, so you can sleep easy.

Mende is about 40 km from Florac where jolly medieval jousting events are held every summer. It's a small village close to Mt Aigoual, 1,565 m at the summit, from where they say you can see one third of France. Further down the valley are charming villages like Valleraugue and La Couvertoirade where you pay for parking and for walking round the ramparts, which are really quite something. They completely enclose the village with towers and walls, and have remained relatively untouched by anything much later than the 13th century. It is advertised as the perfect 'Templar' village.

If it's more drama you crave go to the Cirque de Navacelles. You will stand on the wooded edge of a huge circle 150 m deep, the sides, sheer and treacherous, fall away below you into the chasm. Standing too near the edge gives you butterflies. They say it is the crater of a meteorite, but there are various stories. At the bottom of this great wide pit, is a small hamlet. To live there you might have to consign youself to it forever.

The Languedoc is a big tourist area without the overcrowding of the Riviera. However, the Gard is reckoned to be the hottest summer spot in France. It is also prone to ear bashing storms when nature's illuminations can dazzle the eye for hours on end.

I had the misfortune to be caught in the middle of the devasting storm and floods that swept though the Gard a few years back. The President called it a disaster area, which was a great relief to everyone, as insurance claims would have to be met. It was early September, and driving to a dinner party with two friends, the sky became black and torrential rain exploded over the landscape. Our destinantion was via a route I knew well, and only a few kilometres away. Within five minutes the monsoon was filling the ditches at the sides of unlit country roads, and it became difficult and dangerous to navigate. Meanwhile the thunder was like a bombardment, bouncing off the mountains, and reverberating into the hollow valley below. Continuous fork and sheet lightning was the only illumination in the deep black. The car stalled and stopped. With water half way up the wheels, the monsoon rendering windscreen wipers useless, it was a scary situation. After several more stop-starts, the car limped through cascading water to the village of our rendezvous. Even knowing the place so well visibility was nil, and I took the wrong turning. Finally a tractor appeared and we were towed to the the village hall, where inside were a number of other refugees of the storm. The mayor said it would be impossible to reach our dinner date as the road was impassable, and telephone lines were down. Very soon a village woman arrived with an enormous pan of pasta, cheese and paper plates, which we all fell on, with remarks like 'just like the war' thrown around. Then the mayor brought in a crate of wine bottles and plastic cups and we were told we would have to wait there until the morning, and we should find a place on the floor for the night, as the storm was far from abating. With each newly-arrived, rainsoaked traveller there were more stories of tragedies, perilous situations, and of helicopter rescues. It was like the end of the world, our own Noah's flood, but without the ark. Round about midnight the mayor announced the women would be taken off to an *herbergement* (lodging) for the night.

A large four-wheel drive arrived and squashed in as many as possible, and drove us to a small *château* where we were directed up to corridors of beautiful rooms all done in exquisite taste with *en suites* and towels laid out. Illumination was by candlelight for there was no electricity. The following morning after meeting other refugees over breakfast we learned that our rescuer was Monsieur Guerlain of the famous perfume family. Our genial host and his wife had saved not only the women, M. Guerlain went back to collect the men and any new additions, and beds were found in adjacent wings. They kept us in the *château* fed and warm. Next morning we all set to preparing a meal over the log fire. And there we were, totally different people, from different backgrounds, but all sharing the same experience and all being incorporated as one family at the large dining table, no class divisions; our host sitting paternalistically at the head. For me that *bonhomie* and honest Republicanism has to be the essential spirit of France. No wonder they fought so hard for it.

We left late the following afternoon when the rain finally stopped, but before leaving we refugees clubbed together for a bouquet of flowers to be sent to our rescuers. It was the least we could do.

Others were not so lucky for countless homes had been swept away that night and over three million cars in the Gard alone became heavy insurance claims. Mine was one.

According to a report in a Paris magazine the Hérault has been nominated the best department in which to live. Haut-Garonne came second.

The choice is yours.

Transport-wise the total area has three major autoroutes, the A7 that leads into the A9 at Orange and from thence heads straight for Barcelona via Nîmes and the new A75, Clermont-Ferrand to Béziers. For the interior there are good RN roads. It takes about ten hours by car using autoroutes, from the Normandy coast to the Uzès/Nîmes area. The SNCF provides comprehensive rail links as well as a fabulous TGV service from Nîmes, via Avignon to Paris/Lille and Waterloo. Carcassonne, Perpignan, Nîmes and Montpellier all have airports served by low-cost airline Ryanair.

Examples of properties for sale

Béziers

Villa. 150 sq.m. Garage: 187,000€

Nr Béziers

Country House. 160 sq.m. Land 1,700 sq.m. Pool: 490,000€

Villa. 6 beds. 166 sq.m. Land 13,000 sq.m. with pine forest. Pool, caretaker's house + tennis court: 670,000€

Montpellier area

Country house. 5 beds + office. Terraces. Pool. Garages. Land 1,100 sq,m. Orchard: 494,000€

Villa. 5 beds. 175 sq.m. Land 735 sq.m.: 660,000€

Pézenas

House. Village between Pézenas and Gignac. Renovated. 5 beds. 2 terraces: 276,000€

Bedarieux

House. 120 sq.m. Ex con. Numerous outbuildings. Land 1 hectare. Panoramic views: 350,000€

PERPIGNAN AND REGION

Amélie-les-Bains

House. Village, period. Stone. 3 floors, 240 sq.m. 10/11 rooms. River bank views, close to village centre: 680,000€

House. In village. 224 sq.m. 6 beds. Annexes: 331,500€

Rivesaltes

Villa. New. 146 sq.m. 6 rooms. Pool. Garage. Garden: 305,000€

St Cyprien Plage

Villa. 132 sq.m. Faces 30 m of beach. 2 apartments, 2 beds each. Land 530 sq.m. Terrace facing sea: 633,000€

Canet Plage

House. 140 sq.m. 6 rooms. 300 m from sea: 440,000€

Uzès and region

House. Village. 185 sq.m. Big courtyard: 472 ,000€

House. *Bourgeois*. 3 beds + pool + guest house. All restored. Wells. Garage, cellar. Nr commodities. Land 2,300 sq.m.: 399,000€

Cavaillargues

Farmhouse. Stone. 275 sq.m. 6 beds. 135 sq.m. still to restore. Land 6,000 sq.m. Orchard and vines: 483,000€

Alès

Bungalow. 3 beds. Land 800 sq.m. Pool. Outbuildings: 276,000€

Florac

House. 140 sq.m. Large verandah. Land 15,000 sq.m.: 250,000€

www.maisonsetappartements.fr
Agence Transagri. Tel. 04 67 60 60 80
www.seloger.com
www.lesclesdumidi.com
Immobillier Caroux. Tel. 04 67 95 26 96
Agency Capi Jess Abad. Tel. 04 68 61 54 19, *www.sudimmo.fr*
www.lesclesdumidi.com
www.abonimmo.com
www.provcevimmo.com

22
REGION 10
PROVENCE

Provence starts at Avignon and extends to the Italian border.

It is vast and varied, from the Camargue in the south-west corner to ski resorts in the north-east. Its later history has been war-torn and bloody, with religious and monarchical conflicts along with several foreign occupations; the Greeks being the first to spot Provence's potential. But in the pre-Greek period the country was made up of quiet farming communities that were a mixture of Celtic-Ligurian tribes. The Greeks occupied the coastal zone, and founded Massalia (Marseille) on the left hand side and Niké (Nice) on the right hand side. We know they visited Carpentras to buy skins, honey, wheat and goats, so they were obviously into health foods. It was the Greeks 600BC who brought the first vines to Massalia and their coastal bases. According to legend it was Dionysius who saw a drop of the Gods' blood fall on the soil and immediately sprout a vine. But historically it was the Romans who provided the complete formative occupation, in terms of pretty well everything, especially architecture. In fact the Romans arrived in Provincia by invitation from the Phoenicians to put down the supposedly 'savage' Celtic-Ligurians. So what did they expect, these invaders, bunches of flowers?

For Romans, Provincia was a land of milk and honey, and an important territorial stepping stone on the march to the Spanish provinces. I've often thought what a great posting it must have been for the average Roman squaddie. 'OK Septimus Quintus, it's Glanum for you.' 'Yessir!' (squaddie clicks sandals ecstatically).

They built great roads and one of them, *via Domitia* – linking the Spanish provinces to Rome, through Narbonne *(Narbo Marius)* and Nîmes *(Nemansa)* – is still marked today as you drive along the motorway following the same route. The Aurelian Way ran from Rome to Arles, and again parts of it are still followed from Genoa through Cimiez, Antibes *(Antipolis)* and Fréjus *(Forum Julii)*.

The province is a lush vegetable garden, an orchard, a floral paradise and a vineyard; a place where you may ski in the morning and an hour away at the coast you may sit in the sun. Very easy to understand why it has retained its immense popularity.

There's Avignon, on the River Rhône, where the old *pont* still spans half of the river and whose story we British children trilled in our first French lessons, and where the anti-pope built his sumptuous palace. There are two, possibly three, ways of getting your own palace. Be a royal or related to one, be a high-flown cleric or a conniving ruthless crook or, in the case of Renaissance Italy, all three. So, best to ignore the palaces, think of that small *château* you are going to buy.

Avignon is largely contained within its big, powerful walls that greet you as soon as you step out of the railway station. It is a most attractive city with a fabulous annual summer festival, mostly theatre, when you can never plan to move quickly from one place to another. Crowds, mostly young, come from all over the world, some performing on street corners and in squares. A few years back an impressive new TGV station was built just on the other side of the river, giving Avignon rapid rail links to the rest of Europe. Think back to those hard *couchettes* (they were softer if you weren't travelling steerage), when armed with toothbrush and flannel you had to queue up for the smelly loo, then try to undress in the bunk, contorting your body into a newly invented yoga position, while avoiding the gaze of a drunken lecher on the opposite side. Thanks to the TGV, Avignon to Waterloo via Paris or Lille is only matter of eight hours and there are good deals if you book in plenty of time. If you travel on a Sunday they frequently offer first class accommodation for a few pounds more. Take it. You will glide to your destination on a soft cloud of first class comfort.

Putting your car on the train is always expensive, but if you have a big family it saves hiring a charabanc the other end. And even if your final destination is Cannes or Nice it is still better to book you and the car just to Avignon and drive the rest of the way. For some inexplicable reason, to keep the car on the train down to one of the Riviera hotspots adds on a ridiculous expense.

Historically the Côte d'Azur has been attracting thousands of visitors since the Brits started the pilgrimage to the coast in the 18th century, when it became the health fix for those who could afford it.

Today the Cannes and Monaco Film and television Festivals, the Grand Prix, the Music Festival of Aix-en-Provence, Carnivals and the Arts in every form continue to attract not only holidaying Brits, but also artists in show-biz anxious to get away to the sun whenever possible. One such personality is the delightful Elaine Paige.

Five years ago, after spending regular holidays in the region she decided to buy an apartment near Cannes 'a short hop from London', in order to have a permanent base, primarily because she wanted to escape occasionally from London 'to recharge the batteries'.

Why the Côte d'Azur?

'The warm weather always appeals. When it's cold and grey in London there's usually a welcoming blue sky in Cannes.'

Is there anything that gives you a special *frisson*?

'Oh yes! To sit on the terrace with a lovely glass of French wine and look at the stunning sea view. I can sit there very happily for hours.'

How about your French life style in general?

'Well, life feels much healthier there. The sunshine, the food from the local market – fresh and delicious – I go early each morning and it's such good value. My diet is certainly better.'

Sport?

'Tennis. I love playing tennis and it's a great place to play.'

And hobbies?

'Just recently I've taken up painting. It's the wonderful light – inspirational.'

Did you go to classes?

'I went on a course near St Paul de Vence, and I'd really recommend painting to anyone in need of total relaxation.'

And the social scene?

'Cannes, Antibes, Nice, all great places with high profile events, especially in the summer.'

Doesn't it get a bit too busy sometimes?

'If you just step back from the main areas, you find peace and tranquillity just behind, so you can have the best of both worlds really.'

On the darker side, Avignon has always been a centre for thieves, drop-outs and druggies, especially around the old station. Its very position and accessibility to everywhere is part of the problem, perhaps. I remember sitting on one of our suitcases in the station concourse one morning, waiting for a train to Calais. My husband had wandered away, as they do, leaving me with the children perched nearby on other bits of baggage. Suddenly my 13-year-old leapt to her feet yelling 'Come back you thief! That's my mothers handbag!' Her long legs sprinted after him the length of the concourse, but by now some station staff had gathered at the far end. He gave up and handed back my bag, which was just as well because it contained all our passports and tickets. I must admit I did feel sorry for him; a shabby old tramp in his sixties, rheumy eyed, such a sad human being.

For any wine buff, Châteauneuf-du-Pape is a short distance from Avignon. Here in September the wine tasting starts and I have known quite respectable people become completely legless just by visiting the dozens of open *caves*, tasting, asking the right questions, not buying, but sounding very knowledgable, at first. By the tenth *cave* they are incapable of asking anything except the whereabouts of the car.

There is a delightful hotel facing the square in Châteauneuf that was obviously a favourite with French stage and screen stars. There are large signed photographs of Fernandel, Mistinguette, Josephine Baker, Charles Trenet, Maurice Chevalier, and more, covering the walls. The management may have changed, but I remember the excellent restaurant and floor-to-ceiling windows through which you had a fantastic view of Avignon and the Palace, and so beautiful at night.

The best thing about Orange is the magnificent Roman Amphitheatre. The acoustics are fabulous, as is the ambience. Every year there is a spectacular Opera festival with the singing greats. The stone seating is hard so you either hire a seat pad or take your own.

If Charlemagne had not created the title 'Counts of Orange,' it would never have been passed to the Dutch Royals, William of Orange would not have been an English king and we could well have avoided many of the Irish disputes. But that's history.

Carpentras, not far away, is an attractive town. It was the capital of a Celtic tribe, and later was a Roman base. An interesting fact: it was a refuge for Jews expelled by France, and the Cathedral has a *Porte Juif* through which, on one occasion in the Middle Ages, hundreds of enchained Jews passed, only to be unshackled within the Cathedral having supposedly instantly converted to Christianity. You may draw your own conclusions on that one. The city specialises in truffles, and during the season heavy trading takes place in the Friday market.

Spanning the coastal Bouches du Rhône, is the Camargue.

That magical region of sea salt marshes, where the grains are piled into pyramids; of labyrinthine waterways intersecting vast stretches of flat pampas land; of sugar cane and bamboo plantations; of beehive-shaped reed-roofed huts; of *Camarguaise* bulls rounded up by the Camargue cowboys with their large hats and where magnificent white horses run free through grass and water. Lining the roads leading to the coastal towns of the Camargue are the *manades* (stables) where these elegant creatures munch quietly, waiting for the next riding session when their cowboy owner will take out a group of eager tourists, some very young, through the nature reserve. There is also an ornithological centre containing the only golden eagle I have ever seen. So many were being lost to poachers and their eggs stolen it was decided to keep them in this semi-captivity at least until eggs were hatched and safe. Then there are the glorious flamingoes that at any given moment can rise like a pink cloud into the azure blue.

The Camargue has villages and hamlets tucked away on the banks of these waterways, sometimes needing a ferry-boat for access, sometimes isolated up a narrow lane advertising *'Chambres d'hôte'*.

On the Camargue coast is Les Saintes Maries de la Mer and its beautiful cathedral, the focal point of an annual ritual in May when gypsies from all over Europe congregate to carry statues of the three Marys out to sea along with floats of flowers. The story goes that Mary the mother of Jesus, Mary Magdalen (perhaps her daughter in law and why not?), and their servant a dark skinned Mary Sara, now the patron saint of gypsies, escaped to this part of the coast after Jesus died. It is easy to work out from this legend the basic premise of Dan Browne's *The Da Vinci Code*. So there you go; the plot thickens.

Although this small village has become a little touristy in the proliferating number of trinket and seaside shops, there are moments when it is unbelievably medieval. One summer evening strolling near the cathedral, the sounds of a melody wafted through the warm air. We drew nearer and there in front of the cathedral with an audience of silent, spellbound tourists like us, was a beautiful long haired young man playing a lute. His musical repertoire was Renaissance and he wore jeans. It was only the tabard that was missing for a complete transportation in time.

On another occasion I heard some drum beating coming from one of the dozens of *ruelles* (small steets) that cross the village. What I saw took my breath away: a llama with pretty hat and a collecting bag in his mouth, a pair of steps with upturned bucket, on top of which stood a goat also with pretty hat. Beating the drum was a young man, a gypsy with lean brown face, and standing next to him was perhaps his mother. She could have been Geronimo's mother. Her face was taut, hard and burnt, creased like leather and immobile, set like a mask. She was shaking a tambourine, and then the show started. The drum-beats began in earnest, with specific rhythms. The goat teetered in her dainty high heels on top of the bucket, the audience gasped. Carefully she lifted one leg, to accelerating drum beats, then another leg, louder drum beats, then with three legs suspended in the air, she was standing on the bucket on the ladder balancing on one leg, accompanied by a crescendo of drum beats and gasping applauding audience. Geronimo's mother prodded the llama who delicately nuzzled round the audience with his bag open for financial reward. I'd like to think the goat would have had a share of the spoils, perhaps a good night out? I have never seen anything to match this piece of pure medieval street entertainment.

Further inland is Arles where, alas, Van Gogh's lodgings and street café which he painted are no more. They were bombed by the Allies during

WWII. But just outside the town is his famous bridge, hardly changed.

The Roman past of Arles is strikingly evident, with the theatre, still used for '*spectacles*' (shows) and the wonderfully preserved arena used not only for more '*spectacles*' but for *corridas*. Each April Arles has its *fête* with parades, music and carnival atmosphere. It is quite an attractive town, relying hugely on the Roman antiquities and Van Gogh. If you are looking for *France Profonde*, you won't find it here. Travel a little north to Les Baux and be prepared to gasp in wonderment. To reach Les Baux, if you are travelling from the Nîmes area, you pass through a couple of stunning towns, Beaucaire and Tarascon, built facing – or rather glaring – at each other across the River Rhône and each having a magnificent fortified *château*, owned and defended by Princes of Provence. The two towns had centuries of scrapping, but the Revolution sorted them out. Tributaries flow into the towns providing harbours for small craft alongside working fishing boats. There's a friendly atmosphere in both towns with tree-lined boulevards. It's near to Nîmes for the airport and serious shopping, and near to the coast for a day at the sea.

Once through these towns you approach *Les Alpilles*. I am always amazed why they didn't make Star Wars here, because the landscape is completely lunar. On the other hand Tunisia was cheaper. The white craggy rock formations of this terrain remove it from normal experience. They dazzle brilliantly white in the sun, with vegetation only on the lower levels through which you pass as you climb. *En route* are a number of panoramic view spots that can hold you captive. Below in a half circle is the plain of les Bouches du Rhône and just higher than your eye level is the small citadel of Les Baux perched on a white lunar hilltop. Before you reach this beautiful village you will pass the rather inauspicious entrance to what used to be the old bauxite quarries from which the town gets its name. Quite brilliantly the massive cathedral-like spaces of the quarries have been turned into a most riveting spectacle. The 'Cathédrale des Images' produces stunning *son et lumière* shows right inside these old quarries. At the entrance you are given a poncho to wear because, even on a blistering day (you could cook an egg sometimes on the rock ouside), inside it is very cold. They usually produce two themes each year, all interesting, all different. Of those I have seen the most impressive was the Châteaux of France. The lighting is so clever you think you are walking on old black and white tiles and that you are moving towards an open portico. The specially-composed music adds to the atmosphere. Children love it! You can park outside Les Baux and walk up the tiny twisting streets, lined with period houses, through rather up-market gift shops and interesting clothes shops. The tourist centre offers old posters for sale depicting the first SNCF railway to pass by. At the top is the fortified keep, quite perilous to scramble up, and not for the faint-hearted.

A beautiful location, yes, but what happens here in winter? A question all potential home-buyers have to ask, because it is oh-so-easy to be seduced by the logically inappropriate,

Down to St-Rémy-de-Provence. This is where the Grimaldi sisters used to live and royal spotters used to come here on market day to see them. A delightful place with an exciting summer *fête*. *Abrivados* are held each day and the week culminates in a torchlight trot, canter and gallop through a carefully barricaded town circuit, of two hundred white *Camarguaise* horses, with only a handful of cowboys to keep them in position. The horses are quite magnificent, running free and with each circuit gathering speed. It is both a breathtaking and a moving sight. I once saw a Portuguese bull fight in the arena here, thinking they were not cruel to the bull. Mistake! They don't kill the creature, but it is wounded and if the matador, all dressed up and very aware of him/herself, wounds the bull badly the crowd boos. But nevertheless I found out the bull is slaughtered whatever his condition after the event. How naïve to think there would be a vet on stand by!

Ouside St Remy is Glanum a well-excavated Roman town. In terms of living conditions and household facilities we haven't made much progress since so, as previously suggested, it would have been a good posting.

240

Over many years Terry Kelleher had taken his young family to various parts of France for regular holidays, privately sensing he would 'always end up there,' because he 'loves the French way of life'. He is retired now and lives in a delightful old Provençal market town, much favoured by the Romans. But his was not just an ordinary 'up-sticks' retirement to France.

In the UK Terry was an independent investigative drama-doc filmmaker, but when he developed MS and with it obligatory retirement, a holiday with friends in this same town convinced him, and he decided to stay. So three years ago with his disability, he sold up in the UK, and bought a single storey house with a pool.

I asked him how he found life as a disabled foreigner. He thought attitudes towards disability in France were far more sensitive than in the UK; for example no one takes up a reserved car space; there is always someone who offers to push the trolley at the supermarket, or help in a dozen ways. Whenever he thanks them, the reply is always 'C'est normale'. He says he would be reluctant to display his disability badge on the car in London as it would probably be smashed up, and any goodies sold in the nearest pub.

But not here.

I asked him if he made many friends. 'Anglophones unfortunately', but he added that so many of his Brit friends, anxious to improve their French, become quite cross when they are answered in English by French waiters and shopkeepers anxious to improve their English.

Is life cheaper in the sunny south? He thinks food is more expensive, but he says that is probably because others have to shop for him, so he cannot hunt the special offers, but on the other hand he saves on clothes, living in shorts for half the year.

Was there a downside? Yes, he missed the cultural life of theatres and galleries he was used to in London, but there was plenty of local culture in his town with festivals and traditional *fêtes* that went back centuries. It was just different, that's all.

Terry is a French resident now and has nothing but praise for the standard of health care he receives, particularly with home visits.

Having done so much in the public eye it is hardly surprising that Terry Kelleher's active mind would not take retirement too seriously. In July 2006 he launched an online monthly community magazine for local Anglophones; www.alpillesnews.com. And of course for anyone contemplating a home in Provence, ready-made connections are there at the click of a mouse.

For anyone interested in collecting good *brocante* and antiques, Isle-sur-la-Sorgue is Provence's epicentre. It's a delightful small town crammed with antique shops and warehouses, and surprisingly an English tea-room, more for the dealers than the punters, I imagine. The roads are wide with superb plane trees, and the main boulevard runs alongside the river. There are monthly, weekly and daily markets here, as well as prestigious bi-annual fairs.

To the east are some beautiful Provençal villages – fine examples of the archetypal villages of *France Profonde*, like Gordes on a hilltop near old ochre mines and much beloved of artists of various disciplines. Apparently the village had the highest number of *maquisards* during WWII.

Whilst there are good motorways and rail links, the nearest international airport would be Marseille, although now there are flights from the UK to Avignon.

The towns of this region are probably better known than anywhere else in France: Aix-en-Provence, a beautiful town with a world famous music festival; Draguinon with its wide, tree-lined *boulevards*, around the old medieval *bastide*; Cotignac with its luscious flowers and medieval houses, all worth visiting and considering.

Elayne Murphy of *Provence Grannies* told me she first came to France as an *au pair* working for an Australian diplomatic family and was lucky enough to travel around the country with them. She made a conscious decision never to return to the UK because she had fallen in love with France and later with a Frenchman whom she married. When she divorced a few years later she returned briefly to the UK, but realised her heart was in France and came back. After living in a number of places, she has finally settled in the Vaucluse. I asked her how she came to be a Provence Granny.

It was when her second husband, an Englishman, developed cancer she looked for a job with flexible hours, and came across a Vendée granny who was operating a property search service. They got on so well, the network was born and Elayne became vice president.

'We are now 14 grannies all over France and growing, and yes I am a real granny too!'

I asked what she thought was the absolute essential for any Brit wanting to start up a business in France.

'They **must** speak French. They **must** be prepared for red tape – there are no short cuts. They must have a buffer of money behind them. Social charges alone will kill you in your second year.'

Did she ever feel like relocating?

'Never, ever – I have found my corner of paradise on earth.'

What did she like most about her French life style as opposed to life in the UK?

'The way they take time to enjoy the small things in life especially here in the south. They will drive around in a grotty old car but will spend money on a good steak or a good bottle of wine. Money goes on life not on possessions.'

What irritated her most?

'Red tape.'

Did she have as many French friends as Brit?

'More. Although, of course, there is not the same social pattern. But once you make a friend of a French person they are friends for life. We have regular barbecues and dinner parties with our French friends, but generally the French will invite you for *aperitifs*: easier than inviting you to a meal. But all the Brits I know here make an effort to integrate, always attending their own village functions.'

I wonderd if there were more Brits coming to the south to retire.

'Yes, I think there are. It's the medical care, safer life style, and weather.'

Any advice?

'Do your homework. What looks great as a property set in lavender fields and vineyards could be a nightmare with schools 5 km away. If you couldn't drive for any reason, could you survive without a car?'

Did she think the Côte d'Azur was a real slice of France?

'No, no no. Not unless you go into one of the villages. But then again it takes all sorts and the Côte d'Azur is just one more slice in the many layered cake that is France.'

There is a little narrow gauge train that runs from Nice to Digne-les-Bains called the *Train des Pignes,* the pine-cone train relating to the fuel used in WWI. If you really want to see Provence, take this train: the scenery is breathtaking.

Castellane, like Digne also on the route Napoleon, is now the centre for all activity based tourism; if you want it, they have it, and wherever you are in this region you are close to most activities.

Over to the east, Barcelonette is a superb little town close to the ski stations and surrounded by snow capped Alps. There are ski stations at Auron, St Etienne de Tinée, a neighbouring station, Isola 2000, and Valberg. Skiing here is wonderful because even at half term your family could be quite alone on the slopes. St Etienne is perfect for beginners, our children loved it largely because we were alone and there was no one to witness their first ski steps. Auron has *pistes* at all levels, and is more family-orientated like Valberg. Isola 2000 is for the faster, younger set. There are gondolas and drag-lifts and plenty of ski hire equipment. At St Etienne we did not have to pay for any of the facilities, but maybe they were having a quiet weekend. I should add if you want sophisticated après ski, package holiday stuff you'd better go up into the French Alps.

CÔTE D'AZUR

Probably the most renowned strip of coast in the world is here, the Côte d'Azur. It's true, Nice and some of its hinterland does have a microclimate, but then we are only talking a degree or two for the whole coast. For example Biot between Nice and Antibes can be two degrees lower than Nice. Frankly it is rather a picky exercise when you have generally good temperatures throughout the year and, although you do need a burst of heat during winter evenings, unless there is rain you can generally forget the heating during the late morning and afternoon. I say this because although property is more expensive you save on heating.

I met Dame Vera Lynn, as lovely and as gracious as you would expect, for tea, on the balcony of her delightful apartment in a small town on the Côte d'Azur. We were facing the communal pool set in a tranquil and leafy environment, and as neighbours passed by they waved and exchanged words and smiles with Dame Vera and her daughter Virginia.

Although Virginia speaks very good French, Dame Vera herself regrets not persevering with the language after having been taught the school basics.

'But,' she sighed, 'you get involved with your own work and travelling. I think I could have done quite well in France, had I only bothered, because I sang the kind of songs they like.'

Still, despite the language she knows everyone in the local shops, and manages very well to buy anything she wants. She flashed her famous

245

smile. 'That's my limit. But Virginia speaks, that's why I made sure she stuck to it.'

Dame Vera first came down here 50 years ago when the town was a small village. After a few years of renting apartments, she and her husband decided to buy one of the flats in this new block. That was 30 years ago. When her husband was alive they would spend part of May and the whole of September here, but now she flies down for about three weeks.

I asked her if she had ever considered moving somewhere else.

'No,' she replied. 'I'm a stickler for what I know. Coming down here all those years ago and liking it, I just stuck to it.'

What was the most attractive aspect about her annual sojourn in France?

'The first thing I come for is the weather. I don't need a car here. Buses go past the gates. When I bought the flat I furnished it completely differently from home. No antiques, all modern here. It's a change. I didn't want the same kind of atmosphere. I just don't have to think about it.'

And differences in life style?

'Well, you can't compare it really, so different. We probably go out to eat here more.' She laughed. 'But we are on holiday, after all.'

Nice and Cannes are very attractive cities, but they become very crowded in summer, and the traffic can drive you potty. The best season is either from October to December, or early spring. Antibes, Mandelieu, St Raphael, St Tropez, lovely as they are, suffer from the same overcrowding. A little further along, La Ciotat and Cassis are less crowded. In fact the beaches, shingle from Nice to Antibes, are so crowded that many families budget for their own pools even if they live on the coast. Nice is a very Italienate city and, in fact, did not become part of France until 1860, the year the railway came.

Hilary King and her husband Roy came to Antibes to live permanently fifteen years ago. Roy had just retired and they came to France from various business postings in the Far East. Trained as an actress and teacher, and passionate about theatre, Hilary had run children's theatre companies wherever they were posted.

They first visited Antibes because a friend from the Far East happened to have a flat there. They completely fell in love with the town and finally chose it for Roy's retirement. Hilary sparkles with energy, so when she saw the old theatre in Antibes, already performing French plays for the local population, her theatrical passion took over. Within months she had acquired sponsorship and was renting the theatre for one weekend a month inviting the great and famous from the London theatrical scene to perform in Antibes to the great joy of the huge English-speaking population in the area.

Although they would never go back to England, Hilary needs the buzz of London and the English theatre from time to time. And as she says it's only two hours door to door. Living in France she is very aware of being a guest in someone else's country, and considers it insulting when British residents make no effort with the language (Hilary and Roy did immersion courses in French for two consecutive years).

She feels strongly about people who make 'enclave lives' with other Brit ex-pats, and loves the 'elegant cultural environment' of France, the healthy living with simple foods. Recently Roy developed a condition which immersed them in the French medical scene. The care, which has included regular house visits over past moths, has been excellent. One afternoon they were seeing a specialist, who diagnosed something outside his sphere. Within an hour they were seeing the right man for the problem. As Hilary says you can't get much quicker than that. Yes, it is cheaper to live here than London, and she also believes that being in another culture keeps you mentally on your toes, as it constantly exercises the brain, and obliges you to accept the differences.

What are the down points?

'French bureaucracy, the endless form-filling, and lunchtime closing. But you get used to it.'

Would she want to live anywhere else?

'Emphatically no!' She enjoys living in a Republic, where the plumber and the Mayor are both *Monsieur*, and how could she leave 'the colours, the sun and the most beautiful sea in the world that feast the eyes every day?'

ooOOoo

Richard and Bethan Lewis live two thirds of the year in Cardiff where, before retirement, Richard was a television and film director, and Bethan a French teacher. They have been Francophiles for years, and their children likewise.

It all started with renting holiday homes in St Raphael. For 20 years they had a mobile home near Villeneuve Loubet, 10 km from Nice but, if they visited in February half term, they froze. It was partly as a result of their desire to visit more frequently and to escape their cold lodging, that the search for a bricks and mortar base began. They loved the sun but couldn't afford the Riviera, so instead chose the Charente. Richard is a meteorological aficionado, and says the Charente is the sunniest place in France next to the Riviera, with a micro climate. Fourteen years ago they found a house for £12,000, ready for renovation, 40 minutes south of La Rochelle, and near Bordeaux airport. It was lovely in summer, but always damp with the Atlantic sea air, and needing constant maintenance. Although it was great cycling country and the nearby villagers were lovely, few young people remained. The blazing wood fires helped considerably with the cold winters, but it was 'un bled perdu' – at the back of beyond. With no nearby commerce, nothing for their growing adolescent family, and a flea market only once a year, they decided to sell up. Meanwhile Richard had retired and didn't want to drive much.

They had visited Nice several times and as a family they liked it. They found a perfect flat with small terrace, on the top floor of a prestigious bourgeois building, only a walk from the Promenade, and signed for it in a day. A good investment because, in eight years, their apartment has increased four times in value. They like the fact that they can open it up or close it up, at any time of year. For heat, insurance, water, maintenance and the lift, they pay 1,400 euros per annum.

Bethan, because of her excellent French, makes friends easily, but she still feels many Brits should make more effort with the language, because 'the French really do appreciate it – it doesn't matter about the mistakes'. They would not want to live in Nice permanently because of their grandchildren and because they also love Wales.

The British played quite a part in establishing Nice. Apart from wintering in the city from the 18th century, onwards, the colony decided they would pool contributions to make a little path along the sea front, and the Promenade des Anglais is used to this day, although it is as wide as a boulevard now. Nice is a very lively city with a fabulous bay and a ruined *château* on the hill overlooking the town. There are great restaurants around the port where *moules* and *pommes frites* are a staple diet. And don't let anyone tell you restaurants are more expensive on the Côte. They are not. In fact it can be cheaper to eat out in Nice than in Uzès.

The city is impressive even if you only take into account the people who have lived there. One residential part is the Quartier des Musiciens, where roads are named after visiting musicians, like Rossini, Mozart and Beethoven. A road has been named after Chekhov who lived in Nice for six months, so did Lenin, but there's no road so far for him.

When Angela Rippon talks about France she bubbles.

That mellifluous voice of hers fairly effervesces. There is no doubt she loves the country and her particular corner of it which, at the moment, is an apartment in a charming Cote d'Azur village-town between Antibes and Cannes. She had been a visitor to this region for about 20 years, and loved the place so much that about four years ago she decided to buy something permanent. A friend happened to be selling up and the timing was perfect.

The small town, with easy access to cultural and social activities in nearby Nice and Cannes, and Orange for the opera season, has plenty of shops, a good market and provides a perfect hide-away for long weekends, New Year and the longer summer break.

I asked her what she thought the essential differences were in life style.

'I always feel very relaxed when I'm there. The pace of life is slower, but that's probably because I'm not working,' she laughed. 'Although I do work when I'm there, sitting with my laptop on the terrace. But it's not the same. Life can be so frantic in London.'

And the cost of living?

'Much lower in general.'

As a woman did she feel safer walking alone at night than in the UK?

'Certainly safer than London, yes, and I have never felt threatened. You get a criminal element anywhere, but it's less evident.'

Was it important to find fellow Brits and how easy was integration with French neighbours?

'I knew a number of Brits already, some who live here permanently and there are so many friends who come here for holidays, but I also have French friends whom I know equally well.'

What about the language?

'We have a tennis court and as I play a lot I have tennis partners who don't speak English, so I have to speak French! But in any case I take regular French lessons here in London. It's so important to be understood.'

What was the best aspect of her life in France?

She thought about this for a moment.

'The best aspect is to be able to fit into a different culture. I go there because it's such a complete contrast, and I always feel relaxed, maybe it's the sea air, plus I'm not working at the same pace.'

Were there any irritations?

'Only a mild irritation, bureaucracy I suppose, and all those sheaves of technical papers of such complexity they are a pain. But I do love the way they manage everything surprisingly well. We in the UK slavishly follow the rules of the EU. The French agree, then do their own thing. I love their attitude! Oh yes,' she laughed, 'and everything shuts down in August. You can't get any household jobs and repairs done because everybody goes on holiday!'

Is there anything UK missing from her French life?

'We only miss when denied, and with satellite I can have 'Radio 4' and 'Classic FM', but in any case 'France Classique' is great and 'France Inter' is like Radio 4, so no, I don't miss anything.'

What advice would she give to house-hunting Brits?

'Don't be tempted to buy in the place you know only from summer holidays. Go and visit out of season. It can be completely different without the summer atmosphere. Be sure you know it really well. And if your French isn't really good, find an estate agent who speaks English, and take an ex-pat or builder who knows about renovation/building/repairs with you. My builder has been telling me some horror stories of Brits who have bought badly.'

And the future?

She laughed. 'I can't wait to retire and be able to spend far more time there.'

In Cimiez, higher up the hill, residential, with important Roman artefacts, are to be found the palaces of defunct Romanovs turned into museums or luxury apartments. There are great art collections: Matisse, Dufy, Cheret, Chagall, and many more. The city used to be Queen

Victoria's favourite holiday spot because it was the most convenient place for the annual get together with her dozens of grandchildren peppered across every royal house in Europe. She took over a whole hotel, insisting that it was completely vacated, which was probably going a little too far. However she also brought, along with the vast entourage, her own personal band of the Coldstream Guards so that they could play her usual morning wake up call melodies out on the courtyard. Now that is going too far, especially if the lady was an early riser. They must have heaved sighs of relief when she and her trombones left. Today the hotel has been renamed Hotel Regina.

Nice old town is magic. Narrow streets, 15th–18th century houses with washing hanging out to dry, are reminiscent of Naples. Cours Saleya and the big square at the far end is packed with antique stalls on a Monday and flowers the rest of the week, a place where you will quite often hear more Italian than French. Garibaldi was born in Nice and is commemorated by a statue and a *Place*.

February sees the fantastic Carnival and Battle of the Flowers. Dozens of carnival floats, each one representative of a country with giant sized *papier mâché* figures, all comedic, and usually political, illustrate a cartoon on the chosen theme. The battle of the flowers takes place during the day along the Promenade des Anglais. The flower floats are superbly dressed, some representational, some simply lush. Fantastic costumes, made mostly of flowers, parade to the music of international brass bands. The gorgeous flower maidens on the floats throw out mimosas and gladioli to waiting arms in the crowd below. A must for young and old alike.

Mardi Gras runs for about two weeks with a *spectacle* most days and finishing with the big final floodlit carnival procession when the 'King' is burnt and taken out to sea with a roll of revolutionary drums.

One of the advantages of this neck of the woods is the transport system. First of all there is Nice International airport with flights from several UK companies, and there is a very efficient and cheap bus service to almost anywhere in the Alpes Maritimes region. At the time of writing the bus fare within the served region is 1€30. The train services are excellent and, as it takes only 20 minutes to get to Monaco, it is not worth taking a car. A trip to an Italian market at Ventemiglia or San Remo is easy and very pleasant by train. By car you have traffic, and parking.

Wherever you are thinking of locating, a public transport system becomes more important as time passes, whether or not you have a car.

Some Britons who have lived in France for years are adamant that the Riviera is not France. I can see what they mean, but contained within or just outside the geographical area of the Côte d'Azur are small towns and villages in the hinterland that have preserved a real atmosphere of old Provence. Houses are generally cheaper here, although for how long is another question, as more people are scurrying away from the cosmopolitan areas. For example, St Paul de Vence, a delightful hill village, once the home of actors Roger Moore and Yves Montand, is a colony of arts and crafts and the Maeght Foundation. La Colle sur Loup, is another superb little village. And further up the mountain, Vence, is an old *bastide* town known for its pure air and clinics for respiratory problems where Matisse painted his famous chapel and where DH Lawrence lived and died. There are countless more pretty villages and towns such as Villeneuve-Loubet, Tourettes sur Loup, Le Rouret, La Gaude, St Jeannet, Mougins, Mouans Sartou,Valbonne and, a little further away, Grasse. Although Grasse still has an active reputation for perfume making – and it is undoubtedly a very attractive city set high overlooking the plain, easily accessible to Nice airport with plenty of road transport – there are now certain areas where it is better not to live. I was told this over and over again by estate agents. All cities have certain levels of crime, Nice certainly has, and so, now, does Grasse. High immigrant levels have resulted in unemployment pushing up petty crime and worse. In all cities there are no-go areas, you just have to choose carefully.

Beyond Nice towards Italy is the more expensive Riviera: Eze, Villefranche, Beaulieu-sur-Mer, St Jean Cap-Ferrat, and Menton. Property here is driven by reputation, spellbinding coastal panoramas and fabulous locations, but transport remains cheap.

With so many foreign companies and their employees in the area, there are a number of excellent International Schools. I spent a day in one and was hugely impressed by the quality of the pupils, their maturity, general knowledge and desire to learn. They followed the Baccalaureate curriculum, and although English was the mother tongue of only about 50%, teaching was done in English, most of the pupils being bi-lingual. But the state *Lycées* also follow the Baccalaureate syllabus in French and, following the generally high level of French education, they achieve an all round standard akin to where we were a few decades ago.

International air transport to this region is accessible to most places. Apart from Nice, UK carriers use Marseille, Toulon and Avignon airports.

Examples of properties for sale

Toulon

Loft. 200 sq.m. 2 beds in Haussman building: 390,000€

Le Brusc

House. Village. 6 rms. 155 sq.m.: 370,000€

Castellane

House. To renovate. 5 rooms 129 sq.m. Small garden: 97,000€

Regusse

House. Village. Stone. Beams. Dbl glazing. 70 sq.m. 2 beds: 136,000€

Ampus

House. Village. 123 sq.m. 3 floors. 5 rooms. Land 147 sq.m. totally renovated, ex condition: 205,000€

Draguignan

House. Medieval. Stone, well renovated. 140 sq.m. 5 rooms. Vaulted cellar. Medieval bread oven: 245,000€

Hyères

House. Town, nr shops. 3 floors divided into 3 apartments: 280,000€

Six-Fours Les Plages

Villa. 70 sq.m, 2 beds. Garden 500 sq.m.: 335,000€

St Maxime

House. Nr Centre and sea. 75 sq.m. 2 beds. Land 80 sq.m.: 320,000€

Chalet. 2 rooms, terrace, garden. 300 sq.m. 200 m beach: 195,000€

Vaucluse

Saignon

House. Nearby hamlet, beautifully restored. 85 sq.m. 2 beds: 149,000€

House. Village. 60 sq.m. 2 floors, terrace, verandah. Vaulted basements to develop. Small courtyard + garage and room for renovation: 147,000€

Alpes-Maritimes

Golfe-Juan

House. 5 rooms. 175 sq.m. 15 mins beaches: 1,287,000€

Biot

House. Modern 216 sq.m. 8 rooms. Land 980 sq.m.: 990,000€

Valbonne

Villa. Indiv. In pine forest. Well presented. 3 beds. 82 sq.m. Terrace 40 sq.m. 5 mins Valbonne/Mougins: 445,000€

Grasse

House. Historic centre. 160 sq.m. 5 floors renovated with great taste. Quiet area. Roof terrace: 320,000€

House. 122 sq.m. 3 beds Views. Terrace. Quiet area: 379,000€

Menton

Apprt. Old town. 2 beds. 80 sq.m. to renovate. 1st floor: 180,000€

Apprt. Centre. 3/4 rooms with mezzanine. 3 beds. Big terrace. Nr public gardens: 320,000€

Roquebrune Village

House. 5 rooms facing Château. No garden: 297,000€

HAUT ALPES

Sisteron nr.

House. Village. 150 sq.m. 6 rooms: 165,000€

Isola 2000

Apprt. 32 sq.m. 2 rooms, furnished, balcony, view of pistes: 105,000€

Chalet. 60 sq.m. 2 beds + basement to convert. Furnished. Attractive: 320,000€

Valbonne

Apprt. 2 bed. 90 sq.m. Garden + terrace, peaceful: 350,000€

Le Broc

House. 4 beds. 170 sq.m. Land 2,400 sq.m. 30 mins Nice airport: 580,000€

House. 2 beds. 80 sq.m. Stunning views: 294,000€

Mandelieu

Studio. Panoramic views sea and mountains. Refurbished: 170,000€

GRASSE

St Antoine

House. Semi. 4 rooms. 93 sq.m. Large terrace, small garden: 336,000€

Cannes

House. 170 sq.m. Garden 60 sq.m. Balcony: 561,000€

Vence

Villa. 6 rooms 160 sq.m. + outbuildings to renovate. Very large pool. Land 900 sq.m.: 726,000€

www.orpi.com
www.immovar.com
www.laforet-var.com
www.pierrestradition.fr
www.lesclesdumidi.com
www.actionimmobilier.com
www.seaside-immo.net
www.explorimmo.com
www.seloger.com
info@promotionmozart.com

23

GETTING THERE

ROAD

If you like driving and the distance is not a problem, France is a delight. Excellent motorways intersect the country leaving barely a village more than easy driving distance to join one of them. Motorway tolls have gone up like everything else over the past ten years, but if you can share the cost with passengers they still provide the quickest means of road travel.

The RN (*Route Nationale*) roads were the first free national road network before the motorways. They are always good and are frequently dual carriageways. Roads marked 'D' on the map, indicate they are merely Departmental roads, and not impossible country lanes.

There is no question, avoiding the motorways is the only way to see *France profonde*, so even if your destination is a long way down the Hexagon, consider the drive as part of the vacation and enjoy it.

Three years ago the French were assessed the worst drivers in Europe, and it is true that you will find a generous assortment of the hair-brained variety who need to get from A to B yesterday. But generally they are to be found tearing up urban pathways. Driving in some cities can be a nightmare, so try to avoid rush hours and instead aim for the sacred lunch break when gastric juices are circulating more than traffic.

SEA

If you need a car you'll need to cross the channel! Over recent years there has been a big drop in prices for crossings from Dover but, conversely, the western routes seem to have risen sharply in price. There are many I know who find that it is a cheaper option, and often more relaxing, to take the ferry from Dover or the tunnel from Folkestone and drive thorugh the pleasurably wide-open spaces of the *autoroutes* to Normandy or Brittany.

On the eastern crossings there is a choice of operators and, although on the western crossings the choice is limited, assuming you don't get sea-sick, you do get the chance of a few hours' sleep, which is an advantage if you face a long drive on the French side.

Eastern routes				
Speedferries	**P & O**	**Seafrance**	**Norfolk Lines**	**Eurotunnel**
speedferries.co.uk	*poferries.com*	*seafrance.com*	*norfolkline-ferries.co.uk*	*eurotunnel.co.uk*
Dover to Boulogne	Dover to Calais	Dover to Calais	Dover to Dunkerque	Folkestone to Coquelle

Western routes	
LD Lines	**Brittany Ferries**
ldlines.co.uk	*brittanyferries.co.uk*
Porstmouth to Le Havre, Newhaven to Le Havre	Portsmouth to Caen, Cherbourg, St Malo, Poole to Cherbourg, Plymouth to Roscoff

Rail

Then there are trains, comfortable, cost effective, punctual and clean.

I shall resist the temptation to draw comparisons between Britain and France...

If you are over sixty, you have an immediate ten percent reduction on tickets. With a senior rail card, and you don't have to be French to get one, you will have an immediate 50% off. If train travel is going to be part of your French life, then it is well worth paying out for a rail card.

The TGV (*Train à Grande Vitesse*) has to be the most comfortable method of travel ever. Despite the speed it fairly glides across the terrain and, with the current lengthy check-in times at airports, depending on your destination, many French-bound travellers prefer to go to Waterloo station in London and board the sleek silver bullet instead.

Air

Finally of course the faster travel option is the plane. The only disadvantage is being limited in what you can carry: very important in the early years of creating a French base. There was a time I always drove, even to the south: the car stuffed to the gunwales with things for the house. Conversely I have, over the years, brought back to the UK an assortment of small French furniture and artefacts. At the time, my children always felt I'd be better off with an articulated lorry.

But after 25 years, no more. Apart from being generally cheaper to buy household requirements in France, motoring any distance with a stopover becomes an added expense and an extra drain on energy.

I personally feel, for a destination south of Lyon you should think about a low cost airline flight, unless of course you want to travel by car for some reason.

With luck you will find your French airport has a good bus service, otherwise you will have to bite the bullet and take a taxi. But don't worry, in time you will make friends and airport fetching-and-carrying will become a reciprocal arrangement.

Here are three budget airlines and the French airports they serve. They fly from an assortment of UK bases, including Gatwick, Heathrow, Stansted and Luton.

RYAN AIR	EASY JET	FlyBe
ryanair.com	*easyjet.com*	*flybe.com*
Bergerac	Bordeaux	Angers
Biarritz	Basel-Mulhouse	Avignon
Brest	Grenoble	Bergerac
Carcassonne	Lyon	Bordeaux
Dinard	La Rochelle	Brest
Grenoble	Marseille	Chambéry
Limoges	Nice	Limoges
Marseilles	Paris	Nice
Montpellier	Toulouse	Paris
Nantes		Perpignan
Nîmes		Rennes
Paris		La Rochelle
Pau		Toulouse
Perpignan		
Poitiers		
La Rochelle		
Rodez		
Toulon		
Tours		
Other full-service airlines such as BA and Air France serve Paris, Strasbourg and many major French cities.		

24
CONCLUSION

If you have read thus far and still have no clues where your dreams could take you in this stunning country then maybe you will remain a dreamer, and there's nothing wrong with that. However if you are still undecided, and want to pursue the dream, reconsider the needs for you and the family. If it's sun and ski you want, two areas immediately come tops for me in terms of well-priced housing; they are the Pau Pyrénées region or Franche-Comté.

If you want walks, views, mountains and sun try Northern Provence (the Côte d'Azur hinterland) or Midi Pyrénées.

And if you want the wild open spaces and sun, there's always the glorious Camargue.

If you'd like the country with a city/town close by try Lyon, Nîmes and Bourges.

For small towns with well priced housing try Cognac or Riquewihr.

When you do decide on your spot, look up *www.Angloinfo.com* and find out what really goes on there!

France is a great country. Historically it has given the world a political blueprint, one that is etched on the very mind and soul of all French citizens. A history, initially violent, but finally levelling and maturing, has shaped them. They are a justifiably proud people, and can be reserved until they know you. But once they are friends, they are friends for life. Kindness and generosity in abundance, which you will meet everywhere, is casually dismissed as *normale*.

If we are finally fortunate enough to spend part of our lives in France it is up to us as foreigners to integrate into the community, and become part of its generous heart.

Bon chance !

GLOSSARY

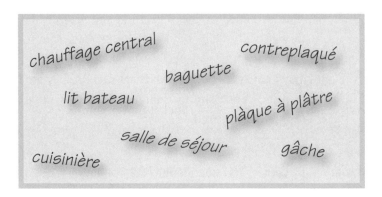

chauffage central

contreplaqué

baguette

lit bateau

plàque à plâtre

salle de séjour

cuisinière

gâche

Here are a few words that may be worth knowing. If you already have a house in France, many of them will be known or at least ring bells. This is not intended to be anything more than a personal selection, so a good dictionary is a sound investment and, perhaps even better, a French manual on *bricolage* (DIY). This way, even if you are not a DIY boffin, you will be able to keep a professional eye on the workforce and its daily progress.

ELECTRICITY

l'alimentation électrique	electrical supply
l'ampère	amp
la baguette	cable cover
le conjoncteur	mains switch
le coupe-circuit à fusible	fuse
le coupe-circuit principal	main fuse
courant alternatif et continu	AC/DC
le courant électrique	electric current
le court-circuit	short circuit
le disjoncteur	circuit-breaker, cut-out switch
le douille	light socket

l'éclairage	lighting
faire sauter les plombs	blow the fuses
la fiche	plug
un fil fusible	fuse wire
une fusible a cartouche	cartridge fuse
la phase	live
une porte fusible	fuse-box
la prise	socket/power point
la prise de terre	earth socket
le neutre	neutral
le socle	insulating base
le télérupteur	light switch
le tension du courant	voltage
la terre	earth
les unités de mesure	units of measure
le volt	volt
le watt	watt

FLOOR COVERINGS

la moquette	carpet
une moquette avec une sous-couche en mousse synthétique	foam-backed carpet
le tapis	rug

FURNITURE

l'armoire	wardrobe
le congelateur	freezer
la cuisinière	cooker
le frigo	fridge
le lit bateau	antique bed with cot sides and shaped ends
le lit de traverse	antique alcove bed, with one decorated cot side

265

les meubles	furniture
le sac à poubelle	refuse bag
le table de toilette	dressing-table
le table de nuit	bedside table
les tiroirs	drawers
les volets	shutters

HEATING

l'accumulateur	storage heater
un boisseau	chimney-flue tile
le cendrier	cinder tray
la chaudière	boiler
la chaudière à gaz	gas-fired boiler
la chaudière au charbon	charcoal-burning boiler
la chaudière au mazout	oil-fired boiler
la chaudière polycombustible	multi-fuel boiler
le chauffage	heating
le chauffage à air pulsé	hot-air heating
le chauffage central	central heating
le chauffeau	water heating
la cheminée	fireplace
le conduit	ventilation shaft
le contre-coeur	fire-back
le convecteur	convector heater
l'energie solaire	solar energy
le foyer (l'âtre)	hearth
le poêle	stove
le poêle-cheminé	modern Scandinavian-type wood-burning stove
le programmateur centralisé	centralised programmer
le réglage de la temperature	temperature control
le robinet thermostatique	thermostatic radiator control
le robinet de purge	air release tap

THE HOUSE

le bureau	study
la chambre	bedroom
le domicile	home
l'escalier	stairs
le cloison contre l'humidité	damp-proof course
la cuisine	kitchen
la fenêtre	window
un grenier	attic, barn
le main courant	banister
le palier	landing
les parois	partition walls
le plafond	ceiling
la porte	door
la ruine	run-down property
le toit	roof
le toiture	roofing
la salle de bains	bathroom
la salle d'eau	shower room
la salle à manger	dining room
la salle de séjour	living room
le sol	floor

HOUSE PROTECTION

la clôture	fencing
l'entrebailleur à chaine	security chain
la fermeture	home security
la gâche	catch of a lock, or striking plate
le grillage	wire-netting
l'haie	hedge
le parterre	flower-bed
la pelouse/gazon	lawn
le portail	gateway

le portillon	gate
le poteau	post
le mur de clôture	boundary wall
un muret en pierre sèches	dry-stone wall
le serrure	lock
le verrou	bolt

INSULATION

le bourrelet en caoutchouc	rubber beading
le calfeutrage	draught-proofing
le chambranle	door frame
la charnière	hinge
les chevrons	rafters
un cloison	dividing wall
les combles	loft area
le double-vitrage	double-glazing
l'isolant	insulating material
l'isolation	insulation
le joint d'étanchéité	waterproof joint
les joints en mousse	foam strips
la laine de verre	fibre-glass
le lambris	panelling, wainscoting
le liège en particules	cork particles
les murs extérieurs	external walls
les planchers bas	floor boards
le plàque à plâtre	plaster board
la plinthe	skirting
les rampants	roof arches
la vermiculite	mica particles

MASONRY

les agrégats	aggregates
le béton	concrete

le béton armé	reinforced concrete
la bétonnière	concrete mixer
un bouclier	plastering hawk
la brique	brick
la brique creuse	hollow brick
la brique réfractaire	fire-proof brick
les cailloux	pebbles
la chaux	lime
le ciment	cement
la dalle	paving stone
l'enduit	plaster coating
le foyer	fireplace
les gravillons	loose chippings, fine gravel
le linteau	lintel
la marche	step
les moellons	quarry stones
le mortier	mortar
le mur	wall
le muret	low wall
le pavage	pavement, paved area
le parpaing	breeze-block
les pierres concassés	crushed stones
le plâtre	plaster
le plâtroir	plastering trowel
le sable	sand
le seau	bucket
le terrassement	excavation
une tranchée	trench, ditch

PLUMBING

une baignoire	bathtub
les colliers	fixing clips
un coulage	substantial leak

une cuvette de w.c.	toilet pan
le débouchage des canalisations	unblocking the drains
une douche	shower
les elements sanitaires	sanitary ware
l'evacuation	waste-water drainage
l'évier	sink
la fosse septique	septic tank
une fuite	leak
un lavabo	wash basin
le manchon	sleeve
un mélangeur	mixer-tap
le raccord coudé	bend joint
les raccords	joints
le robinet	tap
le siphon	trap (of a drain)
tout à l'égout	on main drainage
les tubes de cuivres	copper piping
les tuyaux en PVC	PVC pipework
la vidange	draining

TOOLS

l'atelier	workshop
la bêche	spade
le bédane	mortise chisel
la brosse	brush
la brosse d'encollage	pasting brush
la brosse à maroufler	wallpaper brush
la brosse métallique	wire brush
la burette	oil-can
le ciseau à bois	wood chisel
le ciseau de briqueteur	bricklayer's chisel
la clé à molette	adjustable spanner
le clou	nail

le coupe-verre	glass-cutter
le couteau universel	cutter (Stanley knife)
l'éponge	sponge
l'équerre droite	right angle
l'étau d'établi	fixed vice
la fausse équerre	bevel square
le fer à souder	soldering iron
la ficelle	string
le fil à plomb	plumb-line
le foret pour le metal	metal drill
la forte agrafeuse	staple-gun
le grattoir triangular	triangular scraper
le jeu de clés	set of spanners
la lampe à souder à gaz	blow lamp
la lime	metal file
le maillet en bois	wooden mallet
le marteau	hammer
le marteau d'emballeur	claw-hammer
la mèche	bit, drill
– à bois	wood drill
– à béton	concrete drill
le mètre pliant	folding rule
le mètre-ruban	tape measure
le niveau à bulle	spirit level
la paire de ciseaux	pair of scissors
la pelle	shovel
la perceuse électrique	electric drill
la pince universelle	pliers
la pioche	pick
la ponceuse	sander
le rabot	plane
le rape	rasp
le réglet métallique	metal rule
le rouleau à peinture	paint roller

la roulette à joint	roller for wallpaper joints
la scie	saw
la scie circulaire	circular saw
le tamis	riddle, sieve
la tenaille	pair of pincers
le tournevis	screwdriver
la truelle de maçon	masonry trowel
le trusquin	mortise gauge
le vilebrequin	bit-brace
la vis	screw
la vrille	gimlet

WALL DECORATION

un aspect mat	matt finish
un aspect satiné	eggshell finish
un aspect velouté	silk finish
le carreau de faïence	ceramic tile
le carrelage	tiling
une carelette/un coupe-carreau	tile-cutter
la colle	paste/glue
les dalles de mirroir	mirror tiles
une decolleuse	paper stripper
l'escabeau	step-ladder
la liège	cork
le molleton	flannel, felt
un papier préencollé	ready-pasted wallpaper
le papier peint	wallpaper
la peinture	painting
la soie	silk
la table à encoller	pasting-table
le térébenthine	turpentine
le tissu	fabric covering
la toile de jute	hessian

| *le velour* | velvet |
| *le white spirit* | white spirit |

WOODWORK

les assemblages	joints
– enfouchement	dovetailing
– tenon et mortaise	mortise and tenon
– rainure et languette	tongue and groove
le bois massif	solid wood
la charnière	hinge
le chêne	oak
le contreplaqué	plywood
le hêtre	beech
le pin	pine
la quincaillerie	hardware
le loqueteau	small latch, catch
le vernis	varnish

Don't get caught out when making regular foreign currency transfers

Even once you have bought your property in France you need to make sure that you don't forget about foreign exchange. It's highly likely that you'll need to make regular foreign currency transfers from the UK whether for mortgage payments, maintenance expenditure or transferring pensions or salaries, and you may not realise that using your bank to arrange these transfers isn't always the best option. Low exchange rates, high fees and commission charges all eat away at your money and mean that each time you use your bank you lose out. However, by using Currencies Direct's Overseas Regular Transfer Plan you can get more of your money time after time.

Exchange Rates
Your bank is likely to only offer you a tourist rate of exchange due to the small amounts being transferred. However, Currencies Direct is able to offer you a commercial rate of exchange regardless of the amount that you wish to transfer.

Transfer Charges
Most banks will typically charge between £10 and £40 for every monthly transfer. Currencies Direct is able to offer free transfers, which will save you a considerable amount of money over time.

Commission Charges
When made through a bank transfers are usually liable for a commission charge of around 2%. By using Currencies Direct you can avoid commission charges altogether.

How does it work?
It is very easy to use Currencies Direct. The first thing you need to do is open an account with them. Once this is done all you need to do is set up a direct debit with your bank and confirm with Currencies Direct how much money you would like to send and how often (monthly or quarterly). They will then take the money from your account on a specified day and once they have received the cleared funds transfer it to France at the best possible rate available.

Information provided by Currencies Direct.
Website: *www.currenciesdirect.com*
Email: *info@currenciesdirect.com*
Tel: 0845 389 1729

INDEX